SUPREME PHILOSOPHY OF MAN

s you open this book, you will begin
xciting and inspirational adventure
new realms of self-knowledge and
-fulfillment, exploring the basic laws
nan's nature and his world, the 47
WS OF LIFE.

Here you will find the answers to the
st important questions in life — the
l questions you have asked your-
. Am I getting the most out of life?
at can I contribute? What changes
make my life worthwhile? What are
true values of life? How can I in-
ase the quality and enjoyment of my
?

The 47 LAWS OF LIFE are the es-
tial, unchanging properties of every
n, woven into the web of our being,
o our tissues, our nerve cells, our
ry bloodstream. Invisible and too
en unacknowledged, they are as real
electricity, as explosive a force as the
m bomb.

These laws are tools for living whose
azing power is understood and used
very few. *A mastery of them can
ange your life.* As you learn to apply
em, your world will begin to expand.
ings will start to happen in your life.
oblems and struggles that seemed in-
rmountable will melt away. You will
scover how to harness nature's own
rces and put them to work to achieve
ur every goal.

Unique in concept and in its **direct**
application to the practical business of
living, THE SUPREME PHILOSO-
PHY OF MAN points a clear path
toward building a personal philosophy
that will enable you to become a happier, more effective and courageous person — the exceptional human being who
has learned to call upon all his personal
resources and to live victoriously.

As they cast new light into every corner of man's quest for the good life,
these pages reveal a mother lode of wise
observation and practical experience, a
treasure enriched by a set of personal
values expressed by some of the greatest men in history — PLUS 1001
POINTS ON THE BUSINESS OF
LIVING.

Against the empty, joyless dissatis-
factions so prevalent in modern life,
here is a ringing affirmation of faith in
man's worth and potential greatness, a
powerful philosophy not for the ivory
tower but for the arena of life.

Begin your voyage now. Discover the
unseen forces which govern each man's
life for good or ill. Use the laws of life
to chart your own course toward a rich,
adventurous, successful and dynamic
life — the highest and best life known
to man!

PRENTICE-HALL, INC.
Englewood Cliffs, New Jersey

THIS IS ONE OF THE
BOOKS YOU COUL

D0926262

ACKNOWLEDGMENTS

Sincere thanks are extended to the publishers and individuals for permission to include material in this work. Every effort has been made to assign proper credits. If these have been omitted where they are due, they will be included in subsequent editions. Our grateful acknowledgment to:

HAWTHORN BOOKS, INC., from *Reflections on Life,* by Alexis Carrel, Copyright © 1952 by Hawthorn Books, Inc.

PHILOSOPHICAL RESEARCH SOCIETY, INC., for permission to reprint various excerpts from the works of Manly P. Hall.

SIMON & SCHUSTER, INC., from *Man's Search for Meaning,* by Viktor E. Frankl, © 1963 by Viktor Frankl; from *Be Your Real Self,* by David Harold Fink, M.D., © 1950 by David Harold Fink, both used by permission of Simon & Schuster.

Permit me to acknowledge my great indebtedness to the teachings and influence of all those people whose lives, writings, and counsel have touched my life. My greatest personal indebtedness is to my eminent friend Dr. A. P. Gouthey. To all these I am chiefly indebted for the character and contents of my philosophy.

THE
SUPREME
PHILOSOPHY
OF
MAN

Everyone has a philosophy, and your philosophy is what YOU believe, YOUR eternal pursuit of truth and wisdom.

God's philosophy is brought out in His Natural Laws and in nature. His Laws are SUPREME. His philosophy is LOVE, BEAUTY, RIGHTEOUSNESS . . . this whole world is geared to righteousness. He has given every person free choice.

Free choice, and the Natural Laws, provide the consequences to man's acts.

The environment YOU fashion out of YOUR thoughts, YOUR beliefs, YOUR ideals, YOUR philosophy, is the only climate YOU will ever live in!

LET THERE BE LIGHT

PHILOSOPHY is the art of living. It asks the basic questions—"What is life all about? Who am I? What should I do? What may I hope and believe?" The discovery of truth and the practice of the good life are the two primary goals of philosophy.

THE SUPREME PHILOSOPHY OF MAN spells out THE LAWS OF LIFE and reveals the Dynamic Power of Man's Nature. A new way to personal growth, security and a better life. Life is a matter of DEVELOPMENT or DECAY and in between these two extremes lie the variable degrees which determine the QUALITY OF EACH MAN'S LIFE.

This book presents clearly and concisely: the fundamental principles of rich dynamic living . . . THE ESSENTIAL FACTS OF LIFE . . . THE LAWS OF LIFE . . . THE UNSEEN FORCES THAT MAKE OR BREAK EVERY MAN. LEARN WHAT THESE LAWS HAVE TO TEACH NOW . . . NOT WHEN YOU COME TO DIE AND DISCOVER THAT YOU HAVE NOT LIVED.

Every intelligent person may INCREASE THE QUALITY AND FULLNESS OF HIS LIFE AND LIVE the way he is designed to live. Each person has the opportunity to be a "connoisseur" in the fine art of rich dynamic living. The raw materials are here at hand—the results can be miraculous!

THE SUPREME PHILOSOPHY OF MAN

The Laws of Life

by *Alfred Armand Montapert*

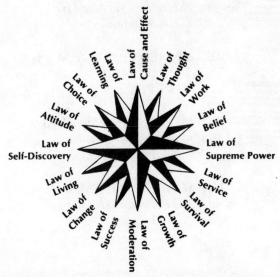

PHILOSOPHY AND PSYCHOLOGY FOR SUCCESSFUL
EVERYDAY LIVING. THESE BASIC LAWS OF MAN'S NA-
TURE REVEAL THE PRINCIPLES THAT DETERMINE THE
QUALITY OF EACH MAN'S LIFE AND GIVE THE ANSWERS
TO THE MOST IMPORTANT QUESTIONS OF LIFE.

REVISED EDITION

ADDITIONAL COPIES MAY BE ORDERED FROM

BOOKS OF VALUE
2458 CHISLEHURST DRIVE
LOS ANGELES, CALIF. 90027

BOOKS BY THE SAME AUTHOR

DISTILLED WISDOM
Thoughts That Successful Men Live By
10th Printing

SUPREME PHILOSOPHY OF MAN
The Laws of Life
9th Printing

PERSONAL PLANNING MANUAL
How to Increase Your Worth
6th Printing

THE WAY TO HAPPINESS
Formulas to a Better and Happier Life
3rd Printing

Printed in the United States of America by
BOOKS OF VALUE

THE LAWS OF LIFE

THE UNSEEN FORCES THAT
MAKE OR BREAK EVERY MAN.

Human nature is governed by Natural Laws . . .
This book will help you discover and benefit from them.

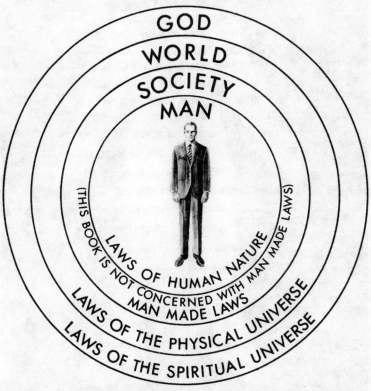

To discover the nature of man and the laws of that nature, marks the highest of human enterprises. For to solve this problem is to open the way to everything which can be of importance to YOU, to humanity, to human welfare and happiness!

THE LAWS OF LIFE

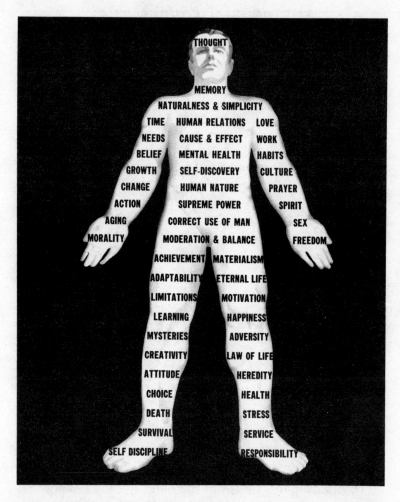

THOUGHT

MEMORY

NATURALNESS & SIMPLICITY

TIME   HUMAN RELATIONS   LOVE

NEEDS   CAUSE & EFFECT   WORK

BELIEF   MENTAL HEALTH   HABITS

GROWTH   SELF-DISCOVERY   CULTURE

CHANGE   HUMAN NATURE   PRAYER

ACTION   SUPREME POWER   SPIRIT

AGING   CORRECT USE OF MAN   SEX

MORALITY   MODERATION & BALANCE   FREEDOM

ACHIEVEMENT   MATERIALISM

ADAPTABILITY   ETERNAL LIFE

LIMITATIONS   MOTIVATION

LEARNING   HAPPINESS

MYSTERIES   ADVERSITY

CREATIVITY   LAW OF LIFE

ATTITUDE   HEREDITY

CHOICE   HEALTH

DEATH   STRESS

SURVIVAL   SERVICE

SELF DISCIPLINE   RESPONSIBILITY

The forty-seven segments of man's nature are each man's sole responsibility for his harmonious development, happiness, health and prosperity. When working in concert like a great symphony orchestra, THE LAWS OF LIFE CAN PRODUCE THE HARMONY, QUALITY AND ENJOYMENT FOR THE HIGHEST AND BEST LIFE KNOWN.

AUTHOR'S FOREWORD

The business of living is the most important business in the world for every one of us. Yet we come into the world unprepared, without a set of instructions for living. We must find the guidelines we need in the observation of life itself, and in the examination of our own human nature.

Unfortunately, in much of society today, the business of living seems to be going bankrupt. Man gropes blindly for new goals, new answers, new solutions to the secrets of life and the meaning of his own existence. In his search he has become a technological giant, while remaining a spiritual pygmy. Even the most casual survey of the world around us—a world torn by anxieties and self-doubt, by depression and despair, by confrontation and alienation, by violence committed in the name of peace—makes it painfully obvious that our enormous technological prowess has brought no clear and certain answers to the most basic and important needs of man's mind and soul.

THE SUPREME PHILOSOPHY OF MAN finds those answers not in technology or fads of popular thought, but in man's own nature, written into the very structure of his being, into his tissues, his nerve cells, his very bloodstream. They are the keys to an abundant, rewarding life. With the understanding and use of these secrets of our nature, despair will give way to hope, confusion to conviction, dissatisfaction to optimism.

For if a man knows how he is designed and for what purposes, all of life's choices and methods for living will then be based upon known, proven, universally applicable truths, laws documented by the whole course of man's history. Acting in accordance with these laws becomes the highest form of wisdom. Man can then actively cooperate with the essential laws of his nature to create for himself the most fruitful, enlightened and wholesome life imaginable. His full potential for personal success will be realized.

Here, then, is a blueprint for man's most important creation: his own life. Here are the fundamental laws of man's nature, forty-seven essential LAWS OF LIFE which are as close to all of us as our hands and feet, but recognized and used by very few. Here are the unseen forces that determine the very quality of life.

Ask yourself: Am I getting the most out of life? What can I contribute to life? What changes do I need to make in myself to make my life worthwhile? What are the true values of life? How can I increase the quality and enjoyment of my life? These are some of the questions THE SUPREME PHILOSO-PHY OF MAN answers for you, finding in the natural laws of life the deepest meanings of human existence.

This is not a philosophy for the ivory tower, remote from everyday living. Rather it is a philosophy for the street and the store, the office and the factory, the home and the school— a practical philosophy that embraces the whole of life. Every man, every day of his life, experiences the effects of these LAWS OF LIFE. The Law of Cause and Effect is as real and practical as the Law of Gravity. So is the Law of Thought, the Law of Belief, the Law of Choice, and the other funda-mental realities of human nature.

Using these LAWS OF LIFE as the foundation for a work-ing philosophy offers you guidance for your judgments, help in your everyday activities, answers to the problems and strug-gles now confronting you in every aspect of your life. When you work in harmony with them, they become your greatest friend; when you work against them, you become your own prosecuting attorney, judge, jury and hangman. Unless a man has learned these basic laws he will always remain ignorant of THE MOST IMPORTANT THING OF ALL . . . HOW TO CONDUCT HIMSELF SO THAT HE MIGHT RICHLY LIVE. A man is RICH or POOR, HAPPY or SAD, depending on how effectively he uses the laws of his own nature.

Man is endowed with certain powers, faculties and abilities. Each man is responsible for their proper use, misuse, or neglect. It is each man's responsibility and duty to himself, to his world, and to the External Power to which he owes his existence, to develop these talents in keeping with the laws of his nature. In so doing he will learn to govern his temper, subdue his appetites, refine his emotions, inform his mind, and increase his understanding.

Experience with thousands of people convinces me that most of us want happiness, peace of mind, health, zestful energy, and financial security. These are the goals to which active co-operation with the LAWS OF LIFE can lead us. When working in concert like a great symphony orchestra, the LAWS OF LIFE can produce the harmony, quality and enjoyment which are the attributes of the highest and best life known.

THE SUPREME PHILOSOPHY OF MAN presents these laws in a unique form, easily understood and applied directly to the business of living. We do not claim our treatment of this monumental subject is complete; the study of man's nature is a lifelong pursuit. But we know from experience that the laws herein unfolded are sound and they work in practice. The LAWS OF LIFE constitute one of the highest and most beneficial studies to which the human mind and soul can turn. These laws should be taught in the schools. TO BUILD A MAN IS THE GREATEST AND NOBLEST PROJECT ON EARTH.

Emerson wrote, "Few men find themselves before they die." This book is dedicated to you in the hope that you may learn from these pages to discover your valuable personal resources while your best years still lie ahead of you, and through that discovery enjoy a useful, happy, gracious and well-ordered life. Our book speaks to your soul and mind . . . but if you would understand it fully you must also bring to it an open heart.

May you LIVE, BE, AND HAVE THE BEST.

CHISLEHURST
1970   *Alfred Armand Montapert*

NATURAL LAWS

When you work within the framework of the natural law, it has to work.

It doesn't matter if it is a physical, mental or spiritual law.

It can be the law of gravity, the law of electricity, the law of chemistry, the law of physics, the law of thought, the law of prayer, the law of aging or the law of death.

The law of Cause and Effect operates in the moral, mental, and spiritual realms, just as surely as it does on the physical plane where we all see and understand it.

TABLE OF CONTENTS

AUTHOR'S FOREWORD 9
TABLE OF CONTENTS 13
PREFACE TO THE LAWS OF LIFE 16

Segment THE FUNDAMENTAL LAWS OF MAN'S NATURE

1	CAUSE AND EFFECT, Action and Reaction	21
2	THOUGHT, Mind	27
3	WORK	33
4	BELIEF, Faith	38
5	ATTITUDE	43
6	SURVIVAL	47
7	GROWTH	53
8	LEARNING, Knowledge, Education	57
9	CHOICE, Judgment	63
10	SUPREME POWER	69
11	SELF-DISCOVERY, Self-Development	75
12	LIVING	81
13	MATERIALISM, Values	87
14	MYSTERIES	93
15	NATURALNESS AND SIMPLICITY	97
16	ADAPTABILITY, Adjustment	100
17	ACTION	105
18	MODERATION	108
19	CORRECT USE OF MAN	113
20	CHANGE	119
21	HABIT	125
22	ADVERSITY, Suffering	130

14

Segment THE FUNDAMENTAL LAWS OF MAN'S NATURE

23	MOTIVATION	135
24	HUMAN NATURE	139
25	SUCCESS, Achievement	145
26	HAPPINESS, Joy	151
27	RESPONSIBILITY	155
28	TIME	159
29	LIMITATIONS	162
30	CREATIVITY	167
31	HEALTH	171
32	CULTURE	175
33	HEREDITY AND ENVIRONMENT	179
34	SERVICE	183
35	MORALITY, Ethics, Conduct	187
36	NEEDS	191
37	SELF-DISCIPLINE	195
38	PRAYER, Meditation	199
39	SEX	203
40	MENTAL HEALTH	207
41	LOVE	211
42	MEMORY	217
43	HUMAN RELATIONS	221
44	SOUL, Spirit	227
45	FREEDOM, Peace, Security	231
46	AGING, Old Age	235
47	DEATH, Eternity	239
48	TO SUM UP	244

THE
SUPREME
PHILOSOPHY
OF
MAN

The QUALITY of every person's life is DETERMINED BY THE KNOWLEDGE OF, and USE OF, the NATURAL LAWS which are built into the very structure of man's nature. To discover and obey these laws is the highest of human enterprises.

Man has to suffer or enjoy the consequences of his acts, as these unseen forces or laws pervade the universe. He may be rewarded or punished — depending upon his actions. God's universe is geared to righteousness.

The life history of every man documents the effect these laws have on our lives.

Of all the studies to which man devotes his time and attention; the Study of Life, the Reason, the Whys and Wherefores of our being, and the Laws that Govern, is by all means the most important. WE NEED TO REVIEW THE NATURAL LAWS OF MAN'S NATURE FOR THEY ARE THE ONLY SOUND STARTING POINT TO THE RIGHT AND BASIC WAY TO EVERY MAN'S BETTERMENT!

PREFACE TO THE LAWS OF LIFE

In today's turbulent world, one question stands out above all the rest: Why can't we find the answers to our growing mass of human problems?

One basic reason is that we tend to deal with effects instead of seeking out and correcting causes.

In his quest to solve his problems, man overlooks the obvious . . . his own nature. All of our problems stem from the nature of man. To solve these problems is to open the way to everything which can be of importance to YOU, to humanity — to human welfare and happiness.

Very few people realize that our whole universe — the sun, the moon, the stars, the earth and everything on earth — is controlled by unseen forces which we call Natural Laws. This book is concerned only with those natural laws which affect MAN'S NATURE. These are the root causes of everything that happens to him, good or bad — success, riches, friendship, happiness — OR disaster.

In this troubled era man looks everywhere except into his own nature in his quest for solutions to his escalating problems. Yet it is in human nature that the answers are to be found for all men everywhere. THE SUPREME PHILOSOPHY OF MAN spells out these basic laws . . . demonstrates in practical language how the precepts of God built into our natures direct our lives and determine our destinies. These LAWS OF LIFE are one of the highest studies to which the human mind can turn, for to BUILD A MAN IS LIFE'S GREATEST PROJECT . . . FOR EACH OF US.

All knowledge, as Plato pointed out, exists only that man shall discover his own Divine Nature. Each individual is responsible for his own spiritual development, which is the foundation for the highest and best life known on this earth.

EACH MAN IS BROUGHT TO TRUE KNOWLEDGE BY THE REFINEMENT AND DISCIPLINE OF HIS OWN NATURE. Every sensible man, in any line of learning, takes advantage of all that has been found and tested.

The favorite exhortation of Socrates, the Greek philosopher of nearly 2500 years ago, was "Know thyself." Aristotle phrased this in a slightly different way when he observed "The best study of man is man." Today the average man knows more about his automobile than he does about himself. WE HAVE LOST OUR CONCEPTION OF OUR NATURE WITH ITS DIVINE DIMENSIONS.

Education has failed to teach that every man is brought to true knowledge by the refinement and discipline of his own nature. In these so-called days of enlightenment very few people know or understand the laws of man's nature. Yet nature's laws are SUPREME. We cannot change them. Ignorance of these laws is responsible for one man's foot on another man's neck. WITH THE TRUE KNOWLEDGE OF NATURE'S LAWS YOU HAVE THE BASIS FOR ALL REAL SUCCESS AND THE KEY TO WISDOM, THE KNOW-HOW FOR BETTER LIVING.

A man is rich or poor, happy or sad, depending how he uses these laws of his own nature. Before the discovery of the law governing the use of electricity, this great force was lying dormant throughout the universe. Man has first to discover and use the law before he could turn it to his advantage. Just so with the Laws of Life.

There is a sense of solidity about the NATURAL LAWS which belongs to nothing else in the world. Here, at last, amid all that is shifting, is one thing sure; one thing outside ourselves, unbiased, unprejudiced, uninfluenced by like or dislike, by doubt or fear; one thing that holds on its way to be eternally incorruptible and undefiled. In these laws one stands face to face with truth, solid and unchangeable.

From time immemorial God's problem has been to get man to look from His viewpoint, obey His unseen forces or Natural Laws. Man's failure in this particular is the reason for the condition of the world today.

This book will give you HOPE, give you the ANSWERS for your own life, in crystal clear language.

THE NATURAL LAWS OF LIFE

1. The whole universe including Man is controlled by unseen forces called Natural Laws. The whole universe is geared to righteousness. All of the natural laws lend themselves to this.

2. The universe is orderly. What if the sun had free choice like man, and would rise at midnight or sleep till noon, or go on strike? Nature, which has no choice, is dependable, responsible. The whole universe operates on Law and Order, the days, the seasons, the sun, moon, stars, gravity, electricity, chemistry, physics, etc.

3. But Man . . . who has the power of free choice, has disobeyed the natural laws and has messed things up badly. Crime, terror, deterioration, and disaster are the result.

4. The only way man will ever get out of this mess is to return to and obey the Natural Laws, which are the basic cure, the answer. BUT the cry today is "Do your own thing!"

5. It is man disobeying Natural Laws and the myriad of man made laws that is causing man to have one foot on the other man's neck. Today we have an infinite network of man made laws managed by a vast hierarchy of attorneys and politicians.

6. If man obeyed the Natural Laws he would not need all the complicated laws and theories which he has built up. Don't fight nature, use it, cooperate with it. Man has gotten further and further away from nature and Natural Laws.

7. When man cooperates and gradually conquers himself, and when all virtues are brought together, we will have a gentle and gracious person, full of love and joy.

This is a book that can be read and reread. The reader clearly sees the difference between POSSESSIONS and TREASURES.

Possessions are outside of you — one can be loaded with possessions and empty inside, even miserable. TREASURES ARE inside of you. You feel the warmth and indwelling Presence of God in your life. "Greater is HE that is in you, than he that is in the world." God is greater than any problem you have, or ever will have. God is the Greatest power in the Universe. There is a BIG DIFFERENCE between POSSESSIONS and HEAVENLY TREASURES, and — like love — they cannot be defined but must be experienced.

Spiritual life is the emancipation of what we are. Through spiritual life we become responsive to God. On that level, and on that level only, does man find release for his highest powers and qualities.

Man today will protest that he has risen from primitive man to the highly civilized, cultured man that he is today. But we ask, what have we accomplished for the good of man's life, for the good of his soul? Have we eased his mind? Have we produced harmony and serenity within?

It is natural for man to overlook the obvious. Goethe said: *"The last law man will learn will be the laws of his own nature."* In our so-called enlightened generation very few people even know the laws of their own nature. Yet most of our problems stem from the nature of man.

TRUE LIVING IS LIFE UNDER LAW. Man flowing through the universe upon the currents of Divine Law, like a ship moving on the great currents of the ocean. The wise man does not desire to escape from Law, but aspires to perfect harmony with it. *"Fishes,"* said Confucius, *"are born in water, man is born in the Law. If fishes find ponds they thrive; if a man lives obediently in the Law he will live his life in peace.*

We are living in a universe of immutable Laws, whether we know them or not, and the unknown is just as lawful as the known.

— *Alfred Armand Montapert*

THIS IS NATURE'S DICTUM:

"Man must live in harmony with the Laws of Life."

HEREIN ARE THE FUNDAMENTAL LAWS OF HUMAN
NATURE . . . THE UNSEEN FORCES THAT
DETERMINE MAN'S LIFE

Segment 1

THE LAW OF CAUSE AND EFFECT....
....ACTION AND REACTION

"WHATSOEVER a man soweth . . . that shall he also reap." Never was there given to the world a more important phrase. "THAT SHALL HE ALSO REAP."

This is the essence of the inexorable, unchangeable law of cause and effect.

IT IS THE ETERNAL LAW OF NATURE THAT THERE CAN BE NO EFFECT WITHOUT A CAUSE.

We must reap what we sow. This is the prime law in our life. This is the keystone of our life. To disregard this law is as stupid as it would be to step off the roof of a forty-story building with the cynical remark, "To hell with the Law of Gravitation." Or to plant sunflower seeds and confidently expect a crop of potatoes.

Things do not just happen, as many people think, they come to pass, and are the result of our thoughts, actions, deeds. If we make mistakes in life we will pay the price. WE ARE THE ARBITERS OF OUR OWN DESTINY. THINGS WHICH WE ALLOW TO LODGE IN HEART AND LIFE ARE THE SEED, AND THE SEED WILL MATURE A HARVEST ACCORDING TO THE LAW OF "LIKE PRODUCES LIKE." The Law of Life is . . . all seed must reproduce according to type.

Our whole world is busy applying Band-Aids to the effects of our problems, when we should be doing major surgery on the causes. Many of us deal with the effect instead of the cause. To eliminate the effect you must remove the cause. Things do not come neatly labeled "cause" and "effect," we have to decide for ourselves where to pin the labels. The answers are spelled out in this book. Remember this, that ALMOST EVERYTHING THAT HAPPENS TO YOU, WAS INITIATED BY YOU.

It is the law of cause and effect which decrees that every action in the universe must be followed by an appropriate reaction, and to this there is no exception of any kind, at any time, for any reason. Everything in the universe is subject to this law, and it correlates and corresponds with every other known and accepted law.

Sir Isaac Newton, in discussing the law of action and reaction, said, "Every action is followed by equal reaction." Whatever we send out returns in kind to punish or bless. The "sent out" is the action, the "return in kind" is the reaction. It means we will get out of life what we put into life, no more and no less. In man and in nature, result always follows thought or activity. WHATEVER YOU DO, THINK, OR FEEL WITHIN YOU, WILL ALWAYS BRING ITS CORRESPONDING AFTERMATH.

THE LAW OF CAUSE AND EFFECT OPERATES IN THE MORAL, MENTAL, AND SPIRITUAL REALMS, JUST AS SURELY AS IT DOES ON THE PHYSICAL PLANE WHERE WE ALL SEE AND UNDERSTAND IT. For example, spiritual laws have to do with our thoughts, beliefs, attitudes, and inner values. We will SINK or SOAR according to the choices we make. The things which we harbor in our hearts will mold us into their own image and there is no escape. Life teaches by cause and effect. You touch fire, and it burns you. You love and you feel happy. You hate and you are miserable. You play the fool and you pay the penalty. You seek and you find. One simple law, and it orders all creation!

MAN SHAPES HIS TOMORROWS BY HIS TODAYS. In the scientific laboratory, the scientist knows that when certain chemicals are mixed together, certain results will follow. The same holds true in the field of electricity, in fact everything in the universe has an underlying cause. It is strange that we spend weeks, months, and years learning some law of mechanics, some physical law, and are unconscious of, or give scant thought to the fact that those who violate the laws of nature, must pay the penalty whether they be Pope, Potentate, or Pauper.

Man never breaks these laws, they break him because they cannot be broken, they are inexorable, immutable, irrevocable. There is no excuse for the ignorance of any law, only penalties, or consequences. BUT THE NATURAL LAWS WHEN OBEYED GUARANTEE THE HIGHEST AND BEST LIFE FOR WHICH WE WERE DESIGNED TO LIVE.

WISDOM IS THE FACULTY OF KNOWING WHAT WILL BE THE EFFECT OF A CAUSE. Those of us who are wiser or more farsighted could foresee the effects we witness today from causes we might have tried to prevent. It is the knowledge of the effect of cause that inspires men to write good and instructive books, to develop a better philosophy, or even to erect an historical monument. They know that every good thought and deed, and every reminder of the good thoughts and good deeds of others, will have its beneficial effect upon the minds of future generations.

Books, motion pictures, television, and radio programs produced today, or at least those listened to, or read, will have their effect on those who do read and listen, for years to come and even on our national conduct and economy. Many writers think only of appealing to poor taste regardless of the effect. The reason, of course, is money, for which some people will cause things to be done regardless of the adverse effect upon others.

There is no easy or royal road to anything that is the best. You must sweat to get to the top. That is what hardens your muscles. You must milk the cow to get the milk. You must fight off the bees to get the honey. It is the same with getting the order. The same way with getting the job done. There is no escape from the law of cause and effect.

THIS IS NOT A DREAM WORLD IN WHICH WE LIVE. IT IS A WORLD OF REALITY. UNDERSTAND THE LAW OF CAUSE AND EFFECT. I WILL SUFFER IF I VIOLATE IT. IT BECOMES MY GREATEST FRIEND IF I UNDERSTAND IT.

IT IS A LAW—YOU GET OUT OF LIFE WHAT YOU PUT INTO IT. No more and no less. The lazy man who sleeps till noon cannot expect to get the rewards of the man who is on the job at seven or eight A.M. Quality of life is another aspect—"cream always rises to the top." You develop your quality through refinements. A man is RICH or POOR, HAPPY or SAD, by the law of his own nature.

If a man is promoted to a better job there is a cause. If he loses his job there is a cause. There are many causes that lead to failure. Such is the inevitable law of cause and effect—one of the great fundamental laws of the universe. It is the law which most of us can easily comprehend, and most gallantly ignore.

Consideration of the law of cause and effect should provoke us to carefully consider every thought and action. Likewise, it should motivate us to do something big and worthwhile that will have a lasting effect. Every great philosopher has had his effect on the generation that followed. Everyone should try to leave the woodpile a little higher than he found it. If a cause contains good and constructive thoughts, it will produce good and constructive results. EVERY ACTION IN LIFE HAS A REACTION . . . THIS IS THE LAW OF CAUSE AND EFFECT.

The law of cause and effect has set its bounds and fixed its standards. Seed determines the type, and the harvest reveals the seed sown. Conduct is the outgrowth of character, and character is the prophetic voice that foretells conduct. If you pull a raw deal you will surely get paid for it; if you do a righteous deed you will surely get paid for it. BOTH VICE AND VIRTUE HAVE THEIR OWN PAYMASTERS. Whatever man sends out in word or deed, will return to him; what he gives, he will receive. If he gives hate, he will receive hate; if he gives love he will receive love; if he gives criticism he will be criticized; if he lies he will be lied to; if he cheats he will be cheated.

People want health, happiness, power, and abundance but they fail to understand that all these things are only effects. The cause lies within themselves, brought into outward manifestation through planning, imagination, work, the power of prayer, perseverance, and development.

How about putting this law to work for you? Begin to reap and to secure the end result that you really want. You can. Just sow the right seed or set up the cause that will bring the desired end result. It's up to you. If your circumstances and your life are crowding you, and you want to change your circumstances, you need only change yourself.

Too often, man has tried to ignore or legislate out of existence the fundamental truth—that one must plant before he reaps, that one must earn before he spends, that one must learn before he understands. CAUSE AND EFFECT. THE GREATEST TEACHER IN SUCH MATTERS IS THE EARTH, NATURE, LIFE ITSELF.

Those who understand the law of cause and effect have learned the truth that makes men free . . . free from the bondage of ignorance which brings about man's own destruction. HAPPY IS HE WHO HAS SUCCEEDED IN LEARNING THE CAUSE OF THINGS.

LAW OF THOUGHT
"As I think - I am."
MAN'S THOUGHTS DECIDE HIS DESTINY.

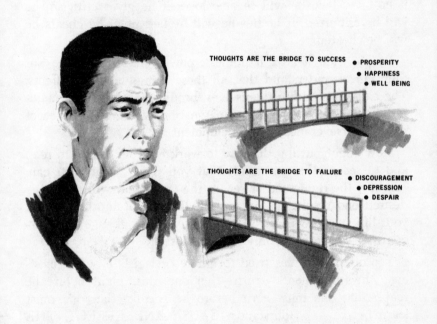

THOUGHTS ARE THE BRIDGE TO SUCCESS
- PROSPERITY
- HAPPINESS
- WELL BEING

THOUGHTS ARE THE BRIDGE TO FAILURE
- DISCOURAGEMENT
- DEPRESSION
- DESPAIR

Thoughts determine success or failure in one's work, study, and daily living. THOUGHTS ARE THE BRIDGE TO SUCCESS OR THE BRIDGE TO FAILURE. We become what we think about. Each of us must live off the fruit of his own thoughts. My present thoughts determine my future.

Segment 2

THE LAW OF THOUGHT

Here is the crux, the core of life . . .
            "AS A MAN THINKETH—SO IS HE."
So simple, but how true, how profound. How few understand
and practice this law of man's nature . . .
            "As you think—so you are."

Life is not determined by outward acts or circumstances.
Each of us creates his own life by his thoughts. Marcus
Aurelius said, "Our life is what our thoughts make it." Emerson
said, "Man is what he thinks." Jesus Christ said, "As a man
thinketh in his heart so is he." A single thought will neither
make nor break a life, BUT A HABIT OF THOUGHT WILL.
We cannot think defeat and be victorious. A fixed habit of
faith is the cure for a worried, troubled heart. We can do more
for or against ourselves than any outside force.

WHAT SETS A MAN APART FROM OTHER FORMS OF
ANIMAL LIFE? It is the ability to think, to reason, to improve his lot. The greatest undeveloped asset in the world
today is man's thinking. Surely it is up to us to at least get our
own thinking on the right basis. No one else can do it for us.

The way you think determines how you live. Every good
thought contributes its share to the ultimate result of your
life. A single thought in the morning may fill the whole day
with joy and sunshine, or with gloom or depression. Many a day
has been dampened by a careless or unkind thought. You will
never be any better or higher than your best thoughts.

That the mind has great power over the body there is not
the slightest doubt. TO CONSCIOUSLY THINK THAT "I
CAN" IMPELS THE SUBCONSCIOUS FACULTIES INTO
ACTION. LIFE IS FORMED FROM THE INSIDE OUT.
WHAT I AM INSIDE DETERMINES THE ISSUES IN THE
BATTLE OF LIFE.

I have heard men say, "THOUGHTS ARE THINGS." THAT IS STOPPING TOO SOON. "THOUGHTS ARE THINGS THAT CHANGE US." THOUGHTS ARE THE TRANSFORMING POWER RELEASED IN OUR LIVES. Otherwise what does the Bible mean when it says, "As a man thinketh in his heart, so is he." He is bound to follow his thoughts. That's why it is mighty important business, when we come to the selecting of our thoughts that we are going to allow to dominate our life.

The Apostle Paul talks about "being transformed ·by the renewing of your mind." There is really no other way to be transformed. When we are exhorted to reconsider—to think differently—he means we are to change our thinking. Why? Because thoughts are the transforming power released in our lives. THIS IS THE ONLY WAY YOU CAN GET YOUR LIFE CHANGED, BY CHANGING YOUR THINKING. THOUGHTS ARE POWER RELEASES. RIGHT OR WRONG, THEY ARE POWER RELEASES. They are bound to mold us and dominate us.

You can not become great and think small—neither can you remain small and think great. THOUGHT IS THE ORIGINAL SOURCE OF ALL WEALTH, ALL SUCCESS, ALL MATERIAL GAIN, ALL GREAT DISCOVERIES AND INVENTIONS, AND OF ALL ACHIEVEMENT. GOOD THOUGHTS MUST BE COUPLED WITH RIGHT METHODS IF WE WOULD ACHIEVE DESIRED RESULTS.

Our personal body chemistry is guided and triggered by our emotions; but thought leads the emotions. YOU CAN MAKE YOURSELF SICK, POOR, AND UNHAPPY BY YOUR HABITUAL THINKING. You can even kill yourself by your thoughts. Dr. Gene Emmet Clark calls negative thoughts "the world's most communicable disease." Worry is an obsession, a mania, a hallucinatory state usually superinduced by—dare I say it?—UNBELIEF. Worry never righted a wrong, dried a tear or lifted a burden. On the contrary, it has slain its tens of thousands. The cure for worry is a heart of faith.

People are probably more careless with their thoughts than anything else. We do not allow friends who visit us at our home to dwell upon the negative. If the subject is controversial we'd rather they discussed it elsewhere. Dwelling upon the negative is not the way to live so that you enjoy life. Change the subject, talk about constructive things, invest your time, don't merely spend it. Life is too short to be little, look at the bright side of life. People do not realize that it is a law that you become what you dwell upon.

Several years ago when my company was building and installing elevators, I had an appointment with the construction company and the owners of the newest and largest hotel in Beverly Hills. This hotel was under construction and was ready to open within a month. I was early for the appointment so I walked through the entire building. During the meeting nothing but the negative was discussed. At the close of the meeting I remarked, "Why doesn't someone say something good about this lovely place? I think it is just fabulous. Why do people talk and complain about the one or two percent that is not perfect, and which can easily be corrected, but do not say a word about the ninety-eight percent that is beautiful and good?" From that meeting on, the owners changed and started talking about the beauty and elegance of the building.

If you would change your condition and situation in life you must change your thinking. Let us accept as truth—"As a man thinketh, so is he." Thoughts can be constructive or destructive. Fear, grief, worry, anger, jealousy, and other negative thoughts are destructive. ALWAYS REMEMBER, THE ONLY PERSON THAT CAN HURT YOU, IS YOU! Thoughts of joy and happiness, and all that is good are constructive. OBEDIENCE PRECEDES AUTHORITY, AND THE LAW OBEYS MAN, WHEN HE OBEYS THE LAW. The law of electricity must be obeyed before it becomes man's servant. When handled ignorantly it becomes man's deadly foe. JUST SO WITH THE LAWS OF MIND.

Never allow yourself to become so anxious about your future that you lose sleep and fall into the grip of fear. Cleanse your mind before sleep, put good thoughts into your mind. The conscious is going out and the unconscious mind is taking over. Victor Hugo put it this way: "When you go to bed at night, have for your pillow these three things—love, confidence, and joy. And you will waken in the morning with a song in your heart." This is one of the reasons I wrote DISTILLED WISDOM, one of the best bed books on the market. By filling the subconscious mind with edifying wholesome thoughts, they are acting upon you while you sleep and becoming part of you. Result: a positive, cultured person.

Napoleon told a group of recruits, who were full of fear, that they were brave and would be strong fighters in the first battle. He encouraged them and encouragement is oxygen to the soul. Tell yourself repeatedly that you can conquer all your difficulties. You become what you strongly think, feel, affirm.

STATE OF MIND IS ALSO A VERY IMPORTANT FACTOR IN SUCCESS. You can condition your mind to a point where it enables or prevents you from going forward and doing things. You can poison your mind and limit your own capacity. The mind is the supreme, originating, constructive force in all human endeavor. Right mental culture is a direct means to refinement and nobility of life. Your mental powers are comprehension, feeling, reflection, conscience, method, observation, comparison, will, intuition, memory, judgment, concentration, imagination, reason, perception, analysis.

The happiness of your life depends upon the quality of your thoughts. Thinking is only a process of talking to oneself intelligently. YOU TALK TO YOURSELF ALL THE TIME, BE CAREFUL WHAT YOU SAY. What can I do to fulfill this law of thought? Think constructive, wholesome thoughts. Be a positive person, not a negative person. WE BECOME WHAT WE THINK. WE BECOME WHAT WE DWELL UPON. THIS IS A LAW OF LIFE.

The Principle: YOU MOVE TOWARD THAT UPON WHICH YOU DWELL. YOU TEND TO BECOME LIKE THAT WHICH YOU THINK ABOUT MOST VIVIDLY, MOST REPEATEDLY, MOST INTENSELY, AND MOST IMAGINATIVELY.

THE MORE WE CONTEMPLATE AND STUDY THOUGHT, THE MORE WE REALIZE WHAT A TER- RIFIC FORCE IT IS, AND HOW UNLIMITED ARE ITS POWERS. Ralph Waldo Emerson declared that the ancestor of every action is thought. When we understand that, we be- gin to comprehend that our world is governed by thought and that everything without had its counterpart originally within the mind. It is just as Buddha said many centuries ago: "ALL THAT WE ARE IS THE RESULT OF WHAT WE HAVE THOUGHT."

All rewards in this life are for right thinking and acting. If we think right we will act right. NO ONE CAN ENJOY LIVING UNLESS HE HAS A POSITIVE STATE OF MIND. How wonderful life is every day when we apply ourselves positively to the task at hand. Maintaining a positive attitude puts you in a position where you can overcome practically all of the negative things that come your way in life.

Never at any time get yourself into a negative state of mind, or allow a friend to lead you to a point of agreeing to anything that is negative. Do not pick up any "hot bricks." The minute you enter into negative thoughts, they have pulled you down. This is a practical law, proven over and over again. Never lose that positive attitude, the positive mind you have. A POSITIVE APPROACH TO LIFE IS A CARDINAL POINT FOR SUC- CESSFUL DYNAMIC LIVING.

MAN'S GREATNESS LIES IN HIS POWER OF THOUGHT. Success is not an accident. Flooding the mind with positive thoughts is an established mental procedure with successful men and women in every walk of life. Acquire the habit of substituting positive ideas for negative ones, and grad- ually your life will become more and more successful.

Man lives in two spheres:

**His vocational
or WORK
LIFE**

**and his
PERSONAL
LIFE.**

There are obviously two educations. One should teach us how to EARN A LIVING and the other HOW TO LIVE. The wise person seeks to achieve harmony between both.

Segment 3

THE LAW OF WORK

"Work is the inevitable condition of human life, the true source of human welfare."—Leo Tolstoy

"LEARN TO LIKE YOUR WORK" IS THE FIRST LAW OF SUCCESS AND HAPPINESS IN LIFE. In life we are all cut out to work. Work is man's divine heritage. If you want food, you must toil for it; if knowledge, you must toil for it; if pleasure you must toil for it; toil is the law.

Work is a kind of psychological glue which holds a man together. There is no state which unconditionally guarantees security. The law of our world, physical, social, mental and spiritual, is the homely, almost crude dictum pronounced upon a certain two-toed animal: ROOT HOG! OR DIE.

Man devotes nearly half his waking hours to work. Work is a paradox, simultaneously a curse, and a blessing. Man works when he is hungry and it is equally obvious that he continues to work when he is well-fed, well-clothed, well-housed. Man cannot free himself from work, nor would he do so, if he could. Abraham Lincoln was not great because he split rails. He was great because he'd split rails rather than be idle while on his way to greatness. A wise man said, "YOUR LIFE'S WORK IS YOUR STATUE. You cannot get away from it. It is beautiful or hideous, lovely or ugly, inspiring or debasing, as you make it."

Eighteen hundred years ago the great Galen observed that doing things with one's hands releases nervous tension and relieves the oppressed mind. Everyone needs the discipline of work. This may or may not be actual physical labor. It is the direction of accomplishment in the cycle of the day, and is necessary for our well being.

Someone asked a successful man the secret of his success.
"I'll tell you," he replied, "it was a small trick I always played
on myself. I pretended that I owned the business. No matter
where I worked, I pretended I owned the place, lock, stock,
and barrel."

V. M. Burrows warns us that "One of the saddest experiences
which can ever come to a human being is to awaken, grey-
haired and wrinkled, near the close of an unproductive career,
to the fact that all through the years he has been using only a
small part of himself."

Sixty years ago there was no automobile industry, there
were no airplanes, no home radios or television, no electric re-
frigerators. Most houses were lit with kerosene lamps or gas.
Time was when most of the people who worked were unskilled workers. Those were the days when life was comparatively simple. Times have changed so much that we find we
have to have specialized training of some kind, in addition to
a good educational background, if we are going to get the
best jobs and the best pay. The big demand today is for skilled
workers. But money isn't everything. You are happiest when
you are doing something you like to do, something you are
good at. And when people are good at something, they usually want to be as good as they can at it. That means special
training.

Why work? Because we need to. It is a need almost as
necessary as physical hunger. I need the discipline of a demanding job. I need to express myself in a meaningful effort.
I need to share with others the products of any skills or
energies I possess. I need to feel needed, so I work, which
engages a man's mind and hand, and is a safeguard against
depraved inclinations. Many benefits are derived from work
well done, it brings the greatest form of happiness and satisfaction one will ever know. Other by-products of work are
health, stability, character, and wealth.

Charles Kingsley writes: "Thank God every morning when you get up that you have something to do which must be done, whether you like it or not. Being forced to work, and forced to do your best, will breed in you temperance, self-control, diligence, strength of will, and a hundred other virtues which the idle never know."

A wise father told his son: "Nothing is ever accomplished without work. If I leave you nothing else but the WILL TO WORK, I leave you the most priceless gift—the joy of work." This father knew enough about life to know that the world did not owe him a living or anything else until he had put the world in debt to him. His was the root-hog-or-die philosophy of life—the only sensible, workable philosophy of life that has ever been written by man. "By the sweat of thy brow" is the established order.

I wonder how many times lately you've used the word "FUN" in talking about your work? It's a pleasure to meet a man who seems to enjoy thoroughly what he is doing.

I've met many men doing challenging jobs they unconsciously expressed as fun. Over the years one learns that in the University of Hard Knocks, there is nothing more substantial than what we know as the joy of accomplishment. Great men are not an accident; they are a result.

I have never known a successful man who achieved his place in life by working at a job he disliked. True, there may be many distasteful duties to perform; long, tedious hours of drudgery to endure, and discouragement piled upon discouragement; but a mature person, who basically enjoys what he is doing, has learned to expect occasional setbacks and will take them in his stride, with never a thought of giving up. When people recognize that careful planning and hard work ARE KEYS TO ACHIEVEMENT—material, intellectual, and spiritual—then it is much easier to overcome the natural aversion to labor that plagues most human beings.

Nature has everywhere written her protest against idleness; everything which ceases to struggle, which remains inactive, rapidly deteriorates. It is the struggle toward an ideal, the constant effort to reach higher and further, which develops manhood and character.

A person planning on retirement must plan to have some hobby or a vocation, something to keep him occupied BOTH mentally and physically. How rapidly a man decays when he retires from active life. The most unhappy people on earth are those who have nothing worthwhile to occupy them, and this applies equally well to the "hobo" at the bottom of the social scale and the wealthy "club woman" at the top. Congenial and useful work is the secret of mental and physical well-being. Anything that is to be kept in good condition must be exercised. Work is the great regulator of the human machine. Idleness has always and everywhere bred mischief—physically, mentally, and morally. Better, my friend, infinitely better, that you attempt a great deal and accomplish half you attempt than to attempt nothing and accomplish—nothing.

We advance in the school of life according to ability and inclination, moved forward by the gentle but insistent proddings of the greatest of all teachers—the law of necessity. At the end of the day when one reflects on a good day's work, it gives one a good feeling and a sense of satisfaction. Work is one of the greatest forms of happiness that can be obtained. Examples: a surgeon laboring to save a life; an electronics engineer after toiling to clear some complicated trouble; a writer finishing a new book; a salesman finally getting the nice orders; a craftsman completing a difficult job; a tired businessman going over all his accomplishments at the end of the day.

BLESSED IS THE MAN WHO HAS SOME CONGENIAL WORK, SOME OCCUPATION IN WHICH HE CAN PUT HIS HEART, AND WHICH AFFORDS A COMPLETE OUTLET TO ALL THE FORCES THAT ARE IN HIM.

MAN COMES INTO THE WORLD IN DEBT AND HE DIES OWING A BIGGER DEBT. He is born in debt because so many have sacrificed for the conditions he has. Doctors, scientists, educators, inventors, workmen have pioneered many of the comforts he enjoys; and there are men who have fought and died for his freedom. His health, his brain, his special capacity, these he has inherited, they are a gift of humanity. He dies with a greater debt because many helped him in his journey through life. He himself is supposed to make a contribution while he is here as a CREATIVE BEING and is supposed to advance the art of living to some degree by having lived.

Render a service if you would succeed. This is the supreme law of life. Be among the great servers, the benefactors for the good of man. It is the only path to success. "Give and it shall be given unto you." Make society your debtor and you may find your place among the immortals.

WHAT DO I CONTRIBUTE IN LIFE TO JUSTIFY MY EXISTENCE? George Bernard Shaw offered this cure for the problem of human society: "A proposal that every citizen should be required to appear at reasonable intervals before a properly qualified jury to justify his existence. If he could not justify it, his existence would be swiftly and efficiently terminated."

The immortal words of St. Paul have been a challenge and great inspiration to all. At the end of the road we all want to be able to feel that "I HAVE FOUGHT A GOOD FIGHT, I HAVE FINISHED THE COURSE—I HAVE KEPT THE FAITH."

THE SUM TOTAL OF EACH MAN'S VALUE IS MEASURED BY THE GOOD HE DOES IN THE WORLD. Let every man be occupied, and occupied in the highest employment of which his nature is capable, and die with the consciousness that he has done his best. Horace Mann says, "BE ASHAMED TO DIE UNTIL YOU HAVE WON SOME VICTORY FOR HUMANITY."

Segment 4

THE LAW OF BELIEF

"In belief lies the secret of all valuable exertion."—Bulwer-Lytton

The Law of Belief will work no matter where it is applied and that goes for everything from bowling to money-making, or success in business. Often belief enables a person to do what others think impossible. IT IS THE ACT OF BELIEVING THAT IS THE STARTING FORCE OR GENERATING POWER THAT LEADS TO ACCOMPLISHMENT.

YOUR BELIEF IS A LAW OR FORCE THAT CAN WORK FOR OR AGAINST YOU. Intelligent, positive belief has the factors that create a good or healthy result. Thus people with strong cheerful resolutions get over illness faster, heal faster and live on against unsurmountable odds. Unintelligent negative belief has the factors that result in distasteful and unhappy results. Intelligent belief makes firm faith. Unintelligent belief always makes for instability.

William James said, "Our belief at the beginning of a doubtful undertaking is the one thing that assures the successful outcome of any venture." Every great achievement in science, in business, in architecture, in art, in education, or in religion has depended a great deal on belief, convictions, and courage.

Faith is one of the greatest forces of life. It is to our human world what electricity is to the physical world. "Obey the law of the power and the power will obey you," is a wise and true saying. To believe is to be happy; to doubt is to be wretched. To believe is to be strong. BELIEF IS POWER. Only so far as a man believes strongly, mightily, can he act cheerfully, or do anything that is worth the doing.

38

Belief will supply the power which will enable you to succeed in everything you undertake. Back your belief with a resolute will and you become unconquerable—a master of men among men—yourself. It's the belief or the basic confidence within you that brings outward or material results.

EXPECTANCY MARKS THE MAN OF FAITH. We draw to us the things which we expect. There is no true prayer without expectancy, and expectancy is prayer uttered or unexpressed. Expect much and you shall receive much. Expect little and your life will remain little, restricted and shallow. IT IS NOT PRAYER BY ITSELF THAT COUNTS, IT IS THE BELIEF AND FAITH THAT THE HEART OF US EXERCISES THAT GETS RESULTS.

Faith is the method of maintaining, or establishing and maintaining contact with God. Just as the light switch on the wall establishes the contact to the source of electric power from the power house, "FAITH" gives to the individual all of God's reserve power. Fact is, it is actually contact with God, and the actual contact is the establishing power released in life. THAT IS FAITH. Apart from faith, the universe is an inexplicable riddle.

Down through the ages faith in God has been an all-powerful force in the lives of men . . . it has been a never failing source of strength in time of trouble. All of the great and lasting movements of civilization have been dedicated to, and founded upon, faith in a Supreme Power.

Recognition of a Supreme Power and dependence upon that power for guidance is contained in the Declaration of Independence and in our national and state constitutions. So strong was their faith in God that our forebears caused to be stamped on our coins the words "In God We Trust." To these founding fathers . . . to these men who signed the Declaration of Independence and the Constitution . . . to these men who pioneered our land . . . this phrase had real meaning.

Faith is absolute confidence that our Creator will guide and care for us under any condition so long as we trust Him and use the divine attributes with which we have been endowed. Paul said, "Now faith is assurance of things hoped for, conviction of things unseen."

The problem which everyone has to face, and the older we grow, the more we find and see the shortness of life, is the problem of trying to bring together a faith that can guide us like a compass. We need this compass to take us through the struggles of everyday living. Our greatest problem is like the problem of Job, in the Bible—to construct a faith. This directional finder is to help us keep a steady and unmovable course, so we know where we are going and recognize the shoals and rocks on which we might flounder. We have had our eyes opened. The answer to our problem is to have this faith which is our compass and directional guide.

Faith marches at the head of the army of progress. It is found beside the most refined life, the freest government, the profoundest philosophy, the noblest poetry, the purest humanity. The late Roger Babson said, "The greatest undeveloped resource in our country is FAITH, the greatest unused power is PRAYER."

Practically all of the outstanding men of history believed in God, in themselves, and in the future of the human race. We are living in an age when people in great numbers have lost their faith. Man has turned to other elements of existence and tried them out as gods; things like capitalism, communism, success, material goals. In frustration man is running away from the simple Biblical faith; and we have chaos, confusion, a spirit of anarchy and nihilism which is frightening. We need faith, faith in ourselves and faith in God. FAITH IS POWER. It moves the inner being, it is confidence in action. The best way to live is to have a strong faith in God. This is much more sustaining than material possessions. THE MOST VALUABLE THING YOU HAVE IS YOUR FAITH IN GOD.

BELIEF and FAITH run beyond an intellectual process and bring the senses in touch, by experience, with a realm beyond the power of the intellect to investigate. Many of the everyday experiences of life are entirely beyond the comprehension of the human intellect. For instance, love, envy, pain, anger, joy, sorrow all belong to, and manifest themselves in the realm of the senses. They are, nevertheless, established as fact. Experience has listed them in the category of classified knowledge.

SCIENCE, BELIEF and FAITH have one thing in common: they deal in facts, and they are concerned exclusively with evidence. This has been worked out in terms of human experience down across the centuries. To you of the scientific turn of mind, let me point out that there is only one thing that establishes a truth as scientific, and that is when it can be so completely demonstrated that you can prove that the law never deviates—then you have science.

The conclusions we come to in this book are the result of PRACTICAL HUMAN EXPERIENCE. In what ways do we arrive at true knowledge? By the law of logic, by the findings of science, and by close observation in the realm of human experience. OF THESE THREE REALMS HUMAN EXPERIENCE IS THE MOST CONCLUSIVE. LIVING EXPERIENCE HAS THE POWER TO COMPEL IDEAS. I am always deeply impressed when someone tells me of things that he has LIVED, instead of offering abstract opinions.

The most scientific of all evidence is experience. Experience is the MOST positive of all knowledge. What we experience we know. There are but three roads over which experience can come to us. We must see, feel, or hear. I have put my sixty years of practical experience with people, problems, and purposes on the line in this book from which all can benefit. There remains one last bit of evidence: the testimony of tens of thousands who have experienced the results of these natural laws in their personal experience.

OUR ATTITUDES CONTROL OUR LIVES

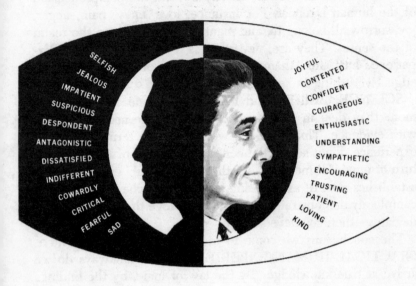

NEGATIVE PERSONALITY RESULTS		POSITIVE PERSONALITY RESULTS	
DRAB	FEAR	ENTHUSIASTIC	SUCCESS
WEAK	WORRY	DECISIVE	RECOGNITION
PESSIMISTIC	TENSION	COURAGEOUS	SECURITY
GREEDY	DESPONDENCY	OPTIMISTIC	ENERGY
IRRITABLE	UNHAPPINESS	CHEERFUL	HAPPINESS
COLD	MOODINESS	CONSIDERATE	HEALTH
RUDE	SICKNESS	COURTEOUS	FRIENDSHIP
INCONSIDERATE	LONELINESS	WARM	LOVE
SOUR	FATIGUE	RELAXED	INNER PEACE

Have a happy loving attitude, a positive attitude is mature
health. This is the best state of psychological and spiritual health
that can be obtained on this earth.

Segment 5

THE LAW OF ATTITUDES

What is attitude? It is basically the way in which you look at life. Everything in your life will depend upon your ATTITUDE. Happiness depends not on things around you, but on your ATTITUDE. This is an important law to remember.

Our attitudes control our lives. Attitudes are a secret power working twenty-four hours a day, for good or bad. It is of paramount importance that we know how to harness and control this great force. MENTAL ATTITUDES ARE MORE IMPORTANT THAN MENTAL CAPACITY. Attitudes affect the body, we create the climate in and around us by our attitudes. Have a beautiful, warm, and friendly attitude.

Seneca, the Roman sage, said: "A man may rule the world and still be unhappy, if he does not FEEL that he is supremely happy."

How beautiful is the world in which you live? Why, it's just as beautiful as your mental attitude. Make up your mind that you are going to have an attitude that is happy, confident, zestful, positive, enthusiastic. Humor, more than anything else in the human make-up, can afford an aloofness and an ability to rise above any situation.

Each individual has a tendency either toward a constructive attitude or a negative one. To maintain positive thinking requires constant vigilance and the nourishment of the character through learning and experience.

As a prisoner of war for six years, Dr. Viktor Frankl found that: "Everything can be taken from a man but one thing: the last of human freedoms—TO CHOOSE ONE'S ATTITUDE IN ANY GIVEN SET OF CIRCUMSTANCES, TO CHOOSE ONE'S OWN WAY."

43

The dominating news of today is helping to create a negative image of man. We read and hear of war, crime, violence, civil disobedience and the deterioration of our worthwhile values. Constant exposure to such news cannot help but have an adverse influence upon our generation. Therefore we should be doubly careful about our attitude, so we do not allow ourselves to be pulled down to a lower level. Our attitude is our most important possession.

Two men fail in business. One shoots himself, the other simply smiles and climbs over the ruin of his failure to a more ultimate and aspiring success. The tests of life are to make, not break us. It is not what happens, but our mental reaction that makes for happiness or misery. WE CANNOT CHOOSE THE THINGS THAT WILL HAPPEN TO US. BUT WE CAN CHOOSE THE ATTITUDE WE WILL TAKE TO-WARD ANYTHING THAT HAPPENS. I believe that one's attitude is nine-tenths of life's battles.

Nothing is easier than fault-finding. No talent, no self-denial, no brains, no character is required to set up in the grumbling business. But those that are moved by genuine desire to do good have little time for murmuring or complaint. Some people are always grumbling; if they had been born in the Garden of Eden they would have found much to complain about. Others are happy anywhere—they see the beauties and blessings all around them.

A person's attitude is his mental and moral disposition. It can be, and has to be, trained the same way as anything else. It starts when we arise in the morning. We can get up with the attitude, "This is going to be a bad day;" and truly it will be. Or, "This is going to be another wonderful day;" and it can be, if we try. One should start off each day with a smile and not a scowl. "Let me do all the good I can today, let me not deter, nor neglect it, for I shall not pass this way again." With these words of wisdom try to meet the challenges of each new day and its many tasks.

Feeling, enthusiasm and earnestness are a vital part of the law of attitude. It is used by all the great virtuosos. It is the greatest secret in speaking, singing, selling, teaching . . . and the emphasis is on feeling, enthusiasm, and positive attitude. Your attitudes include the way you look at things, the way you feel about them, and the way you are prepared to act. Naturally, they are the most important part of you.

Clarence B. Randall writes: "The determining factor in effective communication is conviction. The authoritative voice that carries its message straight into the heart of every listener is that of the man who knows exactly what he believes. His utterance simply will not be denied, because it puts straight out from his spirit. Form does not matter. His sentences may not parse; he may commit crudities of pronunciation; his metaphors may lack polish, but people will listen with rapt attention because he believes so earnestly in his cause."

John Ruskin writes: "The ennobling difference between one man and another is that one feels more than another." I always get a gut feeling when something is wrong. All great discoveries are made by men whose feelings run ahead of their thinking. It is in the area of feeling that genius enters the heart and distinguishes the world's great men.

In all the really fundamental issues of life, the final decision is best left to feelings. Today, earnestness is almost a forgotten quality. In the last analysis; earnestness is born of deep, clear, intelligent convictions. It is a fire that burns, a hammer that breaks, a sword that pierces. It becomes contagious enthusiasm which convinces and moves men to act.

THE WORLD IS WAITING, NOT SO MUCH TO HEAR US, AS TO FEEL US. ONLY HEARTS CAN SPEAK TO HEARTS AND IT IS THE LANGUAGE OF THE HEART FOR WHICH MEN ARE LISTENING. WE CAN MAKE OTHERS FEEL ONLY WHAT WE FEEL.

THE LAW OF SURVIVAL

LIFE IS A STRUGGLE FOR ECONOMIC AND PHYSICAL SURVIVAL. Great trials seem to be a necessary preparation for great duties. Conflict creates character. Soft circumstances usually make soft characters. Rugged opponents are our best benefactors. The hardness they thrust on us gives us the hardness we need until that legend of the rough places fulfills itself at last, "Per Aspera Ad Astra", thru hardship to the stars.

Segment 6

THE LAW OF SURVIVAL

Self-preservation is the first law of nature. Years ago, it meant to keep alive. Now we live in a more sophisticated world—but it still means to keep alive. It means physical and mental health, finances to buy food, clothing, and shelter; to keep our body fit with proper food, water, air and clothes.

Voltaire said, "MY LIFE IS A BATTLE." This is still true today—survival is a fight for life. From the beginning of time man has fought against man. Each era has produced its own methods and systems of fighting. For countless centuries the ingenious minds of men have devised newer, better, more effective ways of fighting. Each combatant has tried to outdo the other. The whole history of mankind can be written in terms of human combat; the struggle to survive, defense and destruction. A nuclear war, or some other cataclysmic event now dims man's hopes for survival.

We live in a world of frustration and despair, whose greatest problem is the very question of SURVIVAL. THE GREATEST THING IN THIS WORLD FOR MANKIND IS A COMPLETE UNDERSTANDING OF THE LAWS OF HUMAN NATURE. SUCH AN UNDERSTANDING IS MAN'S ONLY HOPE FOR SURVIVAL. It is not going to do us much good to unravel the nature of the Universe unless we unravel the nature of man. The LAWS OF LIFE, which reveal the dynamic power of man's nature, are given here as a "life line" back to the firm foundations of individual responsibility and intelligent living. Now almost everything we do is harmful to man and works against his survival. Our destruction of our environment seems endless. One of the most important achievements of this New Decade might be the recognition that growth in population, resources, consumption, and waste production CANNOT GO ON INDEFINITELY. We must come to terms with the FINITE capacity of this planet.

Man has to work the biggest part of his life to obtain food and raiment for himself and his family. A dominant thought in the brain of every human being is the thought of how to make his existence secure. Today the American male is on a squirrel wheel struggling to pay his bills. His future is threatened by inflation, higher taxes, and the demands of his family. He is trapped by easy credit. Even the well-to-do feel poor; they earn more but keep less, and their paycheck is punched full of holes by payroll deductions. Property taxes, the cost of living, social security taxes, sales taxes all keep climbing up and up. The costs of services are high. Many wives are leaving the youngsters with a sitter and taking a job to ease financial worries. Medicine costs more, doctor and hospital costs are three times higher than ten years ago.

People today are financially and emotionally unprepared for the unexpected problems. "If you can swallow a toad every morning before breakfast, you have conditioned yourself for the troubles of the day." This is an Old European proverb that is becoming more and more realistic to Americans. Thirty years ago life was comparatively simple and carefree. Most jobs were unskilled. Now a man has to go to school a third of his life and study for the special skills necessary for his livelihood.

EVERYONE SHOULD UNDERSTAND THAT THEY WILL GO THROUGH PERIODS OF SORROW AND PAIN. Their friends and loved ones will die. There is a vacant chair in many a household, this is the way of life. Accidents are always unexpected, always hard to bear. Trials and heartbreaks caused by divorce and separation leave a scar on one's heart. A man's house can burn down, he can lose all his money. This world is full of trouble. NO MAN IS WITHOUT HIS LOAD OF TROUBLE; therefore, man must cultivate the spiritual qualities of his nature, for there is where his real strength and real wealth come from. These qualities are part of his soul and are everlasting, indestructible, and inexhaustible.

Engineers in planning a structure make provision for an ample reserve factor (or safety factor as it is called); they design it to be able to withstand a strain ten to fifteen times as large as anything to which they expect it to be subjected in the ordinary course of its existence. In the realm of human life, likewise, a large reserve factor is of the utmost importance. The crucial factor in survival is not so much the ability to meet the ordinary demand as to successfully cope with unusual circumstances. It is the crises and special emergencies that eliminate. In times of emergency, stress, and strain, every man has to call upon his reserves of ability and power, and those who do not possess such are wiped out.

The sixties, the incredible sixties are past. It was a different kind of decade, an ironic decade—in many ways a paradox. Knowledge and technological achievement soared to unprecedented heights. World trouble and despair sank to unprecedented lows. And the basic problems confronting humanity remained unsolved. By the end of the sixties more people were disturbed, anxious and apprehensive than at any other time in history. During the seventies it could be decided whether mankind will survive or not. It will be shown whether or not humanity can face up to its mistakes and make the necessary sacrifices and changes required for survival. The real solution will depend upon the change of a very basic but complicated ingredient—HUMAN NATURE.

The causes of insecurity always lie within ourselves, but it is easy to ignore or deny this basic fact. There may be times when it appears that we can get along without religion, but a LIFE WITHOUT FAITH IS DEPRIVED OF ITS GREATEST STRENGTH. THE ONLY REAL SECURITY THAT A MAN CAN HAVE IN THIS WORLD IS A SENSE OF GOD, AND A RESERVE OF KNOWLEDGE, EXPERIENCE, AND ABILITY. NATURE is gently but firmly pointing out there is SOMETHING WRONG WITH US. And we in turn, say THERE IS SOMETHING WRONG WITH THE WORLD.

There is nothing wrong with the world. The delinquent creature is man, *homo-sapiens*. The delinquency began when anthropoid man came to the conclusion that he was God, and knew how to run the Universe. He does not, he has not, and he will not. But he is still obstinately trying.

So long as our way of life is unsound, wars will go on. So long as human beings have the psychosis that the main purpose of human existence is the fulfillment of ambition and the accumulation of wealth, there will be no peace on earth. During the past two decades such words as peace, security, and prosperity have become mere catchwords used for the most part by political propagandists. What they forget and what their deluded hearers forget is that these words indicate spiritual problems, and spiritual results cannot be achieved by mechanical means.

You might as well try to bring about an effect without a cause as to try to make a decent, secure, and peaceful world without changing the nature of men. Security, peace and righteousness are not detached problems. What men are, society will be. Only new men can or will build a new world. The Kingdom of God will appear among us when the Kingdom of God is within us. "From within out of the heart" of men proceedeth both good and bad effects and reactions.

Atom bomb stockpiles are no guarantee of security. Until lust and greed and murder are removed from the hearts of men, there is, there can be, no peace or security. Only supernaturally transformed men can or will give the world an answer to the problems of war and crime and unrighteousness. "OUR GREATEST NEED TODAY IS THE DESPERATE NEED FOR SPIRITUAL DEVELOPMENT." Man is raw and wild and needs the spiritual development to tame and discipline the tyrant, or wild beast, that is within. ONE OF THE GREATEST BY-PRODUCTS OF GENUINE SPIRITUAL DEVELOPMENT IS "A GENTLE, HUMBLE HEART." THIS IS GOD'S GOAL FOR EVERY MAN, AND THE BASIC ANSWER TO OUR PROBLEMS.

Our leaders prescribe and promise money to solve the problems of the nation. They have laughed God out of our schools. We have raised a Godless generation and they are now giving us Hell. Man needs God to temper and transform his nature. You can not have darkness and light in the same place at the same time. Just so with man—you can not have righteousness and evil together, you have one or the other.

If every man found personal meaning for his own life our social problems would be minimized to providing for the mentally retarded and mentally disabled. Poverty has always been merely a negative evaluation of certain environmental conditions. But we know, that THE ONLY POOR ARE THE POOR OF SOUL.

Political activity could be minimized if each man accepted fully the responsibility for his own acts and experiences. THERE WOULD BE MORE INNER STRENGTH, AND LESS OUTER DEPENDENCE. MORE EMPHASIS UPON PLACING DUTY FIRST, THEN RIGHTS.

The Church would once again resume its New Testament function and become a place where we bring the richness of a week full of inner experience, and give joy to God for them, and share them with others that all might grow.

Protection seems to be our modern watchword. We are being educated to depend upon others for almost everything. Lean instead of labor, is our slogan. But over-protection is a peril. THE CURSE OF GIVING PEOPLE SOMETHING FOR NOTHING IS, THEY ALWAYS DEMAND MORE AND MORE ON THE SAME TERMS. Strength is built by struggle. Exposure, more often than not, is good fortune. Character is only built by hardship. Tough fiber is only created by exposure to the storm. Survival is only guaranteed to those who never surrender.

Have courage for the sorrows of life and patience for the small ones; and when you have laboriously accomplished your daily task, go to sleep in peace. God is awake.

LAW OF GROWTH
THE OLD MAN AND THE NEW MAN

PROTOTYPE
OLD MAN

We say
goodbye
to you.

You were........

Lacking confidence
Afraid and worried Shy or
self-conscious Guilty of
indecision Feeling sorry for
yourself Concerned about yourself
Habitually belittle yourself
Accustomed to thinking "I can't".
Inclined to put off doing things
Disorganized in your thinking
and doing Constantly
regretting decisions
you made

PROTOTYPE
NEW MAN

The new you
is to be ....

Ready to think, to do,
to know, to live fully
Broad shouldered
Unaware of yourself
Sure at all times
Confident and fearless
Poised in all
circumstances
Prepared to take
things in stride

Segment 7

THE LAW OF GROWTH

What is life all about? Development—growth. Growth is the natural law of life. When things stop growing they begin to die. This is true of men, business, or nations. Our joy, our happiness, is in our growing. The reward for our development is the release through ourselves of greater potentials for development. We are most content when we are fulfilling our purpose.

The purpose of life is spiritual, mental, and physical growth. The greatest responsibility entrusted to man is that of developing himself. We are born to grow—this is the word which religion, philosophy, literature, and art ceaselessly utter; and we can grow by keeping ourselves in vital communion with the world within us and without. Let each become all that he was created capable of being. Why stay on earth unless it be to grow? Life contains far more than power, wealth, and fame.

"AN ACORN IS NOT AN OAK TREE WHEN IT IS SPROUTED, it must go through long summers and fierce winters; it has to endure all that frost and snow and side-striking winds can bring before it is a full grown oak. These are rough teachers; but rugged school-masters make rugged pupils. SO A MAN IS NOT A MAN WHEN HE IS CREATED, HE HAS ONLY BEGUN. HIS MANHOOD MUST COME FROM YEARS," says Henry Ward Beecher.

The object of man's growth is to take the sick, fearful, ineffective old man and displace him with the creative, happy, productive new man. This is done by showing man the laws by which he can function to attain the full utilization of himself as he was meant to function. There is a correct and perfect use for everything in the universe including man. Man is created perfectly to function in perfect harmony with his design. Each man's job is to find that use and develop it.

"WHY, IN ALL THE AFFAIRS OF LIFE, DO WE SEEM TO GROW BEST UNDER ADVERSITY?" asks Manly Hall. "When a civilization becomes prosperous and self-centered and lazy-minded, that civilization falls; and it nearly always gives way to some young vibrant group that is fighting its way to greater security or greater intelligence or a better way of life. Difficulties seem to be the one thing we all have in common."

Realize that the laws of Nature which put you here seem to be primarily concerned with growth. You are a success to the degree that you grow, and you grow to the degree that you become wiser, more useful, and a more secure person. In other words, WE LIVE TO LEARN, and by this very process we LEARN TO LIVE.

The man who is endeavoring to develop his judgment and growth will profit by imitating an acquaintance of mine. He reads incessantly books produced by the best minds in the country. As he finishes each chapter he analyzes it and makes a condensed digest of it. He picks all of the meat out so that the substance can be read perhaps in five minutes or less. Out of this he has developed an amazing grasp of what men are doing and how they are thinking.

Growth means progress and development. Progress and development means change. Because a thing helped you once is no sure sign it will help you again. Baby food will not sustain the full vigor of manhood. Change of diet calls for adjustment. Ability to make necessary adjustments is the mark of healthy normal growth.

Man, as a total being, is either growing toward something, or his very existence is meaningless. Growth requires a basic recognition of the laws governing the nature of man. "He has changed"—a fine compliment. BERRIES CHANGE FROM GREEN TO RIPENESS. If it were not so they would be useless. All growth means change. The critical point is—did I carry with me essential things in the process of change? If I did I have really grown.

In Texas, years ago, almost all the oil came from surface operations. Then someone got the idea that there were greater sources of supply deeper down. A well was drilled five thousand feet deep. The result? A gusher. Too many of us operate on the surface. We never go deep enough to find supernatural resources. The result is, we never operate at our best. More time and investment is involved to "go deep" but a gusher will pay off.

"God breathed into man's nostrils the breath of life, and man became a living soul." Within this house of sinew, flesh and bones, the soul grows. From infancy the lesson books of life are opened and the mentality and intellect proceed in an ever-expanding circle, producing a consciousness which grasps the profound wisdom of God. The purpose of existence is to develop this consciousness. When the soul has reached maturity it has reached full growth, and should be prepared for immortality and eternal life. Hippocrates stated, "The human soul develops up to death."

THE ONLY REALLY POOR PEOPLE ARE THOSE WHO ARE POOR IN THEIR OWN SOUL, EVEN THOUGH THEY MAY HAVE BOTH HANDS FULL OF WORLDLY GOODS. We are moving away from teaching principles or vital truths that never change. These old established truths are still the starting point for all growth. We must eliminate the conflict between man and himself. To "know thyself" is to understand human nature and keep constantly growing to individual fulfillment.

The nature of man reveals man as a creature of law, who is designed by his Infinite Creator to LIVE and GROW according to law. Man changes by growth—not by magic. Tomorrow's growth depends upon the use we make of today's material and experiences. Nothing is lost upon a man who is bent upon growth; nothing is wasted on one who is always preparing for his work and his life by keeping eyes, mind, and heart open to nature, men, books, and experience.

THE LAW OF LEARNING

Man does not learn certain things until he is ready. Example— a jigsaw puzzle—you cannot put a piece in until you have increased the perimeter so it can absorb this piece. Bluntly; you don't learn until you grow to this point. YOU DON'T LEARN UNTIL YOU ARE READY.

Segment 8

THE LAW OF LEARNING

Learn to live so that you can handle anything that comes your way in life. This is a prime law of life. The first object to any act of learning is that it should serve you in the future. THE REWARD IS YOUR GREATEST INCENTIVE FOR ALL LEARNING.

You can live successfully and die successfully without knowing plenty. Much that we call knowledge is not, in the last analysis, essential knowledge. ESSENTIAL KNOWLEDGE IS THE KNOWLEDGE THAT GIVES POINT AND MEANING TO LIFE ITSELF. Essential knowledge is "indispensable truth" that I must know. ONE OF THE BEST AND FASTEST WAYS OF ACQUIRING KNOWLEDGE IS TO INSIST ON REMAINING IGNORANT ABOUT THINGS THAT ARE NOT WORTH KNOWING.

Man learns from his observation, experience and study. The learning process goes on throughout our entire life span. The quantity and quality of what we learn has a direct bearing on the quality of our life. Life is but one continual course of instruction. Most men already have far more knowledge than they use. They need the inheritance and development of a CHARACTER which will cause them to properly apply this knowledge.

John Lubbock writes, "EDUCATION IS THE HARMONIOUS DEVELOPMENT OF ALL OUR FACULTIES. It begins in the nursery, and goes on at school, but does not end there. It continues through life, whether we will or not. The only question is whether what we learn in life is wisely chosen or picked up haphazardly." A college education does not make an educated man. THE TRUE TEACHER IS LIFE ITSELF, AND THE WORLD IS THE ONLY SCHOOL ROOM IN WHICH WE CAN LEARN WHAT WE SO EVIDENTLY REQUIRE.

Logical thinking and good listening should become a way of life. If you are not listening you are not learning. We need to learn how to THINK and how to LISTEN. Since we absorb only a scant thirty percent of what we hear, we often are faking attention and have our awareness switched off. We cheat ourselves out of an opportunity to learn and grow.

Listening in any form requires concentration, spelled WORK. Learn to listen effectively, to sift, screen, and hunt for something practical which you can use, not just memorize facts. Listen for ideas, work to get the main principles, concepts, or premises. Let the facts fall into place as they will.

You can think much faster than anyone who is speaking to you—three to five times as fast. USE THE RAPID SPEED OF THINKING VERSUS THE SPEED OF SPEECH DIFFERENTIAL, AGGRESSIVELY AND CONSTRUCTIVELY. Weigh what you hear against what you know—and against what the speaker is saying. Pick out the main points. Constantly analyze what is being said, decide what is relevant and what is not. Look ahead to see where the speaker is going.

Thinking ahead also boosts your attention. What is the speaker getting at? Try to guess, then check it against what he actually says. Learn to resist the tendency to dull your attention by assuming you know what is coming next. You can also increase your ability to learn more quickly if you make mental pictures or images of what you are reading, talking about, or studying. See a picture of what you are reading.

I am grateful to the man who can stir my thought, but I insist upon putting it through my own mill. My grist may not be very heavy when I get it ground, but it will be my grist. This is where people are weak today. They are parrots, they are echoes, they are carbon copies. They do NOT think for themselves. LIFE HAS A WAY OF FORCING ONE TO LEARN BY EXPERIENCE—WHEN ONE WILL LEARN NO OTHER WAY.

An educated person is a human being who can deal, with reasonable success, with all of the ordinary situations that are likely to arise in the course of his life. Of all treasure knowledge is the most precious, for it can neither be stolen, given away, nor consumed. Reading seeks, meditation finds, prayer asks, contemplation tastes, knowledge satisfies.

How much education is needed? It is a waste of time and effort to try to make lawyers, teachers, scientists, doctors or preachers out of people who prefer and are better fitted to become foresters, mechanics, farmers, sailors, or chauffeurs. We need skills of every kind. YOU CAN NOT POUR FIVE GALLONS INTO A PINT CAN. THIS IS A LAW OF CAPACITY.

School is but a mental gymnasium. The best thing a school can teach you is how to THINK for yourself. John Lubbock wrote, "Reading and writing, arithmetic, and grammar do not constitute education, anymore than a knife, fork, and spoon constitute a dinner." Education today, more than ever before, MUST SEE CLEARLY THE DUAL OBJECTIVES: EDUCATING FOR EARNING A LIVING, AND EDUCATING ON HOW TO LIVE.

MEN CAN KNOW MORE THAN THEIR ANCESTORS DID IF THEY START WITH A KNOWLEDGE OF WHAT THEIR ANCESTORS HAD ALREADY LEARNED. THIS IS WHY A SOCIETY CAN BE PROGRESSIVE ONLY IF IT CONSERVES ITS TRADITIONS. When ancient opinions and rules of life are taken away, the loss cannot possibly be estimated. From that moment we have no compass to govern us, nor can we know distinctly to what port to steer.

No knowledge we ever acquire is so important as a knowledge of what to say and how to say it; except, perhaps, a knowledge of what not to say, and when not to say it. Lee Du Bridge, former president of Cal-Tech, says, "The scientific man outside of his field is as dumb as the next guy." We are all ignorant, only on different subjects.

The education of the individual in the Western World has been steadily deteriorating. Education and the church are the backbone of this country. So this is what our enemies are out to destroy, using the ignorant people as their method. Education without God gives one but greater capacity to get into trouble. Modern education has put a premium on MATERIAL-ISM. The mere mention of "God" in the classroom provokes laughter and ridicule. Morality has been thrown to the wind!

It should be evident to most parents that the way to a better world lies through their children. Yet how many parents fail to recognize this truism? Ideologies, good or bad, are perpetuated in the mind of the child. Whether the culture implanted in the same mind will be nurtured or starved depends on training. Molding plastic youth into valuable citizenship is the responsibility of both parent and teacher. THE BEST TRAINING ANY PARENT CAN GIVE A CHILD IS TO TEACH THE CHILD TO DEVELOP HIMSELF. YEARS AGO EDUCATION WAS DESIGNED TO DEVELOP SELF-CONTROL, MANNERS, AND DIGNITY.

"The world," wrote Eleanor Roosevelt, "is full of things which no human being can possibly know all about. The intellectually mature are usually anxious to learn and they know that not all wisdom is attained through winning university degrees." You learn until you die no matter what education you have. Life consists in the alternate process of learning and unlearning. But it is often wiser to unlearn than to learn.

Only by learning and obeying the UNWRITTEN LAWS OF HIS OWN NATURE CAN MAN REACH PERFECTION AND FULFILL HIMSELF. These unchanging laws are within the very nature of man, they are written into the very structure of our being, into our nerve cells, our very bloodstream. MOST OF OUR PROBLEMS AND STRUGGLES WILL EVAPO-RATE THROUGH THE UNDERSTANDING AND PROPER USE OF NATURE'S LAWS. IT WILL REQUIRE A REVO-LUTION IN PEOPLE'S HEARTS BUT THIS IS THE AN-SWER TO THE PROBLEMS THAT DOG US.

The rules of efficient learning are: 1. Have a specific purpose in your study. 2. Get at the essential ideas. 3. Criticize as you go along. Supplement the new ideas coming to you with your own thoughts, and apply the best of your previous knowledge and experience. 4. Put the knowledge you gain to use.

It is a costly error into which many men fall of letting their appetite for more information and more new experiences run away with them, and rob them of time which they ought to give to thinking, analyzing, understanding, and applying. The "ITCH TO LEARN" is a great thing, and it cannot be too strong, but it must not be allowed to drown out the "ITCH TO UNDERSTAND" and the "ITCH TO MAKE USE OF" which are even greater. It is not so important to know everything as to know the exact value of everything, to appreciate what we learn, and to arrange what we know. Then to realize IT IS NOT WHAT WE KNOW, BUT WHAT WE USE INTELLIGENTLY THAT COUNTS.

KNOWLEDGE is knowing and consists of facts and experiences which are bound together by memory. You've heard the expression, "Knowledge is power." Knowledge is only potential power. IT BECOMES POWER ONLY WHEN AND IF IT IS ORGANIZED INTO DEFINITE PLANS OF ACTION, AND DIRECTED TO A DEFINITE END.

WISDOM is knowing how to use knowledge, good judgment, plus action. Solomon admonished, "With all thy getting get understanding." Someday science will get around to admitting that God is the measure of the universe, and that man at his best, is an elemental and potential measure and revelation of God. Then, for the first time in several thousand years, we shall have education worthy of the name.

The Creator has so constituted the human intellect that it can only grow by its own action and free will. EVERY MAN MUST, THEREFORE, EDUCATE HIMSELF. His books and teachers are but helps, the work is his.

What is judgment? A knowledge of the fundamental laws of nature and of human nature, combined with the power to apply them to specific cases in order that a correct mode of conduct may be decided upon in advance of an event. We weigh, and balance, then decide what is best.

Segment 9

THE LAW OF CHOICE

To every man is given the power of choice. We live by making choices. CHOICE, NOT CHANCE, DETERMINES HUMAN DESTINY. This power to choose is what makes each one of us an individual, a god in his own right; and our choices determine what happens to us—what our future will be— happy or unhappy, successful or unsuccessful.

Proper choices require reasoning, thinking, common sense and experience. Nothing ranks a man as quickly as his skill in selecting things that are really worthwhile. Every day brings the necessity of keen discrimination. NOT ALWAYS IS IT A CHOICE BETWEEN GOOD AND BAD, BUT OFTEN BETWEEN GOOD AND BEST.

Successful living depends upon the choices we make. You have to know what is important and what is unimportant for you. Intelligent choice implies a realistic sense of values and a realistic sense of proportion.

From infancy to old age this process of choice with acceptance on one hand, and denial on the other, continues. We cannot have everything we want. The businessman in pursuit of financial success often has to neglect his athletic and cultural interests. Men who elect to serve the spiritual, the cultural, or political interests of society—ministers, writers, artists, soldiers, teachers, statesmen, and public servants in general— usually have to relegate monetary well-being to secondary importance.

WITH A LIMITED AMOUNT OF LIFE WE CAN'T BE, OR DO, EVERYTHING. We are constantly faced with a decision as to what and with whom we will spend our time. Even active friendship takes time. We may have to refuse engagements and disappoint many people in order to conserve our time and reach our goals.

Every day we have to make a choice of what is offered on the market. WE CAN'T HAVE THE WHOLE WORLD, NO MORE THAN A YOUNGSTER WITH HIS PENNY CAN BUY ALL THE CANDY IN THE CANDY STORE. This is one of life's great lessons. Here and now we have to make our choice, and destiny is the harvest that grows from the seed of choice. The formula for intelligent choice requires not only that you know yourself truly; you must also assert your true self accurately.

Gracian, the wise monk, said, "KNOW HOW TO CHOOSE WELL. MOST OF LIFE DEPENDS THEREON. It needs good taste and correct judgment, for which neither intellect nor study suffices." Judgment is not the knowledge of fundamental laws, it is knowing how to apply a knowledge of them. This necessitates experience. Good judgment begins with difficulties which force us to think, to recall, to project, to formulate an hypothesis, to test our assumption, to experiment, to observe results, and then to make up our minds and come to a conclusion.

Judgment is one thing you cannot learn in college. You either have it or you do not have it. In this vastly complicated scientific age the one most necessary management skill is "feel." I cannot describe it and you cannot teach it in school. The more surrounded with computers, automation, and the like the more lonely, tragic, vital, and valuable will be that one man with "feel" in each business. All great men are gifted with intuition. They know without reasoning or analysis what they need to know. INTUITION IS THE CLEAR CONCEPTION OF THE WHOLE AT ONCE. INSTINCT IS THE NOSE OF THE MIND. Notice carefully that sound judgment must precede the exercise of initiative.

In reasoning, let's start with what we do know, use logic, but before coming to conclusions, let's reckon with the importance of the unknown. FOR TRUTH WILL BE TRUTH REGARDLESS OF ANY PERSON'S IGNORANCE, DISBELIEF, OR REFUSAL TO TRY TO UNDERSTAND.

Sorbonne professor of philosophy, Jean Guitton writes, "The supreme good of man, according to the sages, lies in refining his act of judgment to the highest degree of purity, in learning to think properly, and in cultivating a good mind, since ALL OUR MISFORTUNES ARE BORN OF OUR INABILITY TO MAKE THE PROPER CHOICES."

It is very poor judgment to expose oneself to the raw sexual pictures and filthy language, to the killings, robberies, and violence performed by criminal heroes on stage and screen that is so prevalent today. Our minds are impressionable and we seldom forget negative and degrading images. We are at war with ourselves, we are destroying ourselves.

THE GREAT PRIZES OF LIFE do not fall to the most brilliant, to the cleverest, to the shrewdest, or to the best educated, but to the most level headed man, TO THE MAN OF SOUNDEST JUDGMENT.

To get the most out of life, not only in the administration of our practical affairs, but also in the cultural, religious, and political sides of our natures, we must always maintain an open mind. WE SHOULD HAVE ENOUGH CONFIDENCE IN OUR OWN JUDGMENT AND DISCRETION NOT TO BE AFRAID OF BEING UNDULY INFLUENCED BY ANYBODY OR ANYTHING.

It always pays to see the other fellow's viewpoint, even if you can't accept his judgment. One cool judgment is worth a thousand hasty councils. The important thing is to know how to take all things quietly, to supply light and not heat. Give your decisions, never your reasons; your decisions may be right, your reasons may be wrong.

The late Felix Frankfurter, distinguished judge of the U.S. Supreme Court, said, "There is hardly a question of any real difficulty before the Supreme Court that does not entail more than one so-called principle. ANYBODY CAN DECIDE A QUESTION IF ONLY A SINGLE PRINCIPLE IS IN CONTROVERSY."

William J. Reilly, business consultant, writes, "But what is good judgment but a product of your mental operations? And if these operations are logical, your judgment will be sound. If illogical, your judgments will be faulty. All kinds of haywire decisions can be arrived at, of course, from perfectly sound facts. So that I should say the statement commonly mouthed, 'A man's judgment is no better than his facts,' should be changed to read, 'A MAN'S JUDGMENT IS NO BETTER THAN HIS LOGICAL ANALYSIS OF THE FACTS.'"

"IN THE AFFAIRS OF THE WORLD JUDGMENT IS THE SUPREME QUALITY," says businessman Lord Beaverbrook. "Judgment is the power to assimilate knowledge and to use it. Many men have brilliant schemes and yet are quite unable to execute them. Through their very brilliancy, unsupported by sound judgment, they stumble upon ruin."

However, a man's judgment may be sound in certain fields of activity, but fail in others. We are apt to believe if a man is clever at one thing, or successful under one set of circumstances, that he must be equally clever at everything and equally successful under all conditions.

To take a practical instance: salesmanship requires above all the spirit of optimism. That same spirit carried into the sphere of finance might ruin a firm. For SOMETIMES YOUR OPTIMISM CAN CHLOROFORM YOUR JUDGMENT. The success in one branch might be the failure in the other, and vice-versa.

A young man may choose the wrong trade or profession. Or he may be in the right business, but the wrong department. It takes time and opportunity for a man to discover in what direction his natural bent lies.

Life is a matter of making wise choices. Most of us can, as we choose, make of this world either a palace or a prison. If we know the right principles and apply them, success is assured because we have eliminated the risks.

Benjamin Franklin's formula for decision making: "When confronted with two courses of action I JOT DOWN ON A PIECE OF PAPER ALL THE ARGUMENTS IN FAVOR OF EACH ONE—THEN ON THE OPPOSITE SIDE I WRITE THE ARGUMENTS AGAINST EACH ONE. Then by weighing the arguments pro and con and cancelling them out, one against the other, I take the course indicated by what remains."

JUDGMENT MAY PROVE STERILE IF IT IS NOT ACCOMPANIED BY ACTION. Action is the basis of all attainment. Unless you act all the knowledge in the world will not help you. Each day you must do something towards the attainment of your goals. Action has to be applied in the right direction—and therefore is the servant of judgment.

OF ALL THE QUALITIES WHICH CAN BE HIRED IN THE MARKET PLACE, SOUND JUDGMENT IS THE SCARCEST. Honesty, loyalty, courtesy are to be had for the asking. But he who would purchase ripe judgment must bid high, for this rare quality is the almost exclusive property of men who possess good observation, long experience, detailed information and analytical habits of thought. It belongs to men who have learned the relation between cause and effect, and have studied all manner of human material reactions; who have continually analyzed situations, asking themselves why and never resting until they found an adequate reason.

Since you are an individual, be yourself and think for yourself. Your conclusions may not always be right, but at least they will be your own. If you find you are mistaken, acknowledge it and correct your mistakes. But never allow another to live in your skin. Your personality is all you have. The person who does not follow his best judgment will incur a penalty. Making a decision and being confident that it is "right" makes life more pleasant. THE GOAL OF ALL DECISIONS: TO FIND VALUE AND THE TRUTH, AND PASS JUDGMENT ACCORDINGLY.

Painting by Michelangelo

God the Supreme Power said: "I have made the earth, and created man upon it; I, even my hands, have stretched out the heavens, and all their host have I commanded."

Segment 10

THE LAW OF SUPREME POWER

"Among the mysteries which become more mysterious the more they are thought about, there will remain the one absolute certainty that we are ever in the presence of an Infinite Power from which all things proceed."—Herbert Spencer

THERE IS ONE SUPREME AND ABSOLUTE POWER AT THE SOURCE OF LIFE, THE CAUSE OF ALL LIVING. This ineffable principle is named God. The Universe in which we live is one of the innumerable manifestations of this supreme power. This eternal power is revealed to us through the laws governing the formation, generation, growth, unfolding, and improvement of all created things.

Every new discovery of science is a further revelation of the order that God has built into His universe. All about us we are constantly reminded of a great power that has set up inexorable laws by which we must abide for our safety and well-being. THE UNIVERSE IS CENTERED ON GOD. HIS INFINITE CARE IS DEMONSTRATED IN THE CAUSE AND EFFECT, ACTION AND REACTION PATTERN BUILT INTO THE UNIVERSE.

NATURE IS BUT A NAME FOR AN EFFECT, WHOSE CAUSE IS GOD.

God is the maker and ruler of everything. He is the Alpha and Omega, the beginning and end, the source. God is at the Center of Man. He will guide us into all truth. We cannot define God or any of the real values of life, but we can experience them. He is the way of life that we were created to live. With Him life has meaning, without Him men exist in a meaningless discord. Man has come to know this Supreme Power through the seeking of his mind and the longings of his heart. To live in harmony and correspondence with this power is LIFE.

69

We live in a universe of law and order. This means the forces that guide the planets are governed by a dependable supreme power. We can predict the appearance of a comet fifty years hence, for the laws that govern the universe are so dependable and accurate.

Since God is a God of law and order He must ever deal with His people on the highest level of intelligent logic. On the principle of cause and effect there must always be spontaneous response to an action both in kind and degree. The fact of God's eternal wedlock to law is the only solid foundation on which our faith and hope can rest. Henry Drummond wrote, "There is a sense of solidity about a Law of Nature which belongs to nothing else in the world. Here, at last, amid all that is shifting, is one thing sure; one thing outside ourselves unbiased, unprejudiced, uninfluenced by like or dislike, by doubt or fear; one thing that holds on its way to me eternally, incorruptible and undefiled."

It is with the heart, NOT the intellect, that you find GOD. Man is spiritual. No belief of ours will change the facts or reverse the laws of the spiritual universe; and it is our first business to discover the laws and to learn how the facts stand. Carl G. Jung, world renowned analyst, scientist, profound student of the human mind, in his Autobiography states, "An experience of God helps man to live and can cure him of his neuroses."

SPIRITUAL things are spiritually discerned. God is entirely beyond the reach of intellectual processes. What men can discover, God does not reveal to them. He only reveals to them what they cannot discover. Discovery is a matter of intellectual adjustment. Revelation is the HOW of spiritual adjustment. No matter how expensive a camera is, it will not take pictures without light. Jesus Christ said, "I am the light." Without Him we remain in total darkness. Reason has its place and function, but it cannot displace revelation.

The mistake of men is, and ever has been, to think of the physical man as the real man and the physical world as the real world. The real man, the Scriptures insist, is the spiritual man, and the real world is the spiritual. The real man does not, because he cannot, live on stocks and bonds, houses and lands, mortgages and commodities. By every scientific test he is built for God and spiritual things. With God he must have fellowship or be in this, and every other world, a bewildered, unhappy, discontented creature. It is not WHERE we are or WHAT we have that makes us happy or unhappy. No generation ever had so much, no generation has so little. We must find God or lose everything.

Materialism has demonstrated conclusively that it cannot protect the well-being of mankind. Facilities directed primarily to the physical aspect of human progress obviously cannot cope with the present emergency in our moral and ethical lives. Man has found he can have millions of dollars and still be unhappy. The material world can bring us much, but we still are faced with the same problems: fear, insecurity, doubt, concern about the reason for existence.

God is a spirit, infinite, eternal, and unchangeable in His being, wisdom, power, holiness, justice, goodness and truth. Man is spirit; it is a natural instinct born in man to have the desire for spiritual development. Man's soul needs spiritual food just as his body needs food, water, and air. In the human species, spiritual development is the Supreme Law.

In the heart of every person there is a hunger, a longing for something that you cannot find in this world. It is the soul that longs for a comforting spirit, a fellowship with God, the Supreme Power. Apart from God, man exists, but does not live. Apart from God and His Word man only guesses and theorizes and gropes and stumbles along in the blindness of his own finite understanding. Augustine said, "We were made for God and we will be dissatisfied until we have God in our hearts."

A great and wise man has well said, "It is absolutely essential that I enjoy God"—essential because time will pass, things will perish, human relationships will cease and the brightest prospects of our most exciting hopes will become blank and barren. Nor is this the musing of frustrated disillusionment. It is the common experience of men everywhere. The reason is easy to find: we were built on so vast a scale that time is not our home, and things are not our goal. Nor do we need better evidence of this truth than the fact that we so soon outgrow the "delights that thrill our little selves." Like Solomon we experience only to say finally, "I have no pleasure in them." If this continues to the end we can but reach a time and place where life will be bankrupt. To experience the Infinite is my ONE HOPE of finding the inexhaustible God, and God alone is the answer to the infinite demands of the infinite me of me.

The great central fact in human life is the coming into a conscious, vital realization of our oneness with Infinite Power, and the opening of ourselves to this divine inflow.

Jesus Christ made no claims as a philosopher; yet what philosopher ever devised a scheme for living worthy to be compared with His teaching? He taught that life must be centered in God—that man's happiness is dependent upon his holiness; that his union with God is his hope of fulfilling the ultimate purpose of his life. This "way of life" teaches man to rule his passions and impulses by reason and right. It teaches him to think God's thoughts, speak His language, and how to live the life he was created to live. By so doing he safeguards himself and the society of which he is a part.

Materialistic education has undermined the belief in God, and has substituted no adequate alternative through which the natural inclination of man to venerate can be properly expressed. We have raised a Godless generation, and it gave us Hell—the hell through which we are now passing. With all our talk about humanity crying for this, that, and the other thing, few listen to the voice: "THIS IS LIFE—TO KNOW GOD."

MAN'S LIFE IS SHORT, AND IF WE WILL TAKE THE THINGS WHICH GOD HAS CREATED AND START FROM THERE, THEN SO MUCH CAN BE ACCOMPLISHED. Each man has access to this Supreme Power, but many shut God out of their lives. This is the unpardonable sin. The worst sin it is possible for any man to commit is to reject God.

There are many things in life for which we do not have a definite, concrete, and clear answer. We just have to take them on faith. I do not know the How or Why or Wherefore of God, but I DO KNOW for sure that I have felt His presence, have seen His power, and that He has changed my life from darkness to light, and that I enjoy His blessings every day.

We have no answer for the question where does electricity come from, or of what is it composed. We know that it is a mighty powerful force, and if used properly can be harnessed to the welfare of man. If not used properly it can bring death and destruction. We cannot see the wind, but we can feel its presence and strength, and we can harness its power and force for our own use. We have to take such things as we find them and put them to our use.

We can see God in everything around us. We live in a universe so great and so wonderful in its creation that there would have to be someone like God, who had a definite plan of creation, in order to make it all so perfect in its operation. NO MERE SERIES OF HAPPENSTANCES COULD HAVE EVER BROUGHT ABOUT SUCH A MARVELOUS RESULT.

From the moment that we know God through experience, life changes for us. THE ONLY LIMIT TO THE SUPREME POWER OF GOD IN OUR LIVES IS THE LIMIT OF OUR BELIEF. If a master craftsman authenticates his work by signing his name, God by the same token, authenticates His work and His word by unmistakably signing His name. "THE HEAVENS DECLARE THE GLORY OF GOD AND THE EARTH SHOWETH HIS HANDIWORK."

THE LAW OF SELF-DISCOVERY

THE GREATEST RESPONSIBILITY ENTRUSTED TO MAN
IS THAT OF DISCOVERING AND DEVELOPING HIMSELF.

Man's total development is the meaning and purpose of life. It is the continual remaking of yourself so that at last you know how to live. To be what you are, and to become what you are capable of becoming. To serve God and humanity. This is the true life and . . . life forever.

THE LAW OF SELF-DISCOVERY

"Know thyself—in talents and capacity, in judgment and in-clination. You cannot master yourself unless you know your-self. There are mirrors for the face but none for the mind. He that knows himself knows how to strengthen his weakness, and the wise man conquers everything, even the stars in their courses."—Gracian

"MAN, KNOW THYSELF"—all wisdom centers here. Self-reflection, then action, is the school of wisdom. The sooner you discover the facts about yourself, the easier will be your journey of life. To get the most out of ourselves we must find out what powers we possess and then cultivate and use them. By control of the emotions a person can overcome almost every handicap that ordinarily mars a joyous life. The handi-cap of poverty can be overcome; illness may be conquered, and physical disability can be offset, bad habits can be sloughed off, most mistakes of life can be rectified.

Socrates admonished: "The unexamined life is not worth living." This ancient maxim which sounds very simple gains richer meaning as we learn more about man's nature. Shake-speare observed, "Of all knowledge, the wise and good seek most to know themselves." Life is a continuous series of ad-justments to reality. You can make your life a victory no matter who you are or where you are or what you are doing. It is not your age or position in life, or bank account that is involved. If you are to live a victorious and dynamic life, your first and most urgent need is to know and understand yourself. Find yourself first! SUCCESS IN ITS FULLEST AND HAP-PIEST SENSE DEPENDS UPON SELF-DISCOVERY. The development of character, faith, self-control, independence, courage, a desire to be of service, and a willingness to make sacrifices, must be our constant aim. By the laws of his own nature every man gravitates to his own level, all it takes is time.

The ideal situation is to live a balanced life developing equally and harmoniously all of the forty-seven segments of man, for these laws are interwoven, each one affects the other. This essential knowledge gives point and meaning to life. You have built a foundation for your life like the foundation for a hundred-story building. With this essential knowledge as your foundation for daily living you can handle anything that comes your way.

We must study quietly, seeking not easy ways and short-cuts, but a vital philosophy that can inspire and lead us to greater efforts in the perfection of ourselves. We must approach the mastery of ourselves with the same determination with which we approach an art or a science. What we must reach for is a conception of continual self-discovery, continual reshaping, in order to realize one's best self, to be the person one could be. It includes not only the intellect, but the emotions, the character, creativeness, adaptability, vitality, moral and spiritual growth. In other words, the continued development of all of one's faculties.

Regardless of how deeply a man feels, how broadly he studies to improve himself outwardly, he's not complete until he has perfected his inner disposition. WHOEVER WISHES TO BETTER EXTERNAL CONDITIONS MUST BEGIN BY IMPROVING THE INNER MAN. When things are not going right I get a distressed "gut" feeling. I sense something is wrong. Sometimes it takes a lot of thinking to find out what is wrong and how to correct it. After I clear it up I feel fine again. Thus proving, "YOUR SENSES WILL TAKE YOU FURTHER THAN YOUR INTELLECT."

Today we can keep ourselves so busy, fill our lives with so many diversions, stuff our heads with so much knowledge, and involve ourselves with so many people, that WE NEVER HAVE TIME TO PROBE THE FEARFUL AND WONDER-FUL WORLD WITHIN. WHEN A MAN BEGINS TO UNDERSTAND HIMSELF HE BEGINS TO LIVE.

How well do we know ourselves and our capabilities? What do you feel are your strongest personal assets or abilities? Describe the image you hold of yourself. What are your values? What is your philosophy? What are your motives? What are your talents, skills? What are your aims, ambitions, desires? What kind of person are you? What do you think of yourself as an individual? Make a complete written analysis. What are your strong points, your weak points?

John Miller writes, "A THING THAT WILL HELP YOUR INNER LIFE IS TO SET UP IN YOUR MIND A STANDARD OF VALUES, SO THAT YOU KNOW WHAT IS REALLY SIGNIFICANT, IMPORTANT, AND VALUABLE."

Have we lost sight of our "sense of values"? The apparent emphasis of the popular news media on the negative side of American life would reinforce the idea that our sense of values is undergoing a change for the worse. The public has become more lax in their responsibilities toward society and themselves, which in turn has lowered values. Where will it all end if we keep breaking the rules?

Moral laxity, disrespect for law and order, a flagrant disregard for authority in any form, and the desire to be a nonconformist seem to have replaced love of home and country, respect for law (even in government officials), and self-respect in our world today. Granted, we live in a world of progress and fantastic scientific achievement, but we must still maintain certain values which the coming generation will respect and admire; otherwise we will lose everything.

The opportunities for acquiring material wealth are greater now than ever before. In our eagerness to attain material things we tend to forget our own ideals and sometimes place too much emphasis on material gain. We do nevertheless come to the realization that there are other things which are even more important. This can be attributed to the average person's strong sense of values.

Albert Einstein wrote, "It is essential that the student acquire AN UNDERSTANDING OF AND A LIVELY FEELING FOR VALUES. HE MUST ACQUIRE A VIVID SENSE OF THE BEAUTIFUL AND OF THE MORALLY GOOD. Otherwise, with his specialized knowledge he more closely resembles a well-trained dog than a harmoniously developed person." In this quotation the phrases "lively feeling for values" and "vivid sense of the beautiful and of the morally good" point out something of the nature of values. They well up from within a man. They are something that is "felt" or "sensed."

Everything that a man does is determined by and is an expression of his values. TRUE WEALTH IS ALWAYS BUILT UPON SOUND VALUES. A person does not have to be thinking about values in order to be acting upon them. On the contrary, a few of them, such as humility, generosity, or spontaneity, would lose their true quality and worth if a person realized at the moment of his action that he was behaving in accord with them.

"In this era of world wars," wrote Boris Pasternak, "in this atomic age, values have changed. We have learned that we are the guests of existence, travelers between two stations. We must discover security within ourselves. During our short span of life we must find our own insights into our relationship with the existence in which we participate so briefly. Otherwise, we cannot live. This means, as I see it, a departure from the materialistic view of the twentieth century. It means a reawakening of the spiritual world of our inner life—of religion. I don't mean religion as a dogma or as a church, but as a vital feeling."

The yesteryear that sired great men was the era of farms, small villages and broad vistas of countryside—of trees and birds and brooks and rivers and lakes—an era when men were more enamored of God than they were of gold, and when they had time to look and listen and pray.

Tennyson wrote, "Self-reverence, self-knowledge, self-control; these three alone lead life to sovereign power." The ancient maxim "know thyself"—so deceptively simple—gains richer meaning as we learn more about man's nature. Research in psychology and psychiatry reveals how closely mental health is bound up in a reasonably objective view of the self, and in acceptance of the self. The "self-image" or the "real self" is a composite of all the attitudes, qualities, and characteristics of a person, the sum total of the experiences and thoughts he has ever known.

Goethe once said that the last creature on earth who could be expected to discover water was the fish who lived in it. It is also understandable that the last of man's discoveries would be the discovery of himself—the discovery of the processes and potentials of his own inherent faculties. The greatest discovery anyone can make is to discover his true self, and develop the latent power that lies within. Discover the power of constructive thought, the value of a cheerful and wholesome attitude. Discover the unlimited inner power. Man has not even scratched the surface of his own nature, and the truth of his own existence. Lt. Gen. A. G. Trudeau reminds us: "Character is something each one of us must build for himself, out of the laws of God and Nature, the example of others, and most of all—out of the trials and errors of daily life. Character is the total of thousands of small daily strivings to live up to the best that is in us."

Most of the ills of the world—and the world is only a mixed collection of individuals like you and me—are not traceable to physical or mental causes, but result from a lack of spiritual power in you and me, caused by the low priority we give to the development of the spiritual side of our being, and to the lack of faith in God. THE IMPORTANT THING FOR MAN IS NOT SO MUCH A COMPREHENSION OF THE TOTALITY OF GOD, IT IS TO DISCOVER THE NECESSITY FOR OUR OWN SPIRITUAL DEVELOPMENT.

THE LAW OF LIVING

Life is not a smooth paved highway, on which one travels from birth until death. It is uphill, downhill, plateaus, valleys, chuck holes, booby traps, like an obstacle course. The road of life can only reveal itself as it is traveled. We must climb the mountain peaks, cross a number of abysses, and chasms, on our journey through life.

THE LAW OF LIVING

The forty-seven segments that are spelled out in this book are some of the most useful laws for living. LIVING itself is an art, in fact, the most important and at the same time the most difficult and complex art, to be practiced by man. Its object is not this or that specialized performance, but the performance of successful everyday living, the process of developing into one's full potential.

The wheel has opened the land to modern travel and the hull has conquered all the seas; the jet has mastered the air and built silver bridges to all countries. The rocket has probed outer space, placed man on the moon, and orbited Mars over thirty million miles from the earth. LIVING IS ALSO A CONTINUOUS ADVENTURE INTO THE UNKNOWN. TODAY THE MOST VITAL FRONTIER LEFT FOR MAN, IS TO INCREASE THE QUALITY OF HIS LIFE, TO DEVELOP HIS OWN NATURE, DEVELOP THE SPIRIT THAT CONNECTS MAN TO LIFE, TO GOD, TO ETERNITY. This development is long past due. It is necessary for the abundant life and to the very SURVIVAL of mankind.

Oscar Wilde said, "TO LIVE IS THE RAREST THING IN THE WORLD. MOST PEOPLE EXIST, THAT IS ALL." Humanity belongs to a class of life which to a large extent determines its own destinies, establishes its own rules of education and conduct, and thus influences every step we are free to take within the structure of our social system. But the power of human beings to determine their own destinies is limited by natural law, Nature's law. It is the counsel of wisdom to discover the laws of nature, including the laws of human nature, and then to live in accordance with them. The opposite is folly. Nature's laws are SUPREME; we cannot change them; we can deviate from them for a while, but the end is evil. That is the lesson we must learn from the history of humanity.

Life Principle: Every little while somebody goes into print to tell us that the mystery of life has been solved. They tell us that they now know all the elements in man's body and are able to reproduce them. It may be true, and they may succeed in doing it, but when they come to this matter of making what they build LIVE, they will find themselves stalled. The scientist in his laboratory can reproduce a hen's egg, shell, yolk, white and all, but the upshot is he cannot put life into it. You can set a hen on it for years but she would hatch nothing. There is no life there.

A professor of biology stood before his class one day holding a seed in his hand. He said, "I know the exact composition of this seed. It is made of hydrogen, carbon, and nitrogen. I can exactly duplicate this seed in the laboratory, all except one thing, the 'life principle' that makes it reproduce itself."

Man cannot manufacture a seed that has within it the power to reproduce its own likeness. All life must come from pre-existing life. And that pre-existing life is the FIRST CAUSE of all life. Dr. Calvin Samuel Page, eminent scientist, says, "WHEN WE COME TO LIFE, WE EVIDENTLY COME TO GOD AND THE FINITE MAY NOT INVESTIGATE THE INFINITE."

Life Definition: Herbert Spencer, a noted scientist, in "Principles of Biology" said, "Life is the definite combination of heterogeneous changes, both simultaneous and successive, in correspondence with external co-existence and sequences." The Bible says, "This is life, and life eternal, that you may know God." To know is to experience, to have fellowship, to enjoy, to appreciate. Life is measured by the number of things you are alive to. Life is effectiveness, life is power, correspondence to environment. I must take the power of God and have inside fellowship with Him. GOD IS NOT ONLY SPIRIT, BUT LIFE ITSELF.

Man, as he stands today, is obsolete and a failure. There are more human beings cast into the junk pile by modern living than ever before in man's history. We have developed a whole new industrial way of life, new gadgets, new processes, but the man in the middle has not grown to a higher state of existence within himself. Man is obsolete today because he has retrogressed by denying the good and the natural, by denying the teachings of the world's great leaders, and of the Scriptures. Even the sciences of man—psychology, sociology, economics, government—are themselves obsolete because they have denied everything that is basic and natural to man and inherent in his constitution. We have two alternatives: we must either face an economy and a world where the one tenth that are sane, sensible and productive are supporting in complete security and vegetable existence the other 90% of humanity; OR we must do something about man himself.

Alexis Carrel wrote, "If we are not to deceive ourselves we must deduce the laws of living from the observation of life itself, just as we have deduced the laws of physics and chemistry from observing inanimate matter." The first lesson in the art of living is to acquire the ability to distinguish the important from the unimportant, and to act accordingly. For life is joy and sorrow, hope and despair, tears and smiles, defeat and victory, success and failure. Only those who have wept know how to smile; only those who have suffered defeat know how to be humbly great in victory, and only those who have been held by the jaws of need know the meaning of plenty.

Omar Bradley writes, "We have grasped the mystery of the atom and rejected the Sermon on the Mount. The world has achieved brilliance without wisdom, power without conscience. Ours is a world of nuclear giants and ethical infants. We know more about war than we do about peace, more about killing than we do about living." THE MOST IMPORTANT THING HAS NOT BEEN LEARNED—HOW TO CONDUCT OURSELVES SO THAT WE MAY LIVE.

IN OUR AGE WE HAVE LOST THE ART OF BUILD-
ING A MAN. A man is strong in proportion to his ability not
only to resist temptation toward unworthy things, but also to
desire worthiness. Our character is really nothing but a composite of our impulses, our ambitions, and our tendencies in
the direction of right and wrong. The whole world is like
the traditional little red school house, and we are all students—
willing or unwilling—learning our ABC's in the school of life.
There can be nothing more useful or necessary to the individual
than a basic philosophy for living, and codes of conduct are
usually founded in religious convictions.

Man today will protest that he has risen from primitive man
to the highly civilized, cultured man that he is today. BUT
WE ASK, WHAT HAVE WE ACCOMPLISHED FOR THE
GOOD OF MAN'S LIFE, FOR THE GOOD OF HIS SOUL?
HAVE WE EASED HIS MIND? HAVE WE PRODUCED
HARMONY AND SERENITY WITHIN?

Spiritual life is the emancipation of what we are. THROUGH
SPIRITUAL LIFE WE BECOME RESPONSIVE TO GOD.
ON THAT LEVEL, AND ON THAT LEVEL ONLY, DOES
MAN FIND RELEASE FOR HIS HIGHEST POWERS AND
QUALITIES. Not only does spiritual experience enable us to
"see God" and release ourselves, but it gives us a proper view
of man. It removes the barrier of perpetual remoteness built
up by self-interest, prejudice and artificial classification which,
in the final analysis, is the world's greatest curse. There is
enough of the eternal quality inherent in even a "bum" to
challenge much more than casual thought when we have eyes
to see. For those who spend their time seeking evidence of
spiritual truth in the outside world I recommend a closer observation of man—through spiritual eyes. True, out there in
nature one is almost certain to stumble upon some super-sensual
phenomenon, but that does not reveal what man most needs
to know. His deepest need is threefold: To know God, to know
himself, and to know man. And the only way to know ourselves
and to know others is to know God.

For the person who thinks of life as merely an opportunity to exploit powers, ambitions, and abilities, life would naturally begin for him at the point where he realizes his personal ambitions. For the person who thinks of life as merely an opportunity to achieve fame and fortune life would naturally begin for him at the point where the accumulation of wealth and power begins. For the person who thinks of life as merely a playground life would naturally begin for him at the point where he could adopt the slogan, "Have fun."

But for the person who is built on a larger scale or takes a more serious view of life than merely an opportunity to make money, achieve fame and fortune, or as a playground in which to "have fun," none of these conceptions will do.

Both his mind and heart would have discovered: that life is more—infinitely more—than eating, drinking, breathing, wearing clothes, having fun and taking up room; that the cradle is not its beginning and the grave is not its end; that he is akin to the centuries past and joined to the centuries to come; that the fire that burns within him is borrowed from the altar of eternal being; that the desires and hopes and longings that keep him ever restless are born of an awareness that the infinitudes are his by right of inheritance; that the stream on which he is being carried along takes its rise beyond the boundary of time and empties into some sea of infinite expanse; that the depths of life are too deep to be filled with gold, its longings are too insistent to be hushed by the trifles of time, and its expanse is too vast to be filled by the slogan "have fun."

To such a one, life must begin at some point of contact with the Infinite God, whose language is the language of life, and whose fellowship is the meaning of life. LIFE BEGINS AT THE POINT WHERE CONTACT IS MADE WITH FULL ENVIRONMENT. THIS IS THE FOUNDATION FOR ALL SUCCESSFUL LIVING, AND IT IS DEMONSTRATED IN THE LIVES OF ALL INTELLIGENT MEN, EVERYWHERE.

VALUES

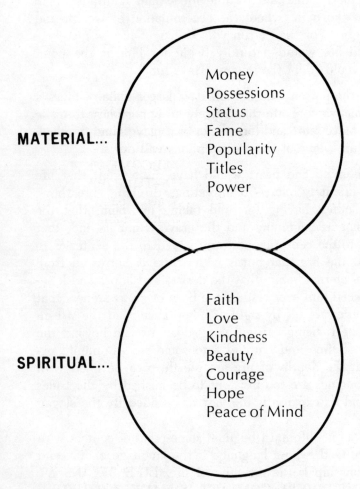

MATERIAL...

Money
Possessions
Status
Fame
Popularity
Titles
Power

SPIRITUAL...

Faith
Love
Kindness
Beauty
Courage
Hope
Peace of Mind

When a man combines GOLD and GOODNESS human nature is at its best.

THE LAW OF MATERIALISM

Webster's Dictionary defines materialism as "a doctrine that the only or the highest values or objectives, lie in material well-being, and in the furtherance of material progress. A preoccupation or stress upon material rather than intellectual or spiritual things."

We live in a materialistic age where the dominant force in the average person's life is possessions. Life has become a mad scramble for gain. We are so busy making a living we forget to make a life. Man is a slave to the material, to the artificial, to the tinsel and glamor. LIFE HAS BECOME A STRUGGLE FOR ECONOMIC SURVIVAL—THIS WE HAVE BROUGHT UPON OURSELVES. We have expanded our desires tenfold or more than necessary. We have built a world in which we must have entirely too many things for the good of most of us.

Material living brings with it a highly competitive life, with each of us trying to outdo the other financially, professionally, in business and in popularity. We expect security and happiness to be derived from the possession of great wealth. Financial independence is supposed to create a state of security, peace, and freedom from care and worry. There are many rich people who are miserable, but we think if WE had money we would really be happy. In spite of our affluence, insecurity and unhappiness are widespread.

When will man wake up and realize that he can live a simpler, freer, happier life when he is not saddled down with an overload of possessions? It is better to be happy, and at least to some degree comfortable, than to hazard everything in a mad scramble for this world's goods. MONEY IS A SERVANT, ITS VALUE IS IN ITS USE, AND NOWHERE ELSE. TRUE WEALTH IS BUILT UPON SOUND VALUES.

Today the glitter of money and possessions has blinded us to the real values of life. Material things do not bring a lasting joy, but only a temporary satisfaction. We cannot safely tie to any material value. The values of all material possessions change continually—sometimes overnight. Too many things can change, there are many reverses, many disappointments. You can lose a fortune overnight due to the stock market, business conditions, accidents, strikes, and many other conditions beyond your control. Money can slip through your fingers like fine sand.

Nothing of this nature has any permanent set value. The real values are those that stay by you, give you happiness and enrich you. When we realize that every material thing is temporary and passing, we can see that our emphasis in life should be on our state of spiritual awareness and growth. This is the foundation for the good life.

Very few realize the high price they pay for some of the material possessions they have. Thoreau said, "The cost of a thing is the amount of what I call life, which is required to be exchanged for it, immediately or in the long run."

One of the biggest sources of trouble with our day is GREED. WHY DOES NOT EVERY WORKER OR BUSINESSMAN AFTER THEY HAVE ACCUMULATED ENOUGH TO FINANCIALLY RETIRE, DO SO? INSTEAD THEY CONTINUE ON THE FANATIC RAT RACE FOR MONEY, UNTIL THEY DROP DEAD IN THEIR BOOTS. Money and possessions can become an obsession and enslave a man. Life is for more than that. Truly successful men are as different from one another as the myriad forms of matter. But these men have this in common: THEY SYSTEMATICALLY AND EFFECTIVELY ATTEND TO CERTAIN FUNDAMENTALS. These fundamentals fall into four groups: physical, financial, mental, and spiritual. THESE FUNDAMENTAL QUALITIES DEVELOPED EQUALLY ARE THE BASIS FOR SUCCESS AND HAPPINESS.

If wisely used, money may do much. Money makes money, interest works twenty-four hours a day, Sunday and holidays included. Money gives us the means of acquiring what we wish. If fresh air, a good house, books, music, are enjoyable, money will buy them; if leisure is an advantage, money enables us to take it; if seeing the world is delightful, it may pay for our journeys; if to help our friends, to relieve those who are in distress, is a privilege, money confers on us this great blessing. "Keep it then," said Swift, "in your head, but not in your heart."

We have no quarrel with money. Financial independence is good, but it does not guarantee happiness, physical health, mental health, spiritual growth, character, or any of the assets of faith, love, truth, confidence, patience, perseverance, joy, hope. These inner qualities are your real wealth. This is the wealth that thieves do not break in and steal.

Materialism has demonstrated conclusively that it cannot protect the well-being of mankind. Will it take a depression to make us satisfied and happier with less of the material and develop more of the inner qualities of life? Why can't we simplify our life today? The world is growing too complex, and it does not make people happier, just the opposite. IF MODERN MAN WERE MORE CONCERNED WITH WHAT HE IS, AND LESS DOMINATED BY WHAT HE HAS, HIS FEARS WOULD DIMINISH.

Irrespective of what is commonly called wealth, there are other riches: riches of courage, of generosity, of kindliness, of gentleness, of truth, of simplicity, and of nobility; riches of love and of loveliness; riches of happiness; and riches of laughter.

The great need of our day is to speed up character building in the home, the school and the church, to keep pace with the scientific and technological advancements. THE SUCCESS AND HAPPINESS OF ANY MAN DEPENDS UPON HIS CHARACTER, MOTIVES, AND IDEALS.

WE MUST CULTIVATE A DEFINITE SET OF VALUES AND LIVE BY THEM. As long as a human being evaluates the material things in life above the moral, the esthetic, and the spiritual, he has no future when it concerns the ways of life that are really and genuinely worthwhile. When man awakens to reality and the lasting values of life, he escapes from his own prison. LIFE IS THE MOST VALUABLE THING ANY PERSON POSSESSES. The art of living consists in distinguishing true values from false. A man's real wealth is within his skin. His inner qualities such as beauty, faith, joy, love, spiritual fiber, courage, confidence, discipline, integrity, self-control, clear thinking, fairness, faithfulness, good will, trust and hope, these are some of the great values of life. We cannot define them, or explain them. WE MUST EXPERIENCE THEM FOR THEY ARE THE MOST STABLE THINGS IN OUR LIVES.

What in life are the things WORTHWHILE? Love, joy, health, faith, peace of mind, work, honesty, positive thinking, optimism, courtesy, friendship, common duties, sorrow.

What in life are the things NOT worthwhile? Worry, pretense, envy, greed, discontent, criticism, resentment, fear, regret, temper, laziness, cynicism, dishonesty, lying, anger.

THERE IS A VALUE CRISIS IN THE WORLD TODAY. The young have not been taught the values of discipline, responsibility, dignity, good-manners, virtue, self-respect, honesty, ethics, love and respect for parents. Students today have little reverence for the past and little hope for the future. They are trying to live in the present. WHEN REMINDED OF OUR GREAT HERITAGE OF VALUES our youth respond in despair and with violence; and with an attitude of intolerance, distrust, and suspicion. EACH GENERATION DOES NOT HAVE TO RE-INVENT THE WHEEL. MUCH GOOD HAS COME OUT OF MAN'S HISTORY. CERTAINLY TEARING DOWN WHAT HAS BEEN ESTABLISHED, THE DESTRUCTION OF THE SOCIETY WE KNOW, IS NOT THE SOLUTION.

For years affluent parents—indoctrinated with the philoso-phy of permissiveness—have been buying off their youth with things. "We gave him everything" is the pathetic defense of bewildered parent after parent in conference with counsellor or police. By which they mean they have given him everything money could buy . . . everything but love . . . everything but themselves . . . everything but spiritual direction. Every-thing except responsibility for his own acts, and respect for the rights and feelings of others. They reared him in a spiritual and moral vacuum—nurtured him in a climate of nihilism—taught him to believe in Nothing. It has been estimated that there are twenty-five million American youths with absolutely no religious influence in their lives. We are beginning to reap as we have sown.

Our mad scramble for things has become the bandit that has looted us clean of the wealth of goodness, and with the loss of genuine goodness has gone our greatness. Our quest for gold has robbed us of our sense of God. Our boasted largeness is rapidly becoming our littleness. Even our religious life has deteriorated into a shallow pretense. We need a revival of the sense of individual worth. BOTH THE CHURCH AND SOCIETY NEED TO SPECIALIZE ON THE PRODUC-TION OF WORTHY MANHOOD. WE HAVE LOST THE ART OF BUILDING A MAN.

The individual who has the courage to live by a worthwhile set of values with tenderness, humility, understanding, and love derives the real wealth of JOY AND FULFILLMENT. It is well that we think often of the words of Henry Van Dyke: "Remember that what you possess in the world, will be found at the day of your death to belong to someone else, but what you are, will be yours forever."

THE ONLY REAL ABIDING SECURITY MAN CAN AT-TAIN IS HAVING A SENSE OF GOD. "TO HAVE EVERY-THING" IS TO HAVE IT ON THE INSIDE AND OUTSIDE BOTH. WHEN A MAN COMBINES WEALTH AND GOD-LINESS, HUMAN NATURE IS AT ITS BEST.

THE LAW OF MYSTERY

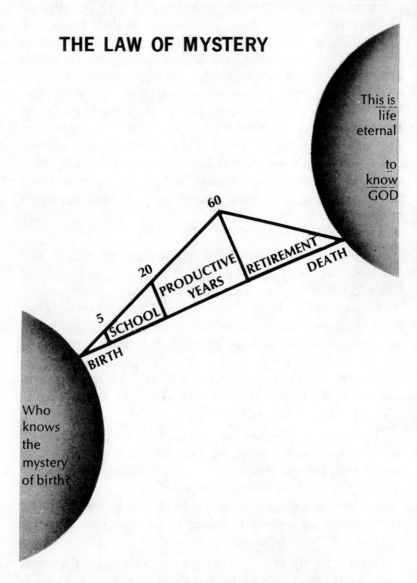

This is
life
eternal

to
know
GOD

Who
knows
the
mystery
of birth?

60

20

5

SCHOOL

PRODUCTIVE
YEARS

RETIREMENT

DEATH

BIRTH

Life begins in mystery and ends in mystery. The journey
through life is a collection of mysteries.

Segment 14

THE LAW OF MYSTERIES

Our life is surrounded by mystery. Mystery surrounds us on all sides, but we must not be impatient with it. The simple mysteries of life are compounded and compounded; so we look and live these mysteries so much that we do not see them. IT IS NOT POSSIBLE TO PROVE EVERYTHING; IT IS ALSO IMPOSSIBLE TO DEFINE EVERYTHING.

Christina Rossetti wrote, "Who has seen the wind? . . . Neither you nor I, . . . But when the trees bow down their heads, . . . The wind is passing by." Who has seen the wind? The fact that you cannot see it directly does not make it less real. Mystery—you cannot see the cause, you can only see the result.

That life has many profound mysteries I will freely admit, but mystery is not an argument against fact. Were it, we would be in a pitiful plight, indeed. IT IS NOT GIVEN TO US TO KNOW ALL THINGS AND TO SOLVE ALL MYSTERIES.

"The most beautiful thing we can experience is the mysterious. It is the source of all true art, science, and religion," says Albert Einstein. Modern man demands to know the HOW of all he accepts. There is no scientist who can explain the mystery of physical birth, the mystery of the electron, the bewildering phenomenon of germination, or the baffling riddle of a lily's growth. Newton discovered the law of gravity but not how it works, no one can. Who can explain with reason and logic why a caterpillar goes into his cocoon and later comes out a beautiful butterfly?

TO THE WISEST OF MEN THE FUTURE IS VEILED. THE SAGE HIMSELF WALKS BLINDFOLDED INTO THE FUTURE. THE PROFOUNDEST SCHOLAR DOES NOT KNOW WHAT A DAY MAY BRING FORTH.

I believe strongly, as did the Spanish philosopher, Santayana, that "MAN IS NOT MADE TO UNDERSTAND LIFE, BUT TO LIVE IT." A great lesson that many persons need to learn is that a man's inability to think things all out, or grasp things completely, should never keep him from living actively.

Ernest Holmes says, "We do not know how it is that an invisible energy causes the sap to flow up in a tree, or how it is that a chicken comes out of an egg. We may only watch the process. No biologist knows what life is, no psychologist knows what the mind is, no philosopher knows what reality is, and no theologian really knows what God is. Yet, put together all of these things, and that is what is meant when the word LIFE is used."

We play with words like world and life, eternity and infinite, beginning and end, but in our hearts we know that these are only the badges of our ignorance; we shall never understand what they ought to mean. A science without mystery is unknown; a religion without mystery is absurd.

Mary Smith writes, "If we could push ajar the gates of life, . . . And stand within, and all God's working see, . . . We could interpret all this doubt and strife, . . . And for each mystery could find a key. . . . But not today. . . . Then be content, poor heart. . . . God's plans, like lilies pure and white, unfold; . . . We must not tear the close-shut leaves apart . . . Time will reveal the calyxes of gold."

We cannot define or explain any of the real values of life, such as love, beauty, truth, friendship, Creation, God. They are the most stable things in our lives and yet we can only experience them. We do not explain . . . we can only state, and this is all we can do with a large proportion of all the facts and truths we know. There is a point, easily reached, where the simplest facts end in mystery, even as they begin in it; as each day lies between two nights. It is not given to man to know all things.

Lest the proclamation of mystery should seem alarming, let us add that this mystery also is scientific. The one subject on which all scientific men are agreed, the one theme on which all alike become eloquent, the one strain of pathos in all their writing, and speaking and thinking, concerns that final uncertainty, that utter blackness bounding their work on every side. Then we may know all that is? By no means. We may only know all that may be known. And that may be very little.

"Man is not born to solve the problems of the universe, but to find out what he has to do; and to restrain himself within the limits of his comprehension," wrote Goethe.

As this chapter is being written man has just landed and walked on the Moon. This is the first time in known history that man has been able to land on the celestial bodies. Perhaps now that we have entered the moon age, the real wisdom from this first journey will be the new perceptions it brings of human nature. If the moon can be grasped, why not the end of hunger, of greed, of warfare, of anxiety? From the standpoint of SCIENCE AND TECHNOLOGY this moon feat is man's greatest achievement. HOWEVER, THE REAL SPACE TO CONQUER LIES WITHIN OUR OWN CONSCIOUSNESS. THE ULTIMATE ACHIEVEMENT FOR EVERY MAN REMAINS THE JOURNEY THROUGH INNER SPACE.

The day of man's greatest scientific venture, could be the day of turning INWARD. Remember that to the person who has fellowship with God, life is not an enigma. Like Job, he will find it easy to believe that life moves forward under Divine convoy. Things do not happen; they come to pass in the purpose of God. Lincoln speaks of God as a "silent partner in our national enterprise." It is a thrilling and mysterious business to be able to justify the entrance of a Divine Leader in the affairs of men. The greatest thought that will ever possess any of us is—"GOD CARES FOR ME."

BENEFICIAL INACTIVITY

To be unhurried, free from burning ambitions and little jealousies, is more than merely a wholesome state of mind —it is positively a blessed state of mind.

Most of us are more in need of a deeper sense of contentment with life as it is, than we are of a deeper understanding of life.

We have been so much with the business of living that we have forgotten how to live.

We have heard so many sermons on life that life itself has become as hazy as the average philosophy about it.

What most of us need is some time free from anxiety. . . .

Time to watch a pair of birds carrying flies and worms to a nest full of young.

Time to watch a squirrel frisk from branch to branch and from log to log with apparently nothing on his mind except to frisk.

Time to watch a hawk make lazy circles on widestretched wings as though practicing some graceful maneuver.

Time to sprawl on the grass or a bed of dry leaves in a patch of sunlight and watch the clouds sail away on mysterious voyages to far places across endless seas of blue sky.

Time to just think and dream of nothing until both heart and mind become so still that God can speak to us again of things that really matter.

THE LAW OF NATURALNESS AND SIMPLICITY

Naturalness is the first law of abiding greatness. How majestic is naturalness. I have never met a man whom I really considered a great man who was not always natural and simple. What is according to nature is best, and what is contrary to nature is always distasteful. Naturalness is the easiest thing in the world to acquire, if you will but be yourself—forget about the impression you are trying to make.

Mankind has moved a long way from his "natural condition." Thoreau has left us a splendid example of the privilege of direct and immediate contact with the living processes of nature. The man who wants to get back to the source of his own vitality cuts through the false fronts of life, and the artificialities of our civilization, which drifts further and further from the realities of life. The wise man seeks to renew himself with the things he can see, hear and feel. By direct contact with nature, by fashioning something with his own two hands.

Few things are as regenerative to the human spirit, to the stress-ridden mind and body, as a few days or weeks of close contact with sun, water, and woods. We are refreshed by the experience of swimming in the ocean, walking on the beach, or climbing the mountains among the tall pine trees, fishing in the stream or lakes, or soaking up some sun on the desert. All these primitive places have not yet been spoiled by man.

Getting away from the cities of concrete and asphalt, can level the frustrations of workaday problems far more meaningfully and effectively than any tranquillizer manufactured by man. These strains are not only real, but they make it imperative that we return from time to time to that well-spring of humanity which we once knew so intimately—the world of nature.

Amid the confusion and anxiety of modern life, our wearied minds dream of simplicity. To aspire to simple living is one of the highest goals man can achieve. Modern man has complicated and confused his life. We are creating our own problems and conflicts and it is making us irritable and very unhappy. The wise man will ever seek to simplify his life.

Oscar Wilde wrote, "Life is not complex, WE ARE complex." Life is simple and the simple thing is the right thing. Our life is frittered away by detail. The haste of modern living is waste in the truest, deepest sense. We are so busy reaching for things beyond us that we miss eternal values which are near at hand.

Man's whole problem today socially, economically, is that he's made his life so complicated he doesn't know how to extricate himself from the mess he has created. He is afraid if he simplifies he will be impeding progress. Yet the human values are far more valuable in the world than any technical progress. Until man can fully injest and use constructively and to his benefit, all this technical progress, perhaps it is time to back-track a little, and regain some of the self-control and self-awareness that is man's true duty on earth.

Thoreau wrote, "I went to the woods because I wished to live deliberately, to face only the essential facts of life and see if I could not learn what it had to teach, and not when I came to die, discover that I had not lived. Let your affairs be as two or three, and not a hundred or a thousand; instead of a million count half a dozen, and keep your accounts on your thumbnail." THE WISE MAN WILL EVER SEEK TO SIMPLIFY HIS LIFE.

We are told in the First Chapter of Genesis that at the close of the sixth day, "God saw everything that He had made and behold, it was very good." Yet how few of us appreciate the beautiful world we live in.

We must learn to simplify our lives. Our wants are endless and can never be satisfied, but our actual needs are few. By simplifying and removing a lot of cares, we automatically increase our happiness and the quality of life.

Simplicity goes hand in hand with the law of survival. People today are going through life with too much baggage. They must have two or three cars in a family, a city home, plus a beach home, and sometimes a mountain home, a boat, an airplane. Life becomes a mad scramble for gain and speed, at the expense of one's health and peace of mind. We live too fast.

Simplicity is making the journey of this life with just baggage enough. The greatest truths are the simplest and so are the greatest men. The more simply you live, the more secure is your fortune; you are less at the mercy of surprises and reverses. Bertrand Russell reminds us that "Forty or fifty years ago things were simpler, people understood life better. The way things are going, getting more complicated, only a few people will run the world in the future; that will take place if man does not wake up and realize there is more to life than scientific progress, and a decay of the natural elements of living."

Whether you are eighty or eighteen, let simplicity govern your life. Use and enjoy what you have, be grateful for present blessings and opportunities. True happiness does not depend upon great material possessions, but emanates largely from a mental attitude of contentment, confidence, serenity, and beneficence. Simplicity of life leads to happiness.

Rhoda Lachar admonishes: "Your life is what you make it. Your life can be simple if you will set it up with simplicity as a goal. IT WILL TAKE COURAGE TO CUT AWAY FROM THE THOUSAND AND ONE HINDRANCES THAT MAKE LIFE COMPLEX, BUT IT CAN BE DONE."

Segment 16

THE LAW OF ADAPTABILITY

Man has within himself and within his environment, everything he needs to fulfill his purpose in this life. He has the potential to solve every problem, and to bear all of life's sufferings and hardships that come his way, all of life's situations —successfully. HE IS ADAPTABLE.

Adaptability is a kind of private revolution. Each time you learn something new you must readjust the whole framework of your knowledge. A principle of happiness is proper adjustment. One is forced to make inner and outer adjustments all one's life; the process never ends.

The pressures of daily life are more likely to spring from relationships between people rather than the relationship between man and his environment. These strains are not only real, but they make it imperative that we adjust. Life is a continuous series of adjustments to reality. MAN'S FREEDOM IS NOT FREEDOM FROM CONDITIONS, BUT RATHER FREEDOM TO TAKE A STAND ON WHATEVER CONDITIONS MIGHT CONFRONT HIM.

Anything can happen today . . . socially, politically, industrially, personally, monetarily, in fact, in every phase of life and living as we have known it. It is a mad, crazy world. The secret is adapting. Not adapting in the sense you become a hippie-dippie, but adapting your life and plans to overcome the confusion and barbarianism of the herd.

In this country we are at war with ourselves; we are in a revolution because people have lost the art of thinking for themselves. If you stand for truth and principle you know what you are FOR and what you are AGAINST. If you stand for NOTHING, you can adapt to EVERYTHING. Adapt yourself around a bad situation, you do not have to adapt to it.

100

ADAPTABILITY IS A GOOD CONCEPT IF IT IS KEPT IN BALANCE. One of the keynotes of Communist propaganda is to accept what comes along in the name of intelligence, and adaptability . . . people become so mesmerized they accept just about anything. If you do not adapt to all the changes that come along, regardless of their source, you are considered unintelligent, unsophisticated, and uncooperative. One surely would not give up the multitudinous benefits of being an American and adapt to Communism just to be a ready adapter. You would have to assassinate your brains first. Changes are brought about by the government, the church, the school, the fashion designers, Madison Avenue, and industry. There is almost a frenzy to see who can adapt to something new the quickest, regardless of how stupid or silly it may be. As you can readily see there is a fine line to adapting. Man can easily adapt to the wrong thing. He can adapt from freedom to slavery, from morality to immorality, and if he does he slowly but surely destroys himself. Reason, logic, truth, sound judgment, principles and ideals must all come into consideration. The public lets many degrading conditions happen because they are not thinking and many politicians base their decisions on the number of votes, not what is right or wrong.

Rhoda Lachar writes, "You are a receiving station for everything depressing, complex, and stupid that goes on in the world, and you accept too much of what comes through to you without censorship. The beauty, brilliance, order, and other wonderful qualities of the world rarely filter through to your station. Why? Because there is nothing sensational about the good things in life so we pass them by unnoticed and take them for granted. There is no news value in goodness, simplicity, love, and optimism; but hate, thoughts of depression, reports of destruction, stories about the rottenness and complexity of life—Ah! these have news value. This is why as a receiving station you are loaded down with everything that is depressing and makes life unbearable. This impossible 'stuff' comes at you from all directions."

"We have a general name for the happenings around us which affect us," writes Harold Fink. "That name is environment. Roughly, environment includes any influence outside us. It might be the weather, the house you live in, the tools you work with, your next door neighbor. All of the things going on with which you interact can be called environment."

We actually create or control our own environment and therefore in a sense, we are adapting to something we created. The ultimate aim in life is to have a completely inner directed life. All the spiritual and moral qualities of character are manufactured right inside our own little skin by what raw materials we let in, by how we refine them, by what application we put them to, and by how we attempt to distribute them to others. What we are, what we get, what we do, and what we reap are all results of how we manufacture the stuff called character.

I have in my mind a picture of perfect adaptability for a human, a goal to strive toward. Its essence is that a person should be able to take whatever comes. He should be able to take each type of person and work himself around in harmony with that person, without trying to change him. We cannot really change anyone else, but if we can get in harmony with them we can reap many benefits from them by understanding them, by accepting the expression they give, and by analyzing their life and the results they have achieved.

This ideal of adaptability includes taking the changes in technology and social thinking in stride, taking the world as it is, not excusing it, but not condemning it either. Just accepting it, as it is—and trying to "brighten the corner where you are."

ADAPTABILITY IN ITS CONSTRUCTIVE SENSE, AND IN THE SENSE WHICH SHOULD BE EMPHASIZED, IS THAT OF "GOING ALONG WITH LIFE," NOT BUCKING THE THINGS YOU CAN'T CHANGE, BUT CHANGING THE THINGS YOU CAN CHANGE.

It all goes back to the basic precept that each individual is responsible for his own self. That the whole stupid evil world can go swirling around you, can take your possessions, can tax you, can draft you in the Army, can infringe on your privacy and on your inherent rights, but yet YOU ARE STILL YOU, AND THE THINGS THAT ARE YOU ARE INSIDE. THIS INNER SPIRIT THAT IS MAN, CAN ADAPT TO ANY CIRCUMSTANCE, IF HIS ATTITUDE, HIS THOUGHTS, HIS INSIGHT, HIS UNDERSTANDING IS PROPER.

Dr. Viktor Frankl's book explains how men adapted to the demoralizing, animal existence in German concentration camps. Those who kept their human dignity, called upon spiritual growth, the memory of love, the willingness to sacrifice for the comfort and safety of their fellows, their willingness to work hard and to continue to believe in their own intrinsic value. THEY MAINTAINED A MEANING FOR THEIR LIFE. It is NOT the physically strong who survive in the concentration camps, or in the arena of life. IT IS ALWAYS THE PEOPLE WHO ARE STRONG INWARDLY.

Adapting doesn't mean just "taking it" whether you like it or not. It is changing your attitude, your way of looking at things so that everything that comes your way is beneficial, and nothing is detrimental. SORROW IS A CHANCE TO GROW, ECONOMIC REVERSES ARE A CHANCE TO PUT THE MATERIAL VALUES IN THEIR PROPER PLACE, CONFLICT WITH OTHER PERSONS IS A CHANCE TO SEE OURSELVES IN ACTION, to analyze our drawbacks, and to work at correcting them. The more we analyze this subject of adapting, the more we realize how vital it is to our everyday well-being.

Your inner strength is the cushion for life's hard knocks. Life asks a continuous series of adjustments to reality. Nothing in life is STATIC, one must learn to make ADJUSTMENTS. But NEVER COMPROMISE A PRINCIPLE OR RELINQUISH A VITAL TRUTH JUST FOR THE SAKE OF ADAPTING.

THE LAW OF ACTION

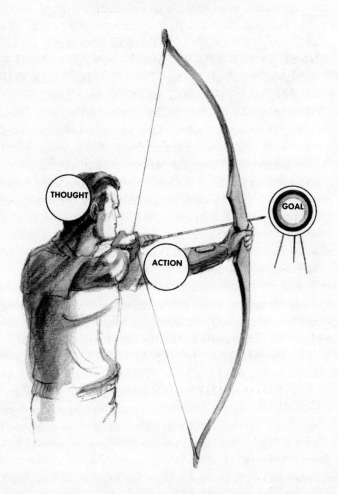

Action is the necessary link between thought and deed. Action is the way to get things done, but the METHOD can be RIGHT or WRONG. It is important to use the RIGHT AND SAFE METHOD.

THE LAW OF ACTION

Man is designed for action. This is a law of man's nature. Everything in his being is built for action. Some people are discontented and dissatisfied in life because they have not learned the basic principle of their being—that they are born for action.

Thought is the seed of action. Thinking is easy, acting is difficult, and to put one's thoughts into action is the most difficult thing in the world. All worthwhile men have good thoughts, good ideas and good intentions—but precious few of them ever translate those into right action.

A FELLOW DOESN'T LAST LONG ON WHAT HE HAS DONE. HE'S GOT TO KEEP DELIVERING AS HE GOES ALONG. IT IS NOT WHAT YOU KNOW, BUT WHAT YOU DO, THAT COUNTS.

There are SAFE and UNSAFE WAYS of doing nearly everything. The knowledge or knack of doing things safely is gained by experience, properly directed. Most of the time we do not learn the methods or techniques necessary for careful and effective action.

YOU CAN HAVE THE RIGHT IDEAS, BUT USE THE WRONG METHOD, AND THEREBY FAIL TO ACCOMPLISH YOUR OBJECTIVE. Like trying to stop a Sherman tank with a bow and arrow, or increasing your capital by betting on the horses. The objective may be fine but the method can be wrong. THE END RESULT ALWAYS PROVES THE CORRECTNESS OF THE METHOD.

Method is PLANNED ACTION. It is the art of obtaining maximum results with the minimum of effort. Lay down a method for everything; it is essential for knowledge, fortune and life. Life begins when you make it begin!

If you want to go fishing you can put the bait on the hook that you like—that's action. But if you want to catch fish you must put the bait on the hook that the fish likes—that's action plus proper method.

It has been said that the height of wisdom for man is that he shall know WHAT TO DO NEXT, and the height of courage is the strength to DO that which should be done. We try to short cut. Action involves learning every step of the way. Everybody wants to be a professional; no one wants to be an amateur. But how do you learn? You learn by doing.

If you really want to do something worthwhile and want to do it hard enough, lay the foundation by doing the preliminary, unimportant, little and big tasks which give you the "know how" and the complete sureness which will carry you right toward your goal. If you are completely absorbed in this doing, you will reach your goals. As you reach each new goal, you will find you have become stronger and more confident. Good luck always seems to line up on the side of the man who gets into action. One of the most insistent things in life is that you are ultimately judged by what you actually accomplish.

Do you keep calm in emergencies, or lose your head and go to pieces? Do you think rapidly, yet clearly and logically, or do you freeze up and go dead? To succeed, you need to cultivate the ability and the habit of remaining unexcited, yet able to leap to action on high tension, reach the right decision, then act on it.

Millions of people throughout the world go through life as failures because they have fallen prey to procrastination and decided to wait, always waiting for the time to be just right to start doing something they already know is good, worthwhile, and should be done at once. Don't delay. The time will never be just right. The only period of time we can act upon is right now. Start today, start right where you stand, and work with whatever tools you now have at your command.

Everything we do from the time we arise to the time we retire at night has something to do with the extent of our success in life. Many great ideas have been allowed to vanish for the lack of action. While we are postponing, life speeds by.

"Nature . . . favors those who are sober, alert, intelligent, and enthusiastic; most of all those who have the courage to take risks and who possess the will to succeed. She smiles on those who are ready to live hard and dangerously. Whoever refuses to take risks pays the penalty of loss of life in one form or another," wrote Alexis Carrel. If you stand up to the human race you lose something called their "good will"; if you kowtow to them you gain . . . their permission to continue kowtowing.

Motion is not progress, activity is not achievement. The squirrel on his revolving treadmill achieves both motion and activity without getting anywhere. The drifter may be intensely active and yet be moving in a backward direction. Omar Bradley says, "In war or peace the naked fact remains the same. We are given one life, we have one span to live it. We can wait for circumstances to make up their mind or we can decide to act, and in acting, live."

Your energy can be dissolved, like so much steam, into the empty air, if you talk too much about your plans. BE A DOER, NOT A TALKER.

"Think it over," yes, but do not dawdle until someone else has thought it over, worked it out, and put it over. A man who has to be convinced to act before he acts is NOT a man of action . . . you must act as you breathe.

Act as though it were impossible to fail. Your actions and your actions alone, determine your worth. IF YOU SIT BACK QUIETLY AND WATCH THE WORLD GO BY—IT WILL. There is no fate that plans men's lives. Whatever comes to us, good or bad, is usually the result of our own action or lack of action. Action is the basis of all attainment.

Segment 18

THE LAW OF MODERATION AND BALANCE

The law of moderation runs through the whole of life. Moderation is strength, not weakness; it requires self-command and self-control. To live in moderation means to follow the middle course as much as possible. AVOID EXTREMES of good or bad, pleasure or sorrow, elation or depression, affluence or poverty.

Moderation is one of the most important words in the dictionary—not too much, not too little. This applies to eating, drinking, sex, work, or play. Every excess has its aftermath, its HANGOVER, EVERYTHING that exceeds the BOUNDS OF MODERATION has an UNSTABLE FOUNDATION.

To learn moderation is the essence of sound sense and real wisdom. Moderation should run through the whole of life. Yet man is ingenious in discovering ways and perfecting means to depart from moderation.

The greatest example of balance and moderation is found in Nature. The entire universe operates in complete balance and harmony with each of its parts. There is just enough of everything to make the whole system work simultaneously and successfully.

In Nature, as in our own lives, when any extreme exists chaos is the result. An extreme of rain causes flood damage, an extreme of alcohol causes brain and liver damage, an extreme of sunshine causes drought, an extreme of physical pleasure causes a deep depression.

To eat or drink too much, to play too much, to work too much, to grumble too much—all of these are equally pernicious. "MODERATION WITH ORDER," should be our motto.

David Swing, lecturing before a Chicago Literary Club, closed his address with the words, "Over almost everything except our virtues there might be written the condemnation, 'Too much.'" Medical science says we eat too much; others claim we drink too much; doctors say we doctor too much; others say we go too much. Overdoing has become an epidemic. Everything is pushed. Life has taken on a jazz tempo and death has speeded up its pace.

Moderation was taught as the supreme moral code by the ancients. Eat not to dullness; drink not to elevation. Moderation is health, excess is disease. Moderation is the secret of survival. Fuller wrote, "Moderation is the silken string running through the pearl-chain of all virtues."

Perhaps the greatest weakness of man is his inability to say NO. This weakness asserts itself in myriad ways—the weakness of not saying no to the temptations, sometimes far from obvious, that come one's way. There's the temptation of working beyond one's strength, the temptation of unworthy ambition, the temptation to be "a good fellow," the temptation to seek or accept office because your friends think you ought to—temptations without end.

It is odd when one thinks of it, that there are people in the world who, having renounced all the laws of God and nature, have themselves made laws which they rigorously obey.

Rome was not conquered by the barbarians, but by its own excesses, which so weakened the constitution of the state that it fell easy prey to a stronger and more vital people. There is a distressed feeling and anxiety in the air today, thinking people are worried about the future. Man appears prosperous, but beneath the surface his whole affluent society is false. People have exchanged their real 24 karat fine gold for fool's gold; in values, in morals, in education, in character, in just about everything. We are going into the dark ages and very few realize it. Industrial science and technology advance, but everything else is deteriorating and depleting.

The forty-seven segments in this Supreme Philosophy are designed to make you aware of the variety and extent of forces and elements in your life. When you finish reading this book you will have a good grasp of how marvelous and complete your life can be if all these segments are kept in balance with each other, and each accorded its proper place and weight in the overall scheme of things.

The way to know if we are on the right track or not, is to take Karl Menninger's approach. When we are out of harmony there will be illness, chaos, foreboding circumstances, mental strain, improper personal relations. When we are in balance there will be harmony, peace of mind, a buoyant feeling of worthwhileness, and a quiet joy with everything working well. More successes than failures, more completed projects than otherwise, more enjoyable relations with family and friends.

Just as the balance of hydrocarbons in your automobile's gasoline determines how smoothly it runs, so your life will run smoothly if the major elements are in balance.

When strain, distress, worry, stomachaches, and headaches, personal conflicts are present in your life—analyze, question— Where am I off balance? What am I doing in excess? What am I neglecting? And of course, what you are doing in excess is automatically causing neglect in the opposite area. If you are working too long hours for your particular physical and mental makeup you are neglecting your rest, fresh air, and exercise. If you are partying too much, drinking too much, you are neglecting cultural and mental pursuits and should spend an evening or two reading or listening to good music to counterbalance the frivolity. When our balance is destroyed, we are unhappy. But when we are in tune with ourselves, we go about our business with every aspect of ourselves, physical and mental, working in harmony. Then we know what happiness is.

Balance should be a key factor in our criteria for choosing friends and associates. People who live unbalanced lives upset or destroy the lives of everyone around them. Unbalanced persons include hypochrondriacs, alcoholics, bores, chronic complainers; those who are frivolous, greedy, selfish, dishonest, conniving, immoral. Many personalities are out of balance in this world and these are the people we dislike, avoid, or push aside when the big assignments come.

Who are the enemies of the world? The unbalanced Hitlers, and Mussolinis, the power crazy, the over-sexed, the lazy, the gluttonous. When evil or negative factors are in excess they produce nothing but excessive evil and negativeness in everything they touch. Excessive pursuit of pleasure leads to indiscriminate sex, artificial stimulation by dope and alcohol; the jag is on and theft, murder, and suicide result. The whole of society can be contaminated by just one imbalanced person.

"Human life is a search for satisfaction," writes Dr. Harold Fink. "Tensions beween organs and tissues drive us to restore balance among them. This urge to restore our integrity, our wholeness, is the root of all progress, all morality, and all nervousness."

The conditions of life enforce on us their own balance. Without hardship there would be no evidence of development; without danger there would be no courage; without need there would never be any effort; without suffering—no compassion.

Lest the task of keeping in balance seem too great an undertaking remember that there is an enabling power in this life that gives us all the power and ability we need to live properly. THE GREATEST BALANCE IN LIFE IS TO BE IN HARMONY WITH THE CREATOR OF LIFE, the Author of the laws that keep the universe, the mind, and the spirit in balance. In a world where things are made to wear out quickly, intelligent men seek personal and spiritual fulfillment and the things that last.

CORRECT USE OF MAN

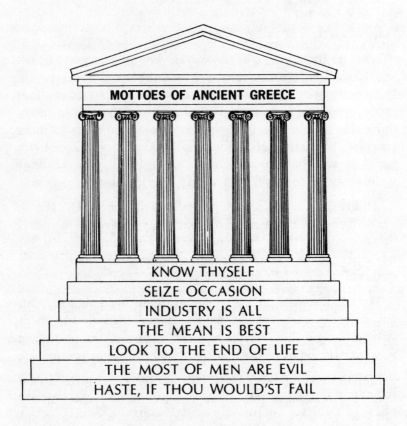

MOTTOES OF ANCIENT GREECE

KNOW THYSELF
SEIZE OCCASION
INDUSTRY IS ALL
THE MEAN IS BEST
LOOK TO THE END OF LIFE
THE MOST OF MEN ARE EVIL
HASTE, IF THOU WOULD'ST FAIL

We have spent much and long upon the science of matter, and the greater our success the greater must be our failure, unless we turn also at long last to an equal advance in the science of man. Most of our deficiencies stem from our spiritual inadequacies.

THE LAW OF CORRECT USE OF MAN

The most important thing to learn in life, is how to live. There is NOTHING men are so anxious to keep as their life . . . and NOTHING they give so little attention to. Happiness and success in life do not depend on our circumstances, but upon ourselves. More men have ruined themselves than have ever been destroyed by others. Of all the ruins, the ruin of man is the saddest, and "a man's worst enemy," as Seneca said, "is the one in the breast."

Some men have a purpose in life, and some have none. Our first objective should be to make as much out of ourselves as can be made out of the stuff that is in us. "The aim of every man," said Humboldt, "shall be to secure the highest and most harmonious development of his powers to a complete and consistent whole." We must not, however, attempt this merely with a selfish objective, or we are foredoomed to failure. For as Bacon said, "No man's private fortune can be an end in any way worthy of his existence." Some of the best and greatest minds—Plato, Aristotle, St. Paul, Buddha—would never have been content to perfect themselves merely for themselves. We are to make the best of ourselves FOR THE SAKE OF OTHERS.

Today we are emphasizing all the wonderful technological and scientific changes that man has developed. The progress of our affluent society, in the sense of material acquisition, is something, but PROGRESS IN THE SENSE OF BEING, IS A GREAT DEAL MORE. TO GROW HIGHER, DEEPER, WIDER, AS THE YEARS GO ON; TO CONQUER DIFFICULTIES, TO FEEL ALL ONE'S FACULTIES UNFOLDING, AND TRUTH DESCENDING INTO THE SOUL . . . THIS MAKES LIFE WORTH LIVING. "It is not brains that matter most," Dostoevski once wrote, "but that which guides them—the character, the heart, the generous qualities."

THE LAW OF USE IS AN INFALLIBLE LAW. WHAT YOU USE INCREASES. WHAT YOU DO NOT USE, OR ABUSE, WILL RECEDE AND REDUCE. For example, if a man is lacking in strength, he can gain strength by using all the energy units he possesses to the fullest extent. For another example, if a problem is too big for one's mentality, one works at it to the fullest extent of one's logic and reason. In so doing, one is consuming the units of intellect. When these units are exhausted, it is a law of life that augments and increases their output, giving one greater mental ability. This law holds good in respect to every function of man. ALL OF MAN'S TALENTS INCREASE OR DECREASE IN PROPORTION TO THE EXTENT TO WHICH HE APPLIES THEM. As much as you think and do, to that degree you develop. What you exercise you develop, and that which you do not exercise will recede. WHAT YOU USE SHALL BE INCREASED, THAT WHICH YOU DO NOT USE, OR MISUSE, SHALL BE TAKEN AWAY. THIS IS A FUNDAMENTAL, BASIC LAW.

Man did make one giant step forward, technologically speaking, when he placed his feet on the moon. How does man make "one giant step forward" on the earth? Man's destiny lies not in the stars or the moon but on earth itself. TO BUILD A BETTER LIFE ON EARTH IS IN OUR OWN HANDS, IN OUR OWN HEARTS. This is infinitely possible. Man has not even scratched the surface of his own nature, nor the truth of his own existence. With the ability to trace human behavior, to measure it, to see it applying itself in life's situations, there is a marvelous challenge for all of us.

THE QUALITY OF LIFE is more important than life itself. Ten qualities that are very important and should be developed by every human being are: ATTITUDE, HABITS, COURAGE, FAITH, CLEAR THINKING, SELF-CONTROL, FAIRNESS, FIDELITY, INTEGRITY, HOPE. THE GLORIOUS MASTERPIECE OF MAN IS TO LIVE PROPERLY. Mirabeau said, "Why should we call ourselves men, unless it be to succeed in everything, everywhere?"

Man is constantly looking for new approaches to live his life "to the full." The basic foundation for the "fullness of life" is established by learning and practicing the fundamental laws of man's nature. When man practices these principles ninety percent of his problems evaporate.

No branch of science is more useful than the knowledge of man. It is of the utmost importance to be able to decide wisely, not only whom you can trust, and whom you cannot; but how far, and in what you can trust them. Envy is a deadly disease, the chagrin or mortification felt because of the good fortune of another. Most other vices have some justification. There is power in ambition even though at times it is misdirected. There is enjoyment in luxury, even though it is sometimes allowed to sink to an unworthy level. There is some dignity in pride, even though it frequently makes itself tall by walking on borrowed stilts. But envy—its only satisfaction will be to die by the poison of its own sting and burn in the hell of its own jealousy. One may meet a fair rival in open combat, but who knows how to meet the coward who smiles and smirks and praises while he drives the knife of envy under one's fifth rib? Success is envy's hell. Failure in others is its heaven. There is no surer way of depriving one's self of the things the successful have than to envy the success of the successful.

Everything that a man does is determined by and is an expression of his values. We must have a definite set of values and live them. Decide what is important, what is relatively important, and what is unimportant. A person does not have to be thinking about values in order to be acting upon them. Values are bound up with the business of living. They provide the bridge by which we cross over to and relate to and communicate with the world of physical objects, animals, other human beings, and God. THE THING THAT WILL HELP YOUR INNER LIFE IS TO SET UP IN YOUR MIND A STANDARD OF VALUES SO THAT YOU KNOW WHAT IS REALLY SIGNIFICANT, IMPORTANT AND VALUABLE.

"How well it would be," said Seneca, "if men would but exercise their brains, as they do their bodies, and take as much pains for virtue as they do for pleasure." A PERSON GETS PAID FOR USING HIS BRAIN, NOT JUST FOR HAVING ONE.

It is impossible to exaggerate the possibilities of man. No unit of measurement will scale the heights to which he may attain. Nor can we reckon the power of his potential might. How pathetic then, that so many of us are content to live on such a mediocre scale.

One of the most important lessons to learn is the fact that we can all improve ourselves. Another important lesson man has to learn is how to guide by his reason the great driving force of his emotions. Man, without controlling his emotions, can get into all kinds of trouble. He can be led by the wrong leader playing on his emotions of hate, anger, greed, to plunder, burn, murder, and do all kinds of disreputable things. Or he can be led by the right leader to do all the things that are fine for himself and society.

Man has been rightly defined as a "worshipping animal." If he does not subscribe to the Biblical statement of the Eternal God he will create a god to which he will render his undivided allegiance. He may not "go to church" but he will, nevertheless, attend a church of his own making. He may call himself an atheist, but he is, in reality, a devout believer. He may flatter himself that he does not "believe in prayer" but he is finally a devout "man of faith." He must worship something. He is built that way. If not the God revealed in the Bible, then the gods of "The State," "Success," "Money," "Power," "Knowledge," "Pleasure." Of course, he does not call them God, but they command the same devotion that a believer renders to the True God—and alas, sometimes even more and better devotion. BUT THE FINAL HOUR OF LIFE WILL BRING DISILLUSIONMENT. HE WILL FIND THAT HIS GOD IS TOO SMALL AND ALTOGETHER INADEQUATE.

Science has given no formulas for easing the tension that invades our modern living. As man takes possession of the laws of his nature he has less need for prescriptions. The ideal life is useful and productive, free from fear and worry, in which one realizes one's nature perfectly. Spiritual faith comforts man, insires him, and gives meaning to his being.

The great scientific discoveries of the past hundred years have been as child's play compared with the titanic forces that will be released when man applies himself to the understanding and mastery of his own nature. CONFLICT CANNOT CEASE IN THE WORLD UNTIL IT CEASES IN MAN.

Dr. Wernher von Braun, the leading space scientist, says, "Only if God is reinstated in the heart of the world will He furnish mankind and its leaders with ethical guidance through dangers and pitfalls of the space age." This is the foundation for a rich dynamic life. It equips us with positive PERSONAL VALUES as anchors against the storms of life.

It isn't merely life that matters, IT IS THE QUALITY OF YOUR LIFE THAT MATTERS. It is the COURAGE, CONFIDENCE, JOY, AND SERVICE YOU BRING TO YOUR LIFE. What does life expect from us? Our answer must consist not in talk and meditation but in RIGHT ACTION AND IN RIGHT CONDUCT.

What we are WITHIN registers itself WITHOUT. A river first digs a channel, then the channel controls the river. Men do not deliberately set out to become villains, drunks, thieves, drug addicts. They gradually become all these things by allowing themselves to become victims of the stream that cuts the channel of living deeper and deeper. We must form high ideals and good habits and control what channels are dug in our lives. The soul must become subordinated to high moral and spiritual ideals until at last such spiritual faculties become the dominating power in our life. Thus, and only thus, can any of us come to his highest and best and fullest living.

THE LAW OF CHANGE

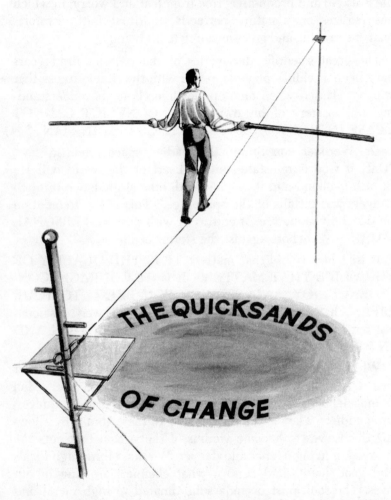

THE QUICKSANDS OF CHANGE

We are living in a world where change is the norm, but all change is not progress. Man is continually walking a tightrope deciding which changes to accept. Truth never changes.

Segment 20

THE LAW OF CHANGE

Everything except the Law of Change is constantly undergoing transformation. "There is nothing permanent except change," said Heraclitus, and this aphorism holds true more than ever in our space age. To be living in the afternoon of the Twentieth Century is to experience one of the most revolutionary periods of history. As bits of colored glass change positions in a kaleidoscope to form new patterns, so the forces of technological progress and social revolution change the patterns of our lives. Today we live in a world much different from that which existed just a few years ago. Tomorrow will bring even more spectacular changes.

The dynamic changes brought about in the lives of men and women in the past seventy years have been almost entirely due to the work of inventors, scientists, and technologists. During the past seventy years, man has done more to change his environment than in all his previous history. He has tunneled through mountains, spanned and harnessed rivers, and converted farm land and forests into modern industrial centers. He has erected high rise office and apartment buildings, laid super highways across continents, and installed efficient manufacturing facilities. In a variety of ways, he has changed the face of his world.

We live in a TECHNOLOGICAL AGE. Our world is changing rapidly. Just imagine, in the last ten years we have put man in space, orbited the earth, walked in space, developed space satellites for instant communication with all the earth, traveled faster than sound. And man's greatest scientific achievement in history was to send men to the moon, walk on the moon and return safely to earth. WHY SHOULD NOT MAN, WHO HAS CONQUERED ENERGY AND MATTER, ESTABLISH THIS SAME MASTERY OVER HIMSELF? WHAT GOOD IS ALL OUR MATERIAL ADVANCEMENT, IF WE DO NOT BECOME BETTER PEOPLE?

119

Drastic and dramatic changes are taking place NOW . . . socially, politically, industrially, personally, and economically; in fact, in every phase of life as we have known it. These changes will be very confusing to the person who lacks personal understanding, and the know-how to meet the future. TIMES CHANGE, PEOPLE CHANGE, CONDITIONS CHANGE, NATIONS CHANGE. There are over ten million people in these United States working everyday on processes and devices to change your life.

Technology has become the common mode of human living, and is invading every institution and activity. It has not only a physical effect in changing man's material way of life, but it brings with it mental upheaval as well. The sudden growth of technology has created social problems of the first magnitude. Old customs have crumbled; the relationships between parents and children, teachers and pupils, employers and workers, all these have been changed. There has been greater change, greater technological improvements, greater scientific progress in the space of a current single lifetime than has taken place in all previous history. 85% of all the scientists that have ever lived are alive at this moment. The jumbo jets will soon be flashing across the oceans at near supersonic speeds, carrying hundreds of intercontinental passengers each trip. The communication satellite program already is making possible instant telecasts between remote parts of the world, and this system is steadily expanding. Science and technology have shrunk our planet.

Man has built a "Frankenstein" of technology that is threatening him. The fumes and odors and contaminants from our factories, power plants, and refineries and automobiles are polluting the air. The chemicals and waste discharges from our cities and industrial complexes are killing the marine life in the rivers, lakes, oceans. He is depleting the natural resources, forests, soil, oil, minerals, air, water.

WE ARE LIVING IN A MAN-MADE ENVIRONMENT. Noisy canyons of concrete-brick-asphalt, cities filled with confusion, violence, and smog. Freeways which are good, but great tension builders. WE HAVE BUILT A SYNTHETIC WORLD. Man has his fists full of synthetic paper money which is worth less and less every day. We are living in a changing world whose tempo is becoming faster every day, and people feel insecure.

Today we have synthetic air conditioning where 90% of the air we breathe is not fresh air, but is old air, either cooled or heated then recirculated. If it is cooled too much it causes the pores of our skin to close up and we get sick.

Synthetic food is one reason so many people are sick. We no longer eat natural foods. What is natural food? Natural food simply means food that still has in it the natural vitamins, enzymes, and minerals that nature put there. But 80% of the food consumed by the average American has had them all taken out. Years ago vitamin pills were unheard of. 40% of your energy comes from the food you eat, and 60% of your energy comes from fresh air.

We want everything push-button, all the conveniences, we complicate our lives with all our contrivances. We should be putting the emphasis on developing the quality of our life. This starts by simplification of our lives, which eliminates confusion and brings enjoyment and contentment. We have allowed our human qualities to wither because we look only for the things that technology makes available and we are willing to become its passive beneficiary.

But have we improved man? We have improved our machines but not ourselves. Man must watch his way of living so that the rapid change does not destroy him, or that he does not destroy himself. We are emphasizing all the wonderful technical and scientific changes, but we do not realize how we are shrinking man's nature and his natural enjoyment of life.

We should develop within ourselves good character, consideration for others, health, peace, joy, happiness, a kindly spirit; and last but not least, the ability to adjust ourselves to constantly changing conditions. When we have learned to do that, we can rise above all our troubles.

If our world were filled with calm and understanding individuals, we would have good families, good schools, good businesses, good governments. Seek peace and principle within and you will have started to change the world. It is the individual that will change the world. There is no magic government which will save our country unless we as individuals are willing to change. We are the government.

We all know that our world is in grave difficulty. Only a few realize, however, that our troubles arise from the natural operations of the law of cause and effect. In the reckless effort to advance progress at all costs, we have broken many laws and abused many privileges. For these mistakes, nature holds us responsible, and penalizes us by undermining our securities and confronting us with unpleasant realities.

We constantly hear that we live in a day of progress and so it is, but it is also a day of confusion. This changing world is drawing all peoples and all nationalities closer and closer together, and making it more imperative each day that we learn to understand each other better and work incessantly toward peaceful solutions to world problems. There is really no other acceptable choice.

What is so wrong about America that we are so frantic to change it? We have by far the most of the highest paid jobs in the world. In the United States everyone can launch any lawful business and if he is willing to work hard enough he can succeed. WHO ARE THESE PEOPLE WHO SCORN IT AND WANT TO CHANGE IT—AND TO WHAT? To change and to change for the better are two different things. BUT TRUTHS NEVER CHANGE.

The fact that a thing is old does not necessarily recommend it to me, but on the other hand THERE ARE SOME THINGS THAT NEVER DO GROW OLD AND THE REASON FOR IT IS THEY ARE THE BASIC PRINCIPLES BY WHICH MEN LIVE. They are neither old nor new. Some things we don't outgrow. The thing so many of us forget is that every change we make is not indicative of progress. It is amazing how many changes you can make and make no progress.

Change carries with it an element of the unknown, the untried, and it usually involves a certain amount of risk. "You have not passed this way before," said Joshua. Each turn in the road brings surprise, not always delight, but at least surprise. There is no such thing as ennui while traveling a new road. Even maps and charts and guideposts do not reveal all. The road of life can only reveal itself as it is traveled. Anticipation must be an ever present traveling companion if life is to be worth living.

Ours is an unusual age. It is an age of unbelievable opportunity on one hand, and seemingly insurmountable obstacles and problems on the other. Whether you find yourself stirred, thrilled, and living a full, worthwhile and creative life, OR bogged down by talk about disorder, chaos, fear, atomic bombings, wars, and the complexity of life is entirely up to you. The choice is yours.

Frankl writes, "The prisoner who had lost faith in the future —his future—was doomed. With his loss of belief in the future, he also lost his spiritual hold; he let himself decline and become subject to mental and physical decay."

None of us knows what is ahead . . . ALL THINGS PASS AWAY, ALL THINGS CHANGE. The important thing is to use today wisely and well, and face tomorrow eagerly and cheerfully. THE SECRET OF COPING WITH OUR CHANGING CONDITIONS IS ADAPTING TO THE LAWS OF MAN'S NATURE.

LAW OF HABIT

*The chains of habit are generally too small to be felt,
until they are too strong to be broken. — Samuel Johnson*

THE LAW OF HABIT

"Habit is the deepest law of human nature."—Carlyle

Life is a habit, a succession of actions that become more or less automatic. Ninety-eight percent of what we do, we do by habit, spontaneously. Each separate act, or habit, good or bad, plays some part in making you what you are.

MAN IS A BUNDLE OF HABITS. Every single qualification for success is acquired through habit. Men form habits and habits form futures. If we do not deliberately form good habits, then we will unconsciously form bad ones. YOU are the kind of person you are because you have formed the habit of being that kind of person—and the only way you can change for the better is through changing your habits.

It is an established fact that "success is a habit." Failure is also a habit. The important point is that man chooses his own pattern of thought. He makes his own blueprints for his future. He selects his own methods. MAN MAKES THE MAN. NO ONE ELSE DOES IT FOR HIM. HE DOES THE JOB HIM-SELF. Man creates his own success, but he also creates his own failure. Success is not an accident. The key is to acquire the right habits.

It is never too late (nor are we ever too old) to change our habits. We can overhaul ourselves just as we can overhaul machinery that develops flaws. One of man's greatest misconceptions is that he can't (or that he is too old to) be made over.

Men do little from reason, much from passion, most from habit. It is always easier to get rid of a bad habit by cultivating a good one.

Silently and imperceptibly you are forming habits that will ultimately determine the degree of your happiness and success. Closely guard the quality of your thoughts, that they may lead to right habits. Use such supreme qualities as courage, faith, humility, loyalty, temperance and integrity. Let these be an active force in your daily work.

William Matthews wrote, "Good habits of industry, consciousness, thoroughness, method, accuracy, and punctuality, once formed by a young man, are a fortune in themselves; inwrought in the very fibers of his being, they become a part of himself, and insure his success as no outward help can possibly do. On the other hand, bad habits, though quickly acquired, hang forever on the wheels of enterprise, and obstruct and defeat all progress, to the ruin and shame of their victim."

Reduce the subject to simple form. Say to yourself: I will make a written list of my faults. I will choose one of them and consider the best way to overcome it. I will take one fault at a time and gradually cover the entire list.

What's good about me? What's bad about me, what old habits can I break, what new habits can I cultivate that will make me a more agreeable and useful person? Am I wasting too much time? Do I talk too much? Am I spending too much? Am I doing as well as I can or am I drifting?

Good habits are man's best friends. They continue to stand up for him when he is not thinking about them. It is just as easy to practice a good habit as a destructive one.

Habits play an important part in man's inner life. Habitual attitudes and tendencies build psychological entities called complexes. First a man has a habit, and later the habit has the man. Habits can easily be broken in the early stages of their growth, but once they have reached the full measure of their intensity, they assume the proportions of psychological obsessions. They completely dominate character and conduct, and if they are bad habits, and are allowed to remain uncorrected, they can ruin the entire life of the person.

WHAT, ESSENTIALLY, IS CHARACTER? A man's character may be described as his manner of action and reaction under all the various conditions and circumstances of life. IT IS THE SUM TOTAL OF HIS HABITS—physical, physiological, mental, moral, intellectual, and emotional.

CHARACTER, THEREFORE, HAS ITS BASIS IN HABITS: AND HABITS ARE THE UNITS OF CHARACTER. Making a certain kind of man means assembling a certain complex of habits. Changing a certain kind of man into another kind of man means breaking down some habits, altering others, and building up still others. The control of character is a problem in the control of habit. SELF-DISCIPLINE IS THE MASTER HABIT OF THE MASTER MAN.

If you are trying to build a good habit, make your desire, your interest in that direction stronger than your interest in other directions. Think of every reason why you should do this and every reason why you should not do the other thing, and this will tend to become your dominant interest. The law of the predominate mental impression is simply that of two impressions in the subconscious mind the stronger wins out, the stronger governs your activities and actions.

HABITS ARE USEFUL, HABITS ARE IMPORTANT, BUT THEY HAVE A FUNDAMENTAL LIMITATION—THEY INTERFERE WITH GROWTH AND ADAPTATION WHEN THEY CANNOT BE CHANGED. The great danger in habits is that, like concrete, they tend to harden and make for the habit-bound man, the man who is so completely in the grip of his habits that he has to stand or fall with them.

There are ten master habits, which, if practiced consistently, will help you realize practically any ambitions that you may have. The habit of faith, or positive mental attitude. The habit of investigation. The habit of purpose. The habit of planning. The habit of economy. The habit of learning. The habit of enthusiasm. The habit of application. The habit of sincerity. The habit of growth.

Most habits are concerned with nervous impulses and the activity of nerve cells and nerve centers, and it is in the nervous system that most habits are founded.

The human nervous system may be described as consisting of some millions of minute nerve cells, each of which has a multitude of extensions in the form of shorter and longer fibers radiating out in every direction and connecting with the fibers from other nerve cells. The whole forms an infinitely complex, interlacing system; comparison with a huge telephone switchboard is not inapt, but it is vastly more complex, more intricate and more subtle than any telephone switchboard in existence.

An impulse, a wave of energy originating in one cell, can follow an infinite variety of paths through the nervous system. Each possible path represents a possible action, whether of the nature of a thought, a feeling, or a movement. What happens in the formation of a habit is that one of these paths is gouged deeper and broader than the others, making it a path of least resistance for the passage of the nervous impulse. Nervous impulses, like all forms of energy, follow the path of least resistance; and so it comes that every time the action is called for, it takes the habitual form.

Habits do not form themselves. Building a life is uphill work, and requires that one be everlastingly on the job. Daily drill and discipline are necessary for the acquisition of right habits. EVERY MAN HAS UNDEVELOPED QUALITIES WITHIN HIMSELF WHICH CAN BE CULTIVATED IN A MARVELOUS WAY BY SYSTEMATIC PRACTICE. If approached in a sensible way it is altogether possible to replace timidity by confidence, indolence by industry, aimlessness by concentration. Suppose you are fighting bashfulness, or carelessness, or lack of thoughtfulness and smiling courtesy. Appoint some friend your confessor, and tell him your every success and failure. As you persist in your efforts, the successes will grow more.

Or, carry a small card in your pocket, with two columns on it, one for the habit of which you wish to rid yourself, the other for the habit you desire to acquire in its place. Place a check in the appropriate column each time you perfect the action. Watch the check marks dwindle in one column, to become all bunched in the other. And above all, always see to it that the teachers under whom you study, the shop or office where you work, the friends you are intimate with, the people with whom you live and work, typify the very best of your ideals in life. So that, when you do the wrong thing, or the right thing not in the right way, you will be made to feel ill at ease. And only by attaining to their level of proficiency will you come to feel at home in the world.

We are slaves to every habit we cannot break. Make good habits and they will make you. Habit is the subconscious functioning. Habit changes into character. Whatever other habits we form, let us form the habit of expectancy, for an expectant frame of mind attracts what we expect.

I AM WISHING FOR YOU THE GIFT OF THE HABIT OF GOOD CHEER. Good cheer spreads more happiness than all the material riches in the world. It comes from the habit of looking at things hopefully—of expecting the best instead of the worst. Everyone should cultivate the habit of happiness, of self-improvement, of trying to become the better person of which he is capable.

God gives us the power to form habits that we may crystal-lize victories. All improvement in the eye of the painter, in the tongue of the orator, in the hand of the artisan, is the gift of habit. It is the channel worn in the substance of the soul, along which our purpose and ability run with increased facility. It has often been said, "What you are, will determine what you do." Not always. You may be much better than your worst act, and you may be much worse than your best act. WHAT YOU HABITUALLY DO IS YOU.

Segment 22

THE LAW OF ADVERSITY

There is a law of man's nature to the effect that the more opposition a person faces the better his chances are of getting ahead. He that wrestles with us strengthens our muscles, and sharpens our skill. The essence of LIFE is struggle. Strength comes from struggle, weakness from ease.

The greatest men of history learned to go against the current by being thrown into the maelstrom, where they had to battle for their life or drown. Only the school of hard knocks graduates men *cum laude* for the business of living. So runs the story through the lives of most of the world's successful men and women.

O. W. Holmes wrote, "If I had a formula for bypassing trouble, I wouldn't pass it around. Wouldn't be doing anybody a favor. Trouble creates a capacity to handle it. I don't say embrace trouble. That's as bad as treating it as an enemy. But I do say, meet it as a friend, for you'll see a lot of it and had better be on speaking terms with it."

Not infrequently do men of promise fail to achieve strong character for want of a great trial. When adversity does come —as it is sure to—they fall all to pieces for want of the fiber that only testing and drudgery can build into them. Many men owe the grandeur of their lives to their tremendous difficulties.

Wealth cannot purchase release from the ills that assail. No house can be built with walls thick enough, no locks can be made strong enough, to keep the ills of life on the outside. They come! They multiply!

Opposition and failure bring out what is in a man. Gold is tried by fire, brave men by adversity.

Adversity does not break men; it makes them.

The fundamental qualities of character are built and matured not by success and ease, but by sacrifice and duties that are irksome. The treadmill is, more often than not, God's providential teacher. Moses became the world's greatest jurist, not amid the luxuries of the palace of Egypt, but amid the solitude of the desert. He was stimulated by a crisis, grew strong by persecution and misunderstanding, and heroic amid the conflict.

EVERY GREAT BOOK HAS BEEN WRITTEN WITH THE AUTHOR'S BLOOD. These are they that have come out of great tribulation. Who was the peerless poet of the Greeks? Homer. That illustrious writer was blind. Who wrote the fadeless dream of Pilgrim's Progress? A prince in royal purple on a couch of ease? No! The trailing splendor of that vision gilded the dingy walls of Old Bedford Jail in which John Bunyan, a princely prisoner, a glorious genius, made a faithful transcript of the scene. Beethoven was almost stone deaf but he wrote some of the greatest symphonies of all time.

John Howard Payne went dejectedly through the streets of Paris toward the garret where he slept. Misfortune and sickness had overtaken him. Darkness had fallen. Sleet and rain drove against his face. The cold chilled him to the bone. His shabbily clothed body shivered convulsively. Suddenly a door opened and light streamed through. Into the arms of the man who stood upon the threshold leaped happy children, and a beaming wife and mother held out her arms. The door closed. Darkness fell again. But that night, sitting beside the table in his attic, shivering with cold, tears streaming down his face, by the light of a flickering candle, he wrote the immortal poem, "There Is No Place Like Home." So distress made an open door through which came a vision splendid.

Helen Keller became deaf, dumb, and blind shortly after birth . . . her entire life has served as evidence that NO ONE EVER IS DEFEATED, UNTIL DEFEAT HAS BEEN ACCEPTED AS A REALITY.

We are all striving for prosperity; adversity is the last thing we want. The paradox is that great men are produced and developed under severe testings and enduring great trials.

"Anyone can carry his burden, however hard, until nightfall," says Robert Louis Stevenson. "Anyone can do his work however hard, for one day. Anyone can live sweetly, patiently, lovingly, purely, till the sun goes down. And this is all that life really means."

No man lives without jostling and being jostled—especially when he is going somewhere. To arrive he'll have to elbow his way through the indolent, self-complacent, indifferent crowd —and in the opinion of such a crowd success is a crime. "I have been a man, and that is to be a fighter," said Goethe.

Pearls are made by oysters, not because the oyster is a creative artist but because a grain of sand gets into its shell and makes it uncomfortable. Affliction is the school in which great virtues are acquired, in which great characters are formed. Life holds one certain quality for every man—SUFFERING. Man must develop inner strength to overcome the vicissitudes of life. Never wish any man a life of prosperity and security, wish instead adventure, struggle, challenge, for these are the developers of all great men.

The modern businessman is like the oyster to this extent: he performs best when he is somewhat irritated. His grain of sand is competition—for markets and for profits. His pearl is many things; good products, fair prices, good jobs, good will, good management, and reinvestment of profits for future growth.

Herbert Casson writes, "The average man takes life as a trouble. He is in a chronic state of irritation at the whole performance. He does not learn to differentiate between troubles and difficulties, usually, until some real trouble bowls him over. He fusses about pinpricks until a mule kicks him. Then he learns the difference."

The time to count your friends is in the day of adversity. Whether you have few or many then the list is complete. "In the world you shall have tribulation." You are not promised everything on a cut-glass plate. Too often we feel that if we could just be without problems our lives would be a utopia. I know of such a place—where there are thousands of people who have no problems, but one would scarcely call it a utopia. It is called Forest Lawn Cemetery.

Hard times are pretty sure to drive us to God. Give us easy times and we drift to the devil. I've watched too many to be mistaken about that. When they're "out of money" they are devoted, prayerful and faithful. When they're "in the money" they are not interested in God and spiritual things. Neglect of, and indifference to the Bible and the Christian Church will empty our churches, fill our jails, increase our crime and destroy us as a nation.

Always remember that you will have some problem or problems, some difficulty, some need, some cross to bear. Whatever your station is in life—rich or poor, you must realize that this stress is necessary for your highest and best good. Struggle is your friend. Only struggle toughens your muscles and your mind.

HE IS A VALIANT MAN INDEED WHO CAN SUFFER WITHOUT TOO MUCH COMPLAINING; who can be patient when misunderstood, who, when maligned, slandered and falsely accused can keep his heart free from resentment and all desire to "get even" and who can patiently wait for time to bring him whatever vindication he needs. THERE IS NO EXPLANATION QUITE SO EFFECTIVE AS SILENCE. Explanations rarely explain. Those who demand explanations usually have their opinions formulated before you begin to explain. IF YOU ARE RIGHT YOUR LIFE WILL DO ITS OWN EXPLAINING. IF YOU ARE WRONG YOU CAN'T EXPLAIN. So, go calmly on your way and forget everything but the business of right living—and let time explain you.

There are two ever present qualities of life—joy and sadness. In a hospital you will find both. Two parents look joyfully at their very first child. In another room a mother is dying with cancer. In another room a middle-aged woman with terminal illness helps her daughter make plans for her approaching wedding. This is our life, one of joy and sadness, tragedy and hope.

Pain and sorrow is almost everyone's lot at some time; the way one meets it and triumphs over it is a test of his FAITH. The problem which everyone has to face is the problem of trying to bring together a FAITH that can guide us like a compass. WE NEED THIS COMPASS TO TAKE US THROUGH THE STRUGGLES OF EVERYDAY LIVING. Poverty, hardship, and misfortune have pressed many a life to moral heroism and spiritual greatness. Difficulty challenges energy and perseverance. It calls into activity the strongest qualities of the soul.

OUR GENERATION IS DOOMED TO LIVE IN A STATE OF PERPETUAL CRISIS . . . HENCE INNER SERENITY MUST BE CULTIVATED IF WE ARE TO SAFEGUARD OUR PERSONAL INTEGRITY, NATIONAL FREEDOM, AND UNIVERSAL VALUES.

WHY DO GOOD MEN SUFFER? The problem of human suffering is one of the deepest problems with which we are faced. Most philosophies teach that suffering is the penalty of sin. Without doubt much suffering in the world is a result of violating the laws of man's nature which make for our highest good.

But suffering, in the case of good men, has entirely another mission. It perfects and ennobles character, enlarges capacity for sympathy and service, and fosters many of the most beautiful virtues and graces such as mercy, sympathy, and human understanding. GOOD MEN SUFFER BECAUSE WITHOUT SUFFERING THERE IS NO SUCH THING AS PERFECTED CHARACTER AND THE RELEASING OF COMPASSION FROM THE DEEPER REALMS OF THE SOUL.

THE LAW OF MOTIVATION

Move out, Man! Life is fleeting by.
Do something worthwhile, before you die.
Leave behind a work sublime
That will outlive you, and time.

There is a law of nature known as the law of inertia. When something is in a state of being it tends to continue in that state of being, whether resting or moving. The same law applies to human beings. You can make inertia work FOR you just as well as AGAINST you.

Man is a mass of matter that is at rest and does not always want to get moving. But when we put the heat on ourselves, and actually get moving, then we find that inertia is like a jet power plant within us . . . it's a hundred times easier to keep going once you are under way, than to make that first real start getting off the ground. Motivation and drive make the difference in people. Let a man conceive an ambition, recognize a duty, espouse a cause, and how every organ in his body and every faculty of his mind begins to function smoothly and effectively as never before!

T. H. Huxley in his "Lay Sermons" writes, "Perhaps the most valuable result of all education is the ability to make yourself do the thing you have to do, when it has to be done. Whether you like it or not, it is the first lesson which ought to be learned and, however early a man's training begins, it is probably the last he learns thoroughly."

Paul Speicher writes, "Give yourself the courage to crash into each day's problems and do the things today that have to be done. The curse of life is procrastination, under the spell of which some men sit and wait for fairer days, wasting life as they wait, while its beads slip unchecked through listless fingers."

Goals give meaning and purpose to life, they make each day interesting, constructive, worthwhile and profitable. Many waste their lives in useless living. The individual must learn that each day is a little life and when they set purposeful constructive goals and make it a daily habit to attain them, their lives will have meaning and purpose. PROMISE YOURSELF REWARDS—SMALL REWARDS FOR SMALL ACCOMPLISHMENTS, BIG REWARDS FOR BIG ACCOMPLISHMENTS.

In our book *Success Planning Manual* we spell out twenty-four ways to motivate yourself to your full potential. Some men are not self-starters, someone must wind them up. Companies are people, and they are constantly searching for techniques to keep motivation and drive instilled in their workers. People are how they get the job done. They invest a great deal of money and time in training them, and making them valuable assets. However, the one quality that really distinguishes all successful people is this internal impetus . . . this DRIVE. Drive can make the difference between outstanding or mediocre performance, success or failure.

We must realize that high motivation in a person is, in most cases, a more precious commodity than talent. I would much rather employ a person who is highly motivated with little talent than an apathetic genius.

Incentive! What a little word, but oh! what big things it can do. It furnishes the strongest driving force known to man. It creates a real interest in doing things. If we could discover a formula to arouse in all of us a real interest in doing the right sort of things, we would revolutionize the world. There would be no such thing as laziness, lack of will power or boredom. Just watch anyone, when he is sufficiently interested in something, get up and go. About 90% of the success in doing anything depends on a real willingness to try. Newton wrote, "NOTHING MOVES, WITHOUT A MOVER."

We all have the problem of motivating others. A valuable technique used by leaders to motivate others is best explained by the French word *detente*, which means "the end of strained relations."

Of course there is no motivation, no friendliness, no good will, no persuasiveness if there are strained relations existing between you and another person. We meet people of all kinds every day. Some are cross. Some are belligerent. Others are pleasant and reasonable. It is our job as motivators to have *detente* with all of them; and that can be quite a job. You meet somebody who is ugly, cross, insulting, unhappy. If you react to him, if you become ugly, cross, insulting, unhappy, there is no *detente*. There is no motivation. Your job is to change them and prevent them from changing you. You remain calm, pleasant, cheerful. When *detente* enters, motivation proceeds.

All great men have the artistic mind. The seed, or germ, of all successful effort is in a trained imagination. If you can't picture your goal, you won't have the courage to start. Your imagination is working with you or against you every minute of every hour of every week of every year of your life.

Life would not be complete without dreams, the daytime hopes and ambitions that fill our lives from earliest childhood through adulthood—the dreams that spur us on to accomplishment—getting the job done, obtaining financial independence, having a happy home life. One goal of every man should be to accumulate enough money so that, as early as possible in life, he can buy some leisure time and do the things he has always wanted to do. We have to come up with the motivation that changes these dreams into reality. Call it drive or urge or desire to do, there is that something within you which alternately prompts and pushes you to do, and then scolds because you do not do.

THE MOST IMPELLING URGE IN OUR LIFE SHOULD BE OUR MOTIVATION AND DRIVE TO SELF-FULFILL-MENT AND SELF-REALIZATION.

THE LAW OF HUMAN NATURE

There is a wolf in man, possibly a whole zoo. HELP US TO SEE IT IS THESE WILD THINGS WITHIN US, THE NATURE OF US, THAT WE HAVE TO BATTLE. Each individual has within himself the seeds of fear and faith, anger and love, anxiety and peace of mind, despair and hope. We are strange mixtures of good and evil, and as a result we are inside of ourselves, a battle ground.

Segment 24

THE LAW OF HUMAN NATURE

The greatest scientific discoveries of the past hundred years have been as child's play compared with the titanic forces that will be released when man applies himself to the understanding and mastery of his own nature.

The real science and the real study for man, is man himself. The study of his nature is the noblest study the world affords. Human nature includes the whole realm of personal attributes, many of which are included in these forty-seven laws of life. To build a man is the greatest project on earth. Marcus Aurelius wrote, "Let men see, let men know, a real man, who lives as he was meant to live."

Modern man has everything going for him. He has both hands full of money, food, possessions, and the prizes of life. You would think he would be happier than any past generation. But he isn't. This is the day of the complainer, the griper. Man should be enjoying himself but he gets too greedy. We may be the last generation of men on earth with access to a better future.

THE THING FOR US TO FEAR TODAY IS NOT THE ATOM, BUT THE NATURE OF MAN. The struggle of humanity is of man with man. Man's nature has a spiritual basis but today we are deifying man and humanizing God. Where will human nature be tomorrow? We may be at the beginning of another Dark Age. The church is preaching the humanities instead of the spiritual values. The humanities are a by-product of Christianity.

Man is the favorite of nature, not in the sense that nature has done everything for him, but that she has given him the power of doing everything for himself. THE NATURE OF MAN IS ALWAYS THE SAME: IT IS HIS HABITS, PERSONAL ATTRIBUTES, ATTITUDES, AND PERSONALITY THAT SEPARATE ONE FROM ANOTHER.

We, of this day, have classified, arranged and pigeonholed a vast amount of knowledge on almost every conceivable subject—that is, every conceivable subject except the BASIC question of life. What is my TRUE nature? Where did I COME FROM? Where am I GOING? What is the TRUE MEANING OF LIFE? We know more about the physical world around us than we know about the spiritual world within us. We hear and talk much about the "conflict between nations" but fail utterly to understand that OUR BASIC CONFLICT IS BETWEEN MAN AND HIMSELF.

What one misses most today is the evidence of widespread personal determination to develop a character that will in itself, given any reasonable odds, make for happiness. Our whole emphasis is on the reform of living conditions, of increased wages, of controls on the economic structure—the government approach—rather than on improving man's nature.

Why do we have to live in fear rather than in hope, in antagonism and distrust rather than in harmony and cooperation? U Thant writes, "Human nature is popularly held to be responsible for this deplorable state of affairs, the assumption being that human nature is in some way a force which can not possibly be controlled or improved. Men should aspire to be the masters of their fate, rather than the victims of their own nature. If we presume, as we do, to change and improve everything else in nature, why do we leave ourselves out of the process?" Modern man must wake up and realize that ALL OF OUR PROBLEMS STEM FROM THE NATURE OF MAN.

According to Albert Einstein, "The real problem is in the hearts and minds of men. It is not a problem of physics but of ethics. It is easier to denature plutonium than to denature the evil spirit of man." In all of the development of life, we have emphasized the growth of skills, but we have never matured in terms of right decision and right action. We have let this self in us run riot, and it has given us wars, inquisitions, and disasters of all kinds.

In his poem "Wilderness," Carl Sandburg says, "THERE IS A WOLF IN ME." There are other animals within all of us. Who has not heard the lion in his rage roar in a fit of temper? Who has not heard the restless tread of the panther of envy? Who has not heard the snarls of the tiger of jealousy? Who has not listened to the lonesome cry of the jackal of criticism as he snarls and tears the reputation, faults and failures of others? According to Jesus Christ the heart of man UNCHANGED is literally a zoo. He was the first in the field with the startling disclosure that this zoo within man is filled with wild ferocious things which cannot be tamed or managed. HELP US TO SEE CLEARLY IT IS NOT OUR CIRCUMSTANCES, IT IS NOT OUR CONDITION THAT WE HAVE TO BATTLE, IT IS THESE WILD THINGS WITHIN US, THE NATURE OF US!

Many people have allowed savage impulses to govern their moods and passions. Crimes, murders, rapes and robberies are at an all time high rate. The streets in our cities and towns are not safe at night. Social standards too have changed. The animal instinct seems to come first with those individuals who claim they have a right to construe "morality" in their own way. The reading of pornographic literature, or the viewing of obscene movies, is defended as a natural pastime.

MAN'S SPIRITUAL DECLINE IS THE REASON FOR ALL OF THIS. IF WE WOULD REVERSE THE TREND, WE MUST RETURN TO SPIRITUAL VALUES. We can expect more and more trouble since we are removing any reference to God in our schools. Paul Tournier writes, "It is not necessary to be a great scholar to see that our world today is not in good health. What is the disease from which it is suffering? The typical sickness of our age is neurosis. A neurosis is an inner conflict. What distinguishes a neurosis in the first place is anxiety. The cause of it is that our materialistic and unmoral civilization no longer answers the deeper needs of the soul. The farther away from God man moves, the more neurotic he becomes."

Do I know, REALLY KNOW, all the powers that are in me?
St. Paul's tripartite division of human nature into physical,
mental, spiritual is psychologically true. Our spirit is the divine
part of our nature which connects to God. The GREAT-
EST ACHIEVEMENT FOR EACH MAN IS TO KEEP
HIS PHYSICAL, MENTAL, SPIRITUAL NATURES DE-
VELOPED EQUALLY, AND IN GOOD REPAIR. Spiritual
values bring us light and joy. Man's cheating, lying, adultery,
stealing, even murder can be forgiven. SHUTTING GOD OUT
OF OUR LIFE IS THE UNPARDONABLE SIN.

The new concept of today is that man has now so advanced
and accumulated knowledge and is so familiar with the laws
that manage the earth, that he does not need God. Man has
needs that cannot be filled by himself or his fellow creatures.
Man has demonstrated this fact through the ages by his almost
universal effort to find something to live by, to believe in,
some source of strength. The notion that he has risen or is
about to rise above these needs is preposterous.

Modern religion says, suppress this wild beast within you,
make him tame. Keep him locked behind iron bars, suppress
him. That is a strange paradox when modern education is
saying to the whole present generation, do not suppress anything. No part of our nature must be suppressed for fear of
inhibitions. Turn it all loose.

The New Testament gives the answer, the remedy: "If any
man be in Christ, he is a new Creation, old things are passed,
behold all things are new." Only God can work the miracle
that gives the heart of us the essential change which it must
experience before we shall realize what victorious living means.
IT IS THE POWER OF GOD IN MAN WHICH TAMES
THE TYRANT OR BEAST, WHICH GIVES MAN A GEN-
TLE, HUMBLE HEART, WHICH SATISFIES HIS NA-
TURE AND MAKES HIM ACT AND BEHAVE AS HE
SHOULD. But God cannot do anything unless man asks Him
to. Give us the wisdom to fill that purpose and accomplish our
God-given task.

The study of man as a whole human being in a world created for his use, can be the science of the new space age. It is the only hope we have of ushering man into an era of growth, purpose, progress, instead of into an era of decay, depravity, and destruction. Man is the key to his own destiny. His destiny is built within his own design and function. There is a law of biology that a creature can only investigate the environment for which he is made. Augustine said, "We were made for God and we will be dissatisfied until we have God in our hearts." In the heart of every person there is a hunger, a longing for something that you cannot find in this world. It is the soul that longs for a comforting spirit, a fellowship with God. This is man's real lasting joy, and true personal fulfillment.

"Let men formulate what philosophy of life they may, they can never give men the assurance of hope which they need," commented Socrates some 400 years before Jesus Christ came to give us final words about life and death, time and eternity, and how the present is related to the future. The words of Socrates are as apropos now as when they were first spoken. TIME HAS NOT CHANGED THE NATURE OF GOD, THE NATURE OF MAN, OR THE ESSENTIAL NATURE OF TRUTH.

Let modern man draw what inspiration he can from nature —and there is much to be drawn; let him glean what evidence he can from scientific research—and there is much to be gleaned; the fact still remains, if man was made for God, then there is a part of him that must find and keep correspondence with God or he does not live. That is what Jesus meant when He said, "I am come that they might have life, and that they might have it more abundantly." The real man is the spiritual man and this part of man is fully capable of perfecting an adjustment to God and maintaining that adjustment indefinitely. To experience the infinite then, is my one hope of finding the inexhaustible. God, and God alone, is the answer to the infinite demands of the infinite me of me.

there are two spheres of SUCCESS --
INNER AND OUTER

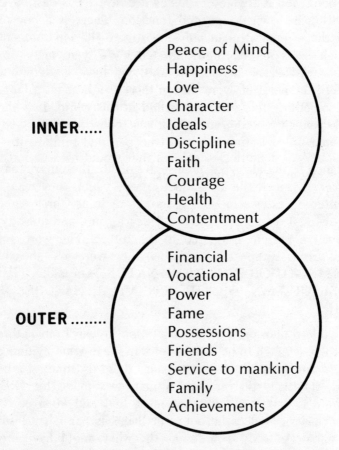

INNER.....

Peace of Mind
Happiness
Love
Character
Ideals
Discipline
Faith
Courage
Health
Contentment

OUTER ....

Financial
Vocational
Power
Fame
Possessions
Friends
Service to mankind
Family
Achievements

Success is not limited to the material realm of making money, although this is vital and every man should stand on his own two feet. There are mental, personal, and spiritual achievements. Life's greatest achievement is the continual remaking of yourself so that at last you know how to live.

Segment 25

THE LAW OF SUCCESS

Success is the achievement of anything that is worthwhile to you. It may be having peace of mind and happiness; home and family unity; enjoying the work you are doing; financial independence; joy and satisfaction from serving others; the development of the constructive forces inherent in man; enjoying life and being satisfied with your character, ideals, and achievements.

"A complete definition of success that would be satisfactory to all persons, has perhaps, never been found," wrote Zu Tavern. "Each person has his own idea of what success would mean to him, and this idea keeps changing with the passing of time. To some persons success means fame; to some it means fortune in money; to others it means only love and happiness."

It is a law of man's nature to achieve, to earn respect, to be a constructive worker and builder, to leave the world a little better than he found it. Man is designed for achievement. The greatest satisfaction in life comes from achievement. This is proved by his physical, mental and moral makeup. When he is doing something—serving, accomplishing—he is happy and feels worthwhile.

The desire to achieve is born in us. We want to do something worthwhile, to attain something that we do not have, to have some of our ideals fulfilled. The cornerstone of success and achievement is DESIRE. Ambition is the force behind our striving. The moment we permit pleasure or hardship to neutralize this force, the moment we stop pushing forward, the moment ambition dies, that moment we, also, are dead. REAL SUCCESS IN LIFE WAS MEANT TO BE ATTAINED ON ALL THREE PLANES OF YOUR BEING— THE PHYSICAL, MENTAL, AND SPIRITUAL.

Well-intentioned persons who have never succeeded in managing their private affairs are ready to take over the destinies of worlds. Our society today seems to have sympathetic concern only for the bum, the misfit, the pervert, the drug addict, the criminal, the loser.

I am for the ACHIEVER whether he is rich or poor. It is better to win than to lose, better to get an "A" in college than a "C." WE WILL NEVER CREATE A GOOD SOCIETY, MUCH LESS A GREAT ONE, UNTIL INDIVIDUAL EXCELLENCE AND ACHIEVEMENT ARE NOT ONLY RESPECTED BUT ALSO ENCOURAGED.

Our future and our hope lies with those who take seriously their responsibility for achievement and self-development. THE GREATEST RESPONSIBILITY ENTRUSTED TO EACH MAN IS THAT OF DEVELOPING HIMSELF. Everything you do, from the time you arise, to the time you retire at night, has something to do with the extent of your success in life.

The common denominator of success—the secret of success of every man who has ever been successful—lies in the fact that he formed the habit of doing things that failures don't like to do. It's just as true as it sounds and it's just as simple as it seems. You can hold it up to the light, you can put it to the acid test, and you can kick it around until it's worn out, but when you are all through with it, it will still be the common denominator of success, whether we like it or not.

The biographies of men who have left their mark upon the world are a record of incessant work. In times recent and contemporary, as well as in times ancient, this has always been the law of the universe, that outstanding success can be achieved only at the cost of great effort and much sacrifice. Longfellow wrote, "Lives of great men all remind us . . . We can make our lives sublime . . . And, departing, leave behind us . . . Footprints on the sands of time."

After thirty years of analyzing the causes of success and failure, Roger Babson concluded, "Experience has taught me that financial success, job success, and happiness in human relations are, in the main, the result of physical well-being; constant effort to develop one's personal assets; setting up and working toward a series of life goals; allowing time for meditation and spiritual regeneration."

Men can be successful in certain fields of activity and fail in others. Some who have been successful in many walks of life have tried politics and failed, and vice-versa. We are too apt to believe that if a man is clever at one thing or successful under one set of circumstances, he must be equally clever at everything and equally successful under all conditions.

In business a man with the capacity for action is worth any number of talkers. In practical affairs it is not deep thought that wins but the eagle's eye. The qualities that make for success are judgment, action, and health. The measure of any executive is his ABILITY TO GET THINGS DONE.

Many people have the mistaken belief that success is synonymous with the accumulation of money. While ultimate success includes money, it is far more than that. It is a mental and spiritual attitude—a state of consciousness—of which money is an incidental by-product. Success is a way of life. WE ARE HERE IN THIS WORLD TO SUCCEED AS HUMAN BEINGS. A successful person is one who has achieved peace of mind, one who is satisfied with the talents God has given him, and is happy to be able to use and develop them to his best advantage. The quest for a better life, and the achievement of a worthwhile goal, is the most satisfying pursuit of men.

FEW OF US HAVE EVER RISEN EQUAL TO OUR BEST VISION. THE PLACE AT THE TOP IS ONLY WON BY THE BRAVE AND THE AVERAGE PERSON'S COURAGE LEAKS OUT BEFORE HE REACHES THE TOP.

Shakespeare was a real man, who was born in a different but exciting age. He lived and loved like all of us, and he spent his enormous energies doing the things that he loved best. The result is a treasure that will last as long as people do. Can we say the same about our lives? Will the sum of your work survive a little while after you? We hope so. We hope you spend a little time, once in a while, thinking about things that will outlast you.

Find a reason for your own existence. Unless you believe in something bigger than yourself, have some purpose more vital than accumulation or advancement in business or society, you are only existing, not living. It is better to fail in a thing that will ultimately succeed, than to succeed in a thing that will ultimately fail. TO DO FOR THE WORLD MORE THAN THE WORLD DOES FOR YOU, THAT IS SUCCESS.

All progress calls for greater thought, action, and personal sacrifice. As with all other phases of life, so with financial advancement, or any advancement; results can only equal the investment. Man is intelligent, having an ability to reason, through which he sees, observes, deduces, analyzes, and acts, and benefits or suffers from his actions. The five principal sources which supply you with a stock of ideas are reading, writing, conversation, observation, reflection.

I have this motto over my desk. I read and allow it to judge me often: FOR WHEN THE ONE GREAT SCORER COMES TO WRITE AGAINST YOUR NAME HE WRITES—NOT THAT YOU WON OR LOST—BUT HOW YOU PLAYED THE GAME.

A successful life is not an easy life. It is built upon strong qualities, sacrifice, endeavor, loyalty and integrity. The race is not always to the swift nor the battle to the strong; often victory goes to the adventurous and the persistent. The biggest handicap to success is not lack of brains, not lack of character, or willingness. With most people it is the inability to get things done.

To live successfully one must have a definite plan and be aware that there is a limited time in which to get the job done. Best living depends upon elimination as well as upon accumulation. We get so full of little things that we finally have no room for big things. You must know what to eliminate. A waste basket is as necessary to successful living as a storage bin. Dr. William Osler, famous Canadian surgeon, said his success was due to the fact that he found the best and easiest way to do each thing he had to do.

In the arena of business, it is a man's business acumen that counts. The successful man knows when to grasp opportunity and act on it. In fact he makes opportunity. TO GET PROFIT WITHOUT RISK, EXPERIENCE WITHOUT DANGER, AND REWARD WITHOUT WORK IS AS IMPOSSIBLE AS IT IS TO LIVE WITHOUT BEING BORN. Successful men usually snatch success from seeming failure. If they know there is such a word as failure they will not admit it. They may be whipped, but they are not aware of it. That is why they succeed.

MOST FAILURES AND MISERIES CAN BE TRACED DIRECTLY BACK TO A LACK OF WISE THINKING BEFOREHAND. Your success depends upon you. You must make your own decisions. You must abide by the consequences of your acts. You may have spread before you the wisdom of the ages, but unless you assimilate it you derive no benefit from it. You are the creator of your own personality. You have to write your own record.

Day by day we write our own destiny; for inexorably we become what we do. This is the supreme logic and the law of life. No matter who has gone ahead of you, follow behind them and do the job better than the one you are following. Always try to do a better job than the other fellow.

YOU HAD BETTER LIVE YOUR BEST, THINK YOUR BEST, AND DO YOUR BEST TODAY—FOR TODAY WILL SOON BE TOMORROW, AND TOMORROW WILL SOON BE FOREVER.

THE LAW OF HAPPINESS

    A life of earthly success is full of perils and anxieties. If a man does not have the elements of happiness within himself, not all of the beauty and variety, the pleasures and interests of the whole world can give it to him.

Segment 26

THE LAW OF HAPPINESS

In undertaking to describe some of the laws of life that are working on us every day of our lives, one might get the impression that life is such a serious business that we should be every moment churning our minds over every move we make.

It is a law of nature to desire happiness. This law is not local, but universal; not temporary, but eternal. Marcus Aurelius wrote, "The end of man is to live comfortably to nature and he will thus obtain happiness, tranquility of mind, and contentment."

To find happiness, we must search our hearts, for it comes from within, through our own efforts and beliefs. HAPPINESS DEPENDS NOT ON THINGS AROUND US, BUT ON OUR ATTITUDE. Everything in our lives will depend on our attitude.

Happiness is found in little things: a baby's smile, a letter from a friend, the song of a bird, a light in the window. Happiness does not depend upon a full pocketbook, but upon a mind full of rich thoughts and a heart full of rich emotions. Real happiness comes from contentment of mind and spirit. It comes entirely from the kind of thoughts we think. Often those without the material comforts of life get great joy out of living.

Happiness and contentment are not commodities which we import; neither do they depend upon "the abundance of things" which we possess. It is not where we are, what we have, or what we possess, that makes us happy or unhappy. WHAT WE ARE DETERMINES OUR STATE. A very poor man can be immensely wealthy and a very rich man can be abjectly miserable. Existence is a strange bargain. Life owes us little, we owe it everything. The only true happiness comes from squandering ourselves for a worthy purpose.

When the French writer, Colette, was being interviewed by newsmen, she exclaimed, "What a wonderful life I've had, those were my happiest days." Then after a sigh of remorse she added, "I only wish I'd realized it sooner."

How much is a sunset worth? There are things such as a sunset or a beautiful sunrise that have no price. Their only value is what they do for you, or to you. Each one of us has only so many sunsets and sunrises. LET US LEARN TO ENJOY THEM EACH DAY TO THE FULLEST.

Cheerfulness is the great lubricant of the wheels of life. It lightens labor, diminishes difficulties, and mitigates misfortunes. Cheerfulness gives a creative power which the pessimist never possesses. A sunny, hopeful, optimistic disposition sweetens life, lightens its inevitable drudgery, and eases the jolts along the road.

Every day should be a happy day for thoughtful people. To be thankful to be alive and enjoy the real values of life, health, family, and friendship. To see, enjoy, appreciate all the handiwork of nature. There is so much to live for and so much to do. We are living in an age in which technology has made life much easier physically and provided many comforts and pleasures that our ancestors could have never imagined. It is our own fault if we do not enjoy life. "All men," said Ruskin, "may enjoy though few can achieve."

In our generation multitudes of people have had so much given to them, and done for them, that they have lost the grateful heart. Each year we should be more joyful than ever before, because we have fewer years ahead in which to be joyful. Joy lends itself to our best physical and mental health. Joyous people are not only the happiest, but the longest lived, the most useful, and the most successful. Nature has given the opportunity of happiness to all, if we but knew how to use it.

Happiness consists in being perfectly satisfied not only with what we have, but also with what we do not have. IT IS NOT HOW MUCH WE HAVE, BUT HOW MUCH WE ENJOY THAT CREATES HAPPINESS.

Someone has said, "ALL THE WORLD IS SEEKING HAP-PINESS." Actually, all the world is in search of something infinitely deeper and more abiding than mere happiness. THAT SOMETHING IS JOY. Joy is contentment that fills the soul, A STATE OF HEART.

The difference between happiness and joy is more than a mere play on words. JOY IS THE ABIDING FELLOWSHIP WITH GOD, WHICH EXPERIENCES NO CHANGE AMID THE VICISSITUDES OF LIFE. Happiness can be a super-ficial happiness which depends upon an abundance of things one possesses which evaporate. JOY IS DEEP, ABIDING SPIRITUAL UNION WITH THE UNCHANGING GOD.

"A man's life," said Jesus Christ, "is not fulfilled, nor is it filled full of, nor by, the abundance of things which he pos-sesses." Here is one of the most important statements ever given a bewildered, heart hungry world. The shallowness and futility of superficial happiness is its dependence upon things —congenial companions, good clothes, a bank balance, a com-fortable home. These things, of course, contribute to the sum of life, but the point is THEY ARE NOT THE FIRST NEEDS OF LIFE. JOY IS A LIVING SPRING HIDDEN DEEP IN THE INNER LIFE that is not dependent upon things. We live in a rough-and-tumble world. "In the world," Christ said, "ye shall have tribulation," but He further added, "Be of good cheer."

WHAT IS THE PRACTICAL VALUE OF SEEKING JOY AS WELL AS HAPPINESS? Joy is strength. The Old Testa-ment writer said, "The joy of the Lord is your strength." The joyful person will surpass all others in spiritual strength, poise, and usefulness. Joy is content, and contentment is the positive, constructive, creative force on which life depends for both health and happiness. JOY IS SPIRITUAL PROSPERITY. "Rest in the Lord," and lo, joy will come out of its hiding and if you will live quietly and confidently, in prayerful fellow-ship with God, it will abide with you forever.

RESPONSIBILITY

I am responsible for the 24 hours of every day. How I use them and whether I abuse them concerns others as well as myself. Time is God given; I cannot do with it as I please. It belongs to all and I must share time with others. I am responsible for property, for money and for those things bought and sold, used and enjoyed, given and received. I did not create them; others have helped me to obtain them. I cannot use them alone; others are concerned. I am responsible for the development of my mental powers. My mind is my kingdom of opportunities, I am responsible for my religious development. I am spirit as well as flesh. Into me God breathed the breath of life; I am His breath. In Him I live and move and have my being. I am responsible for others. I cannot live in a vacuum. I must live among people my own age, among those who are younger, in the presence of those who are older. We live together; therefore we have responsibilities toward one another. I am responsible for seeking to help to find my way through life. My help is friends, in literature, in the Bible, in communion with the Divine. All these will help me and I shall help others. I am a responsible human being.

—William M. Elder

Segment 27

THE LAW OF RESPONSIBILITY

"Man is fully responsible for his nature and his choices."
—Jean Paul Sartre

Life is the acceptance of responsibilities or their evasion; it is a business of meeting obligations or avoiding them. To every man the choice is continually being offered, and by the manner of his choosing you may fairly well measure him.

We are born in this world to perform our duty. It is up to us to find it and do it. Goethe wrote: "Do thy duty. What is thy duty? The day's demands." Our greatest duty in life is to know and obey the natural laws of life, to develop ourselves to the fullest, then choose and fight to maintain right and good, lawfulness and charity, responsibility and Godliness. Our first responsibility in life is to take care of ourselves. And in taking care of ourselves we will relieve anyone and everyone else from the task of taking care of us, so they can take care of themselves. If everyone takes care of himself everyone can be productive, healthy, and meet his needs satisfactorily.

Dr. Albert Schweitzer wrote, "Man must cease attributing his problems to his environment, and learn again to exercise his will—his personal responsibility in the realm of faith and morals." A criminal is responsible for his own acts—not society. There are just as many honest and upright and resourceful people who come from the other side of the tracks as there are criminals and degenerates. And the same is true for this side of the tracks. The increase in crime, violence, and drug addiction in middle and upper class neighborhoods, just re-emphasizes the fact that each man is responsible for his own life.

155

In this mystery of existence, nature has provided each creature with the power to solve its own problems. Nature's evolution, therefore, is planned upon the principles of continually demanding that the individual use his own resources, becoming strong by personal growth, by self-discipline, and by the dedication of all that he knows to the strengthening of his moral consciousness and his ethical character.

WE HAVE A RESPONSIBILITY TO MAKE OUR OWN LIFE BETTER, to keep the corner lighted where we are. If we want outside conditions to improve we must improve ourselves. If we want a society of law and order, honesty and just dealing, friendliness, then we must first be that way ourselves. No strong character can be developed unless emphasis be laid upon the thought of personal responsibility. RESPONSIBILITY EDUCATES. Freudianism has moved us toward dependence upon the state. We must get back our concept of individual responsibility.

The great threat to the future of our nation—to our freedom —is not foreign military aggression, nor internal communistic subversion, but the growing dependence of the people on a paternalistic government. A nation is no stronger than its people, and the best measure of their strength is how they accept responsibility. There will never be a great society unless the materialism of the welfare state is replaced by individual initiative and responsibility. Beware of any theory of government, religious creed or doctrine, or philosophy of life that incapacitates you for independent thinking and action.

Mankind has learned from bitter experience that it can never trust the individual who cannot control himself. A man cannot be given authority over other men until that man has learned to accept authority from others graciously and constructively. Most tyrants in this world were rebels against authority in early life; parental guidance was either lacking or it was not sufficiently firm and enlightened.

Each one of us is completely responsible for the quality of our life and the effect we have on others—whether we build or tear down others—either by example or by direct influence. It is serious business to live. We are so built that we must curse or bless everyone we touch. Those who know me intimately will be better for having known me or they will be worse, and that is true of you.

"Just as the tradesman keeps his account books and the scientist his experimental notebook," wrote Alexis Carrel, "so every single individual ought to register every day the good and evil for which he has been responsible. Above all he should record the amount of joy or sorrow, anxiety or peace, hate or love, which he has given his family and his neighbors. It is by the patient application of these techniques that the transformation of our bodies and souls will gradually become a reality."

The human being is ready, willing, and anxious to control everything except himself. Our generation has been raised on the idea of "self-expression" which, being translated negatively, means there should never be any self-restraint. Dr. William Glasser writes, "People do not act irresponsibly because they are ill, they are ill because they act irresponsibly. A RESPONSIBLE PERSON DOES THAT WHICH GIVES HIM A FEELING OF SELF-WORTH AND A FEELING THAT HE IS WORTHWHILE TO OTHERS. How does one satisfy his needs? By doing what is REALISTIC, RESPONSIBLE, RIGHT."

People run away from responsibility, and that is one thing which makes them sick. They think that by evading or avoiding, it will disappear. THE BASIS OF DEVELOPMENT IS RESPONSIBILITY. Responsibility is the price we pay for the right to make our own choices. RESPONSIBILITY IS ONLY ANOTHER WORD FOR OPPORTUNITY. And we become forever rich or poor as we use or neglect opportunity.

THE LAW OF TIME

IT'S LATER
THAN
YOU THINK !!

TIME GOES, YOU SAY? AH NO! TIME STAYS, *WE GO.*
Each moment is precious — use it!
Time is our greatest asset.

THE LAW OF TIME

Time. One of the most valuable elements of life. TIME, THE ELUSIVE VALUE, THAT GOVERNS, DOMINATES AND LIMITS MAN'S VERY EXISTENCE. Today, in a modern world racing toward tomorrow, and tomorrow, time is a constant challenge. No matter how old you are you have never lived THIS day. This day is a new piece of road. EACH MORNING PUTS A MAN ON TRIAL AND EACH EVENING PASSES JUDGMENT.

One of the marvelous mysteries of the universe is time. Like a perpetual caravan, it moves on and on past the great mileposts of history, and on into the future eons of eternity. It moves eternally with God, and is indefinable.

Time plays no favorites. It levels us. It bestows its favors impartially; 60 seconds to the minute, 60 minutes to the hour, 8760 hours to the year. Each man, be he poor or wealthy, young or old, great or unknown, shares equally in the allocation of time. His twenty-four hour day is no shorter or longer than that of his fellow man. This time is his to spend, second by second, hour by hour, day by day, year by year, as he alone chooses. It is his to spend wisely or foolishly, in daydreams or productivity, in hate or love, in fear or happiness, in selfishness or contribution.

LIVE A DAY AT A TIME. Too many people spend half their lives living in the future. They dissipate their time, their energy, their thoughts, reacting to situations which probably will never occur. This "dream world" saps their creativity. Life is simply a succession of small units called days. What I do today is very important because I am exchanging a day of my life for it. THE COST OF A THING IS THE AMOUNT OF MY LIFE I SPEND OBTAINING IT. In order that I shall not forget the price I paid for it, I must do my best to make it profitable.

With a limited amount of time we can't be, or do, everything we want to do. A PERSON IS CONSTANTLY FACED WITH A DECISION AS TO WHOM, OR TO WHAT, HE WANTS TO GIVE HIS TIME. Everything takes time and our choices determine our destiny. THIS IS ONE OF LIFE'S GREATEST LESSONS.

I regret the many times I have had to refuse to go out to meetings or visit with friends. With several books in my system and a limited amount of time, I had to cut off all social affairs. But without this trait I would not have reached some of my goals. And so I am disappointed and not disappointed. It is said that "time and tide wait for no man," only another way of saying, the passing hours, days, and years bring OPPORTUNITIES WHICH WILL QUICKLY PASS TO COME NO MORE FOREVER. Accept and use them now or lose them.

Don't be fooled by the calendar. There are only as many days in the year AS YOU MAKE USE OF. One man gets only a week's value out of a year, while another man gets a full year's value out of a week. If before going to bed every night, you will tear a page from the calendar and remark, "There goes another day of my life never to return," you will soon become TIME CONSCIOUS.

DECIDE what you want from your time. Plan carefully, on paper, each day, or at least each week, how you will use your time. Put time in where it counts most. Delegate well. Concentrate on the job at hand. Respect time. TIME INDEED IS A SACRED GIFT, AND EACH DAY IS A LITTLE LIFE.

To get all there is out of living, we must employ our time wisely; NEVER TO BE IN TOO MUCH OF A HURRY TO STOP AND SIP THE SWEETS OF LIFE, BUT NEVER TO LOSE OUR SENSE OF THE ENORMOUS VALUE OF A SINGLE MOMENT. John Lubbock wrote: "We must fill up our time as well and wisely as we may, even the most fortunate of us must leave many things undone, many books unread, many a glorious sight unseen, many a country unvisited."

These are the days of hurry up and get there fast. For years we have been coming to it. Speed and more speed has been our slogan for several decades. Quantity and not quality has been the master passion. And this in spite of the fact that history shows that the greatest men are the product of hard, slow, painstaking work.

IF LIFE HAS TAUGHT ME ANYTHING, IT HAS TAUGHT ME TO LIVE IN THE PRESENT! ONLY ONE PERSON IN A THOUSAND KNOWS THE TRICK OF REALLY LIVING IN THE PRESENT. This is one of the key points for abundant dynamic living. Most of us spend fifty minutes an hour living in the past with regret for lost joys, or shame for things badly done; OR in a future which we either long for or dread.

Man's days are numbered. "Teach us to number our days that we may apply our hearts unto wisdom." In other words help us to realize that we have only so many heartbeats and we must be wise in how we use our time. IT IS HOW PEOPLE SPEND THEIR TIME THAT DETERMINES HOW WELL OFF THEY ARE. Associate with people where you invest your time, not merely spend it. To waste my own time is bad enough, but to waste the time of others while wasting my own time, is unpardonable.

TIME IS THE ONLY SURE TEST OF ANYTHING. It is not only the severest critic of all, it is the only accurate critic. You cannot judge the value of this or that on the spur of the moment, for only time can determine that. TIME WILL HONOR YOU FOR WHAT YOU ARE. The year of a man's birth is marked in the calendar, but THE CALENDAR FAILS TO TELL US HOW MANY YEARS A MAN HAS TRULY LIVED. One really lives in terms of desire and passion, joy and sorrow, vision and prayer. WE MUST DO OUR BEST TO LEAVE THE WORLD A LITTLE BETTER FOR OUR STAY IN IT. Time steals the strength from a man's muscles and the youthful beauty from a woman's face. Time robs us of our health and strips us at last of everything we have.

Segment 29

THE LAW OF LIMITATIONS

MAN IS GREAT OR SMALL ACCORDING TO THE WAY HE THINKS AND LIMITS HIMSELF. THE GREATEST DISCOVERY A MAN CAN MAKE IS HIS OWN LIMITATIONS. Strength, true strength, is as much an awareness of limitation as it is of ability. The person who is not aware of his limitations will soon overreach himself and his strength will become weakness. To say, I cannot, or I do not know, from a sincere appreciation of limitation is at once a mark of bigness, dignity, and personal power.

Every person has his limitations. A heavy person would not make a jockey, a physically weak individual would not make a wrestler or boxer. If you have an average intelligence you can't be a space scientist. If you are over 50 you can't be an astronaut. Everyone cannot run a four minute mile. No man can be anything he wishes, nor can he do anything he wishes. We are limited by our physical stature, mental capacity, sex, health, and cultural background.

Each man is given physical and mental advantages, capacities, and talents. People differ in capacity, skill, health, strength, and unequal fortune is a necessary result of unequal condition. Such inequality is far from being disadvantageous either to individuals or to the community.

In America, we all grow up subject to the misleading ideals and dreams presented in the movies, TV, books and plays. But we all have our limitations. We do not all have the capacity to be a millionaire, the looks or voice to be a movie star, the physical stamina to be a cowboy, the self-control to be a saint. Some men are going to be limited, they have not the brains, they have not the initiative, they have not the skills, they have not the knowledge, they have not the same capacity that other men have.

162

Some people are gifted with their hands, some people are gifted in the realm of art or music, some people are gifted in the realm of abstract ideas. Almost no one is gifted in all three realms. We are all limited, and we must accept ourselves with our limitations, recognizing that we can do what others cannot do, that we can contribute where others cannot contribute.

The design of an airplane determines the altitude it can attain. That's called its ceiling. Some can go thousands of feet higher than others. The pilot can, at his will, take his plane from the ground level to the ceiling made possible by the designer. Nature is the designer of every man. She may have fixed each one's ceiling, but she has MADE MAN HIS OWN PILOT. MAN CAN STAY ON THE GROUND, OR BY DEVELOPING HIMSELF, RISE TO THE LIMIT OF HIS CEILING.

You may have the capacity of a 1000 kilowatt generator, but if you are only using 100 kilowatts you are limiting yourself to ten percent of your capacity. This works both ways. A person must have the capacity; you can't pour five gallons into a pint can. Rhoda Lachar writes, "THE ONLY LIMITING FACTORS MAN IS SUBJECT TO ARE HIS OWN LAZINESS, HIS LACK OF FAITH IN GOD AND HIMSELF, AND HIS LACK OF KNOW-HOW IN EVERY AREA OF HIS LIFE. We should develop faith and begin to do some digging which gives us knowledge and understanding of God, the Universe, other human beings, ourselves. Thus we will find our true and unlimited self."

Perhaps the greatest need of all is for self-realization. As Ibsen said, "So to conduct one's life as to realize oneself— this seems to me the highest attainment possible to a human being." Wake up your greatness. Don't hide your light under a mask of dejection and degradation. No person has the right to feel fearful, shameful, or worthless. EACH MAN'S RESOURCES AND PRIVILEGES ARE LIMITED ONLY BY HIMSELF.

The moment one vitally grasps the fact that he can rise he will rise, and he can have absolutely no limitations other than the limitations he sets to himself. Cream always rises to the top. It rises simply because it is the nature of cream to rise. Study, and you will rise to the highest standard.

Maxwell Maltz writes, "If we are to be somebody we must learn to accept ourselves for what we are and do what we can do within the limits of our capabilities. And this does not mean limiting ourselves."

When we fear our inability to succeed at any undertaking, that very fear of failure causes worry and anxiety. It puts a doubt in our minds which destroys our efficiency, paralyzes our abilities and causes the failure we fear. When a man has put a limit on what he will do, he has put a limit on what he can do.

We know that every phenomenon in Nature has its own peculiar properties. Glass is different from wood. Gold is different from steel. We are never provoked because glass won't do what gold will do. Or if wood won't do what steel will do.

People too are a phenomenon of nature, and people too have their qualities, their properties, their limitations. Each one of us has his special properties or characteristics. God is the Creator of man as well as the universe and there must be a purpose and design in every attribute of every individual.

If the sickly and feeble can get so much done, what can limit the healthy person except himself? Michelangelo, the master painter, was blind part of his life. Deformed Steinmetz developed his mind to the point where he was regarded as a genius. Milton in his blindness saw more beautiful visions, and Beethoven in his deafness heard more heavenly music, than most of us can ever hope to enjoy. TO BECOME WHAT WE ARE CAPABLE OF BECOMING IS THE ONLY END IN LIFE.

There are only two classes who never make a mistake; the dead and the unborn. The greatest mistake you can ever make is to be continually fearing you will make a mistake. Do something—right or wrong. If it is wrong, correct the mistake, but for goodness sake, do something!

Dr. David Harold Fink writes, "Limitations are part of the nature of things as cracks are part of a pitcher and scars and blemishes part of the body. Wisdom comes from knowledge of one's limitations. HAPPINESS COMES WITH CHEERFUL ACCEPTANCE OF THOSE LIMITATIONS."

Within our capabilities of self-confidence the future is limitless. This realization is the initial step in the development of an adequate image of ourselves: when we know that we can be more than we think we are, when we neither underestimate nor overestimate ourselves, when we do not feel superior or inferior.

The most direct route to finding our place in life and to determine our purpose for having been born is to discover our limitations as early as possible. Name them and begin to draw a boundary around our lives. THEN and only then can we begin to concentrate on what WE CAN DO. When we know what we can do, and we develop those talents and abilities to our full capacity, then we are living successful, purposeful lives. The only way you can ever be happy and mentally healthy in this world, the way it and you are made, IS TO FIND WHAT YOU CAN DO BEST, AND THEN DO IT.

Less than one hundred people produced BOTH the Renaissance and the Reformation. Ten people were responsible for the Federal Union of America. Twelve men—and let this astound, bewilder, and amaze you—began the Christian Era. And they, for the most part, were just ordinary men. But they **were potential miracles. SO ARE YOU!**

CREATIVITY

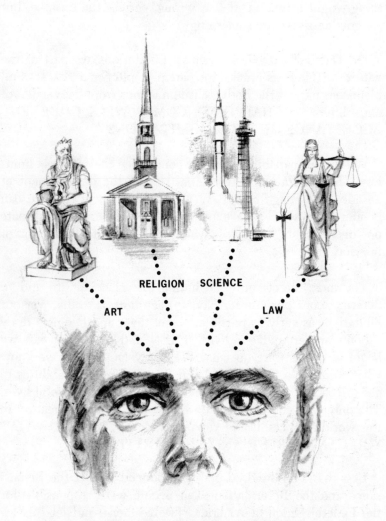

The power to create, provided man by his Creator,
is a force by which man controls his life.

THE LAW OF CREATIVITY

Each single individual has a creative ability. The more creative imagination we apply to our everyday living, the more effective and happy we are going to be, and the more friction and problems can be reduced.

"Creativity is the ability to see (or be aware) and to respond," says Erich Fromm. "Man is a creative creature, and it is this attribute that has been the sole cause of his being able to carve a civilization out of a wilderness, great manufacturing metropolises out of a wide place in the road." Man has adapted himself and the elements of nature to every conceivable use for his benefit.

There is a happiness which comes from creative effort. The joy of dreaming, creating, building, whether in painting a picture, writing an epic, singing a song, devising a new invention, or creating a vast industry. "IMAGINATION," said Albert Einstein, "IS MORE IMPORTANT THAN KNOWLEDGE. For knowledge is limited, whereas imagination embraces the whole world."

Man gets his best ideas when he is completely relaxed. In such moments of relaxation the mind seems to open and give birth to new ideas. It is true that it takes a lot of hard work to develop an idea and win acceptance for it, but as a rule the idea itself comes easily and like a flash.

The potential power of creative imagination is all but limitless. For example, Jules Verne hardly ever left the quiet of his home; and yet he found that his imagination could take him around the world, 20,000 leagues under the sea, and even to the moon. To those who scoffed at his ideas, Jules Verne retorted, "Whatever one man is capable of conceiving, other men will be able to achieve."

The successful man has imagination. The greatest thing in man is soul. The greatest thing in soul is that which creates—imagination. All progress, all achievement is the story of imagination. All religion, all art, all finance, all business, every ship at sea, every bridge that spans the gulf, and every discovery in the great world of science owes its origin, its inception, its first impulse to the exercise of that strange gift, imagination—a power to make images.

A person should save his best thoughts or ideas, some of which may be very valuable in future work. Some authors keep a box near their desk at home in which to toss a note of any idea or thought which they may have and possibly need later. It takes a moment to jot down a thought on a slip of paper and toss it into the box. Good ideas may flash through the mind and soon disappear—perhaps never to return; therefore, it is a good plan to record them in writing as reminders.

Years ago when I was in business all the good ideas came out of the shop or from the men in the field. There was little or no research, only part-time testing crews.

Alex F. Osborn, outstanding leader in the creative field, wrote: "Education is not a vital factor. Many highly trained persons are sterile creatively, while others accomplish outstanding results in spite of an almost total lack of formal instruction.

"Our creative thinking calls for a positive attitude. We have to be hopeful. We need enthusiasm. We have to encourage ourselves to the point of self-confidence. The principle of brainstorming boils down to this: When driving for ideas you go further faster if you keep your foot off the brake.

"From a functional standpoint our mental capacities might be over-simplified as follows: 1. Absorptive—the ability to observe, and to apply attention. 2. Retentive—the ability to memorize and to recall. 3. Reasoning—the ability to analyze and to judge. 4. Creative—the ability to visualize, to foresee, and to generate ideas."

We don't know, of course, just where you happen to be at this moment, but chances are that you are in a man-made environment: your office, your home, a schoolroom, library, or public vehicle where you have time to read. Glance about and you will see that almost everything surrounding you has been invented and designed by someone else, some person at some time engaged in a creative act, and the sum total of those acts makes up the world you live in. This applies not only to your physical environment, but your mental one as well—your mind is filled almost entirely by symbols originally formed by creative persons.

Imagination plays an important part in all great success. It is a prerequisite of all great invention, construction, industry, art, literature, music and drama. The five principal sources which will supply you with a stock of ideas are reading, writing, conversation, observation, and reflection. A man is no greater than his dream, his ideal, his hope, and his plan. Man dreams the dream—fulfilling it, the dream makes the man.

"Imagination rules the world" is the way a great scholar evaluates that soul quality on which all progress must depend for its light and inspiration. When the lamp of imagination ceases to burn, enthusiasm dies. Imagination fathers vision and where no vision is there can be no life or progress. That person is bound to perish who never experiences the driving power of a great dream. Vision beyond the present pioneers the way for new and better tomorrows. Georges Clemenceau said, "The thing that gives people courage is IDEAS."

In his creative aspect, man shares with God a portion of His infinite power and eternal life. This power is most vividly displayed in man's ability to imagine things not imagined before, and to create things not created before. It is seen in his art, his music, and his literature. Thank God for the creative ideas that enrich life by adding your own creative contributions to human progress.

SEVEN ESSENTIALS OF HEALTH

Fresh air

Sunshine

Pure water

Exercise

Good food

Rest

Power of the mind

Segment 31

THE LAW OF HEALTH

The more man follows nature and is obedient to her laws, the longer he will live; the further he deviates from these, the shorter will be his existence. HEALTH IS NATURE'S RE-WARD FOR GETTING INTO HARMONY WITH HER LAWS.

IT IS A LAW OF LIFE TO MAINTAIN ONE'S HEALTH OR SUFFER THE CONSEQUENCES. We can use the body to its greatest usefulness and purpose by doing everything beneficial for it, by learning to use techniques of discipline, health, sanitation, exercise, proper eating, to produce a radiant, healthful life.

Today life has become so changed and so complex that the tendency is to make the physical, mental, and moral health subordinate to the acquisition of wealth, social standing, power and fame, and political position. As a consequence, the preservation of health has largely become of secondary consideration.

But it doesn't take a genius to see that the vast difference in humans is mostly a matter of physical energy—the driving power that gives certain persons the capacity to do vigorous, sustained and active work.

It has been said that a woman is as old as she looks; Oliver Wendell Holmes said, "A man is as old as he feels," but the assertion of the eminent French physiologist, "A MAN IS AS OLD AS HIS ARTERIES," is more correct. Youthfulness or age is expressed in the condition of the blood vessels that form the channels of communication in the body; through which circulates the blood. Many individuals are prematurely old—older at forty-five than they should be at seventy. Their age is measured—not by years, but by the manner in which they have spent their lives.

171

The seven essentials of health are: fresh air, good food, pure water, sunshine, exercise, abundant rest, power of the mind. NATURE is God's physician.

These gifts of Mother Nature, if put to use as they should be, would not only help solve the world's health problems, but would also revolutionize our present-day civilization. In adopting these divinely appointed principles of correct living, man would be practicing PREVENTATIVE MEDICINE in its highest form, and would also be introducing to a sick world the superlative benefits of creative medicine—which to my way of thinking is tenfold more important than our present-day orthodox practice of CURATIVE MEDICINE.

Dr. Henry Bieler, in his outstanding book, *Food Is Your Best Medicine*, gives us valuable advice. Briefly stated: IMPROPER FOODS CAUSE DISEASE; PROPER FOODS CURE DISEASE. Nature does the real healing, utilizing the natural defenses of the body. Literally, we are what we eat. The body is a chemical substance that is constantly changing. Each second old cells die as new cells form. These new cells are created from the chemicals in food, and we have to eat right to provide the proper building materials. HEALTH CAN BE FOUND ONLY BY OBEYING THE CLEAR-CUT LAWS OF NATURE.

"The study of the human body and its requirements for optimal health, should be made a basic principle in all educational effort," writes Dr. Frederick Rossiter, "and that each individual should regard his health as sacredly as his character." Every man is not only the architect of his own character, but he is also THE BUILDER AND CUSTODIAN OF HIS OWN HEALTH AND PHYSICAL WELL-BEING.

Every man is a builder of a temple called his body. No investment in the future can be as important as an investment in health and physical fitness. Health, happiness, peace of mind, and long life will be the inevitable reward. HEALTH IS CERTAINLY MORE VALUABLE THAN MONEY, BECAUSE IT IS BY HEALTH THAT MONEY IS PRODUCED.

The conditions of our life render the study of health now especially important. Our ancestors lived more in the country, more in the open air, more in agricultural operations. We are to a much greater extent concentrated in cities, work much more in houses, shops, offices and factories; our occupations are sedentary and stooping, and are a greater tax on the brain and nervous system. OUR BODIES ARE NOT AS YET ADJUSTED TO A SEDENTARY FORM OF LIFE.

We now have smog in many cities. The importance of breathing proper air and the effect of air on the health and efficiency of individuals is forcefully realized by this fact: FOOD SUPPLIES ONLY FORTY PERCENT OF A MAN'S DAILY ENERGY, THE AIR HE BREATHES SUPPLIES SIXTY PERCENT.

Americans following the warning voices of televised drug commercials and newspaper ads, consider health something that can be purchased in bottles at the drugstore. Why don't we realize that MOST OF OUR ILLS COME FROM OUR OWN WRONG ACTS AND WRONG THINKING, and that Nature is the great physician?

Weight watchers and dieting have expanded into a great American dilemma. Generally, when a person consumes more calories in the form of food than he burns up as energy, fat accumulates. Our automated, push-button way of life is incredibly fattening. Automobiles have almost eliminated walking. Modern conveniences have lightened the load of housekeeping, lawn mowers move by power. Electronic push button garage doors and remote control TV hardly flex a single muscle. And for some the weekly golf game can be enjoyed while riding in an electric cart.

Thoughts produce energy. Thoughts can also rob you of energy. UNNECESSARY FEARS AND WORRIES WASTE OUR ENERGIES. Fear takes a thousand forms. Each time we feel fear, our bodies are fortified for action just as they are by anger. Like anger, fear is in most cases a spendthrift emotion.

Life is ended for every person by one of four causes: disease, accident, suicide, or old age. By far the greatest cause of death is disease. Dr. Joe D. Nichols writes, "There are six chief causes of disease: emotional, nutritional, poisons, infections, accidents, inherited. THE GREATEST CAUSE OF DISEASE IS, WITHOUT A DOUBT, EMOTIONAL. Worry, fear, anxiety, hate, envy, jealousy—these are the great killers. When any of these emotions take hold of us, we get a conflict and that conflict leads to tensions.

"Heart disease is the leading cause of death in America today. How do these adverse emotions affect the heart? Conflict and tension cause the coronary vessels to constrict; the heart muscle itself does not get enough blood, and that heart cries out in pain. We call this symptom angina, which is functional or inorganic. If the conflict persists, and other factors of disease are present, the patient gets coronary thrombosis. All organic disease is made worse by emotional upset." EMOTIONALLY INDUCED ILLNESS BECOMES MORE PREVALENT AS ONE GOES UP THE LADDER OF HUMAN RESPONSIBILITY, MENTAL ALERTNESS, AND CAPACITY.

Travel provides a change of climate and scenery which is often more necessary for certain ailments than medicine. You will find that you have not only gained in health, but your cares, troubles, and anxieties are greatly reduced.

"I WOULD NOT EXCHANGE MY LEISURE HOURS FOR ALL THE WEALTH IN THE WORLD," wrote Mirabeau. We are losing our sense of leisure. In a frenzy, we rush through the days and weeks, not living life, but consuming it. Commercialism so dominates us that we are mere animated machines doomed to the slavery of goods and bonds and business. "I DO NOT HAVE TIME," is the most frequently heard excuse for neglecting health, happiness, necessary recreation, and even worship. Well, WE HAD BETTER TAKE TIME, OR TIME WILL TAKE US!

THE LAW OF CULTURE

THE FIRST LAW OF CULTURE IS, LET EACH BE-
COME ALL THAT HE WAS CREATED CAPABLE OF BE-
ING; EXPAND, IF POSSIBLE, TO HIS FULL GROWTH.
"THE VALUE OF CULTURE IS ITS EFFECT ON CHAR-
ACTER," admonishes Somerset Maugham. "It avails nothing
unless it ennobles and strengthens that. ITS USE IS FOR
LIFE. ITS AIM IS NOT BEAUTY, BUT GOODNESS."

Culture is like wealth; it makes us more ourselves, it enables
us to express ourselves. Culture is not so much something we
have as it is something we have absorbed, and that has become
a part of us. It is a state rather than a possession.

PERSONAL CULTURE CAN BE THE REFINING OF
A MAN SO THAT ALL THE ROUGH EDGES ARE
SMOOTHED OFF. The cultured man is mature, well in-
formed, enjoys and appreciates beauty, music, art and the refinements of life. He is decent to others, understanding, com-
passionate. He is polite, well-mannered, considerate. In other
words, it is the concept of man as his highest self. It makes a
difference to the world and to yourself how cultured you can
become, because civilization depends on cultured people—people who are honest, trustworthy, dependable, conscientious.
It's not just being an art critic, or understanding music, it is a
COMPLETE MAN FUNCTIONING AT HIS GREATEST
POTENTIAL. Recognize with Thoreau that there is a place in
life for culture, as well as for work, and that education to that
end can become as important in business as the most technical
education.

Advice from a father to his son: "My boy, treat everybody
with politeness, even those who are rude to you. For remember
that YOU SHOW COURTESY TO OTHERS NOT BECAUSE
THEY ARE GENTLEMEN, BUT BECAUSE YOU ARE
ONE."

Edward Markham put it poetically, "We are all blind until we see that in the human plan, . . . NOTHING IS WORTH THE MAKING, IF IT DOESN'T MAKE THE MAN. . . . Why build those cities glorious . . . If man unbuilded goes? . . . In vain we build the work, unless . . . The builder also grows." There is only one way to attain culture in the true sense—be natural, be sincere, be honest, have no pretense, be true to the best that is in you. Then culture will become second nature to you. Seek always to do some good, somewhere. EVERY MAN HAS TO SEEK IN HIS OWN WAY TO MAKE HIS OWN SELF MORE NOBLE AND TO REALIZE HIS OWN TRUE WORTH.

What do you mean by culture? It means refinement. It means, that which you add to the raw material, in any direction, by skill and labor. Here is a short analogy. Remove a piece of crude iron ore out of the mine, smelt it, convert it into pig iron. You have cultivated it out of a lower stage into a higher. Take your piece of pig iron and convert it into steel. By the process of culture, the application of skill and labor, you have lifted it into another grade. Now take your piece of steel and manufacture with it the highest and the finest and the most beautiful things that can be constructed out of such material. You have cultivated it still further.

This is true of another kind of material—YOU. Likewise you can cultivate any part of your body. You can set your destiny by what you make of yourself. So, in any direction precisely the same illustration will hold. A man cultivates his hand when he learns a trade, or when he learns to play on a piano. Culture comes from the contemplation of Nature; from the study of great literature and art, also noble architecture; and from personal knowledge of the emotional realities of existence. It is a system of values, or worths, different from those which belong to the spheres dominated by science and commerce. We live in a culture where success is measured by material possessions. Gaining material objectives is important, but being a mature, well-balanced, cultured person is more important.

Culture, like the Kingdom of Heaven, lies within us, and not in foreign galleries. It means gentleness of spirit, and the founding of a good character. THE FULLNESS OF LIFE DOES NOT COME FROM THE THINGS OUTSIDE OF US; WE OURSELVES MUST CREATE THE BEAUTY IN WHICH WE LIVE.

"Though we travel the world over to find the beautiful, WE MUST CARRY IT WITH US or we find it not," wrote Emerson. One man will derive the keenest delight from scenery, trees, and foliage, fruit and flowers, the blue sky, the fleecy clouds, the sparkling sea, the ripple on the lake, the gleam on the river, the shadows on the grass, the moon and stars at night. To another the beauty of nature is nothing. The moon and stars shine in vain; birds and insects, trees and flowers, river and lake and sea, sun, moon, and stars give him no pleasure. ANYONE WHO WANTS TO LEAD A RICHER LIFE HAS ONLY TO REALIZE THAT IT IS UP TO HIM TO RECOGNIZE ALL TYPES OF BEAUTY AND CULTIVATE THE LOVE OF IT WITHIN HIS OWN SOUL.

A gentleman is much harder to find than a genius. The most distinctive mark of a cultured mind is the ability to take another's point of view; to put one's self in another's place, and see life and its problems from a point of view different from one's own. To be willing to test a new idea; to be able to live on the edge of difference in all matters intellectually; to examine without heat the burning questions of the day; to have imaginative sympathy, openness and flexibility of mind, steadiness and poise of feeling, cool calmness of judgment, is to have culture.

NO KNOWLEDGE THAT WE EVER ACQUIRE IS SO IMPORTANT AS A KNOWLEDGE OF WHAT TO SAY, HOW TO SAY IT, OR WHAT TO DO AND HOW TO DO IT. It is one of the secrets of success. It is the Golden Key that opens the door of opportunity. It gives ease and poise to an individual that no amount of learning can give and it carries more conviction than the strongest moral principles.

True beauty in a person has nothing to do with physical characteristics or charming personality. True beauty is an inner quality that radiates from the inner soul of the ugliest peasant, or the plainest saint, or the most humble seeker after truth. Wise Solomon prayed for an understanding heart, and the immortal Socrates asked God to make him beautiful within. Emerson referred to beauty as God's handwriting, and urged his readers to welcome it in every fair face and flower.

Cultivate poise. It is power under control. Poise stores up energy and holds it in reserve for special use. Poise is the art of raising the eyebrows instead of the roof. It keeps you calm and deliberate under varied circumstances. Poise does not mean weakness, vacuity, listlessness, or indifference. In its highest form it suggests self-confidence, independence, and mastership. The man of poise rules. Work done in poise is best because it is thorough, painstaking and intelligent. It exercises a great influence over other men. It suggests immense stores of power in reserve. POISE IS POWER PROPERLY CONTROLLED AND DIRECTED. POISE CONSERVES WASTE OF VITAL ENERGY, AND GIVES BALANCE TO ALL THE POWERS.

IT IS POSSIBLE FOR EVERY MAN TO ACHIEVE BETTERMENT IN THE QUALITY OF HIS LIFE. To be tolerant, gentle, generous and forgiving, and yet never to have compromised a principle, or relinquished a vital truth or conviction, is to have achieved true greatness. In all ranks of life the human heart yearns for the beautiful; and the beautiful things that God makes are his gift to all alike. Broaden your horizon, develop an interest in all that is fine, beautiful, and purposeful. Great internal good comes from the love of music, art, great literature, broad philosophy, and simple faith. Strengthen the inside of your nature, and the outside will be better. NO ONE CAN HAVE REALLY BEAUTIFUL THOUGHTS IN HIS SOUL WITHOUT HAVING HIS LIFE BEAUTIFUL THEREBY.

THE LAW OF HEREDITY AND ENVIRONMENT

It is a law of life. We inherit from our family line physical characteristics, looks, body shape, skin color, hair type, color of eyes; and inclination to certain kinds of natures; tendencies to have certain kinds of diseases such as diabetes, heart trouble, pneumonia, tendency toward alcoholism. WE ARE WHAT OUR CHROMOSOMES MAKE US. These are the microscopic filaments of cell division, and are derived from the parents. They carry the genes that determine heredity. So say the biologists.

Some one has well said, "A MAN'S ORIGINAL CAPITAL COMES THROUGH HIS ANCESTRY." Nature invests in the child the accumulated values of the generations preceding him. Oliver Wendell Holmes thought that a man's value is determined a hundred years before his birth. One thing is certain: the ancestral ground slopes upward by way of an ancestry big of heart, large of mind, and serious of soul. Great men never appear suddenly. It required the combined investment of seven generations to produce an Emerson. The Bach family included one hundred and twenty musicians. Socrates was unique because he was the offshoot of Sophroniscus.

Multiplied thousands are moral and physical paupers because of an unworthy parentage. Many a modern lad is not so much born, as damned into the world. "Blood tells," says science. We accept and heed that in all manner of stock raising— except the human. SCIENTISTS BELIEVE THAT HEREDITY IS THE GREAT DETERMINING FACTOR IN LIFE. In their extensive laboratory investigations and experiments with cattle, hogs, monkeys, rabbits, etc., they know that they can breed almost any characteristic by proper mating. They believe that WE ARE LARGELY WHAT OUR ANCESTORS ARE, AND THAT WE ARE BORN WITH DEFINITE CHARACTERISTICS VERY DIFFICULT TO CHANGE.

Albert Edward Wiggam, authority on heredity, writes: "When we study, not men's rights, but men's natures and capacities, nothing is more obvious than that all men are unequal; they are born unequal, they will always be unequal; nature intended them to be unequal; and no system of government, social control, or education has yet been devised or ever will be devised, that will make them equal. Indeed, the astonishing and delightful discovery of modern psychology and biology is, that the more you educate men the more unequal you make them. The more you equalize opportunity, the more you unequalize men. The more nearly you treat men alike, the more unlike they become. Birth, talent, labor, virtue, and education are forever making differences in people. Some must command, and some must follow. It is a law of life."

The differences among men, therefore, are almost entirely due to their differences in natural powers and aptitudes. But none of this remotely discourages us from stimulating and educating those powers and aptitudes, NOR SHOULD IT DISCOURAGE THE INDIVIDUAL FROM DEVELOPING HIS OWN INNER NATURAL CAPACITIES AND TENDENCIES TO THE UTMOST. TO DO THIS IS THE ONLY WAY TO ATTAIN HIS PRIZE IN LIFE. And whether he starts with one talent, two, five, or a hundred, makes very little difference.

To recognize that heredity shapes much in life leads to understanding and acceptance and wise direction, not to fatalism or despair. The problem for each is to make the most of his heredity, and shape efforts and training accordingly. Therefore, the young person who appraises his personal chances for health, intelligence, vitality, longevity, and other characteristics of his life, is faced with only one question. He can do nothing about his heredity. That is settled. His personal problem is, WHAT CAN I DO TO STRENGTHEN MY WEAKNESSES AND DEVELOP TO THE MAXIMUM THE POWERS I HAVE? Few men during their lifetime come anywhere near exhausting the resources dwelling within them.

Clement Stone, financial wizard of Chicago, writes, "You are the product of your: heredity, environment, physical body, conscious and subconscious mind, experience, and particular position and direction in time and space . . . and something more, including powers known and unknown. You have the power to affect, use, control, or harmonize with all of them. And you can direct your thoughts, control your emotions and ordain your destiny."

"Man must quickly learn to control the increasing human population," said the Harvard Scientist, Ernst Mayr. "The only practical way of improving the human race is to use 'positive eugenics'—to see to it that those with superior genes have more children and that those with inferior genes have fewer. Practicing eugenics is compared with breeding cattle. Man must make an effort to improve himself as well as to limit his number."

If some of the philanthropic endeavor now directed toward alleviating the condition of the unfit, should be directed to enlarging the opportunity of the fit, greater good would result in the end. WE WILL NEVER CREATE A GOOD SOCIETY, MUCH LESS A GREAT ONE, UNTIL INDIVIDUAL EXCELLENCE AND ACHIEVEMENT ARE NOT ONLY RESPECTED, BUT ENCOURAGED.

While some are shouting they need this and that, the crying need of the hour—if there is to be any future—is GODLY MOTHERS AND PRAYERFUL, GOD-FEARING FATHERS. Without doubt, a man mothered by a godly woman will inherit a worthy theme for living, and become the expression of a worthy sentiment. He will inherit a robust fury against wrong and injustice, persistence in a righteous cause, and patient devotion to high ideals. HE WILL CARRY WITH HIM TO HIS LATEST BREATH, THE ENVIRONMENT THAT ONLY A GOOD MOTHER CAN WILL TO AN INTELLIGENT, DEVOTED SON—and amid the shadows of a fading day, he will thank God that he was born of a good mother and inherited the riches of her heart. NOBLE PARENTS HAVE NOBLE CHILDREN.

SCIENTIFIC RESEARCH SHOWS THAT, UNDER IDENTICAL ENVIRONMENT, ONE MAN WILL GO FORWARD WHILE ANOTHER GOES BACKWARD. At the present moment, we live in a world that is hostile to life. We exist in an environment ill-adapted to the real needs of our bodies and souls; among the crowd which wants, above all, to continue the regime of go-as-you-please, laziness and immoralism.

THE ENVIRONMENT YOU FASHION OUT OF YOUR THOUGHTS, YOUR BELIEFS, YOUR IDEALS, YOUR PHILOSOPHY, IS THE ONLY ONE YOU WILL EVER LIVE IN. We should seek the atmosphere and the surroundings which call forth the best that is in us. Why should we think upon things that are lovely? Because thinking determines life. It is a common habit to blame life upon environment. Environment modifies life but does not govern life. The soul is stronger than its surroundings.

Dr. Harold Fink writes, "If you don't like the way you feel about things, you can help yourself by changing your environment. Going on a diet means a change in the environment of your digestive tract. Better tools, better books, better friends, mean a better opportunity for coping with your problems." In the long run we shape our lives, and we shape ourselves. The process never ends until we die. And the choices we make are ultimately our own responsibility. This is a cold world in which we live. It is coldly calculating, frigidly selfish, freezingly thoughtless and frostily unconcerned.

MAN, NOT HIS ENVIRONMENT, MAKES CIVILIZATION. Man has proved over and over again his capacity to rise above all natural obstacles if he is so determined. Therefore, IT REMAINS IN EACH OF US TO PURSUE A PATH LEADING EVER UPWARD TO A GOLDEN DAWN, OR DOWNWARD TO OBLIVION—AND NOT BECAUSE OF LACK OF ENVIRONMENT OR HERITAGE, BUT BECAUSE OF WHAT WE DO OR FAIL TO DO WITH WHAT WE HAVE AND ARE NOW. This is the lesson of history, the challenge of today and tomorrow.

THE LAW OF SERVICE

RENDER A SERVICE IF YOU WOULD SUCCEED. Be among the great servers, the benefactors. It is the only path to success. "Give, and it shall be given unto you." MAKE SOCIETY YOUR DEBTOR AND YOU MAY FIND YOUR PLACE AMONG THE IMMORTALS.

"I don't know what your destiny will be," wrote Albert Schweitzer, "but one thing I know; THE ONLY ONES AMONG YOU WHO WILL BE REALLY HAPPY, ARE THOSE WHO HAVE SOUGHT AND FOUND HOW TO SERVE."

"HE THAT WILL BE GREATEST AMONG YOU LET HIM BE SERVANT OF ALL," is Christ's way of putting it. HE BEST SERVES HIMSELF WHO LOOKS FOR PRIVILEGES OF SERVICE. Rewards cannot be gratuitously handed out. They are compensation for service. By "looking out for number one" we promote selfishness, which is only another word for suicide. To save at the expense of service is to lose what we attempt to save. Any other way of life is to forfeit life itself. TO GIVE IS TO GET. THIS IS A FIXED LAW OF THE UNIVERSE. THIS LAW WILL EITHER MAKE OR BREAK US.

This law is demonstrated wonderfully in people's lives every day of the year. Those who give freely have a pleasant, loving personality. Their sacrificial desire to serve, to help others along the road, brings them the greatest blessings in feelings of self-fulfillment, and in most cases their needs are provided for. What they give to others returns to them ten or a hundred fold. MEN ARE RICH ONLY AS THEY GIVE. Action and reaction are always equal. GIVE LARGELY AND RECEIVE LARGELY—whether it be money, friendship, faith or confidence. Your giving may be betrayed, squandered or unappreciated but you are bigger and better for having given.

One of the major problems of our life today is that we have too many people who want to be on the receiving end and not enough on the giving end of service.

Service in its true meaning involves contributing more to life than you take from it. Anyone who sincerely tries to leave the world a bit better than he found it, is serving regardless of his occupation. Perhaps the noblest way of serving God lies in nobly serving one's fellow men. TO AFFECT THE QUALITY OF THE DAY, THAT IS THE HIGHEST OF ARTS.

The brotherhood of man is just a dream. Understanding, maybe, but not true brotherhood, because people are too different. Men have their different customs and ways, they have their likes and dislikes. Each man is an individualist, he is unique, he is not manufactured on the production line like broomsticks. Each man is to develop himself, and has a right to his own beliefs and customs. However, if every man had a change of heart and was Christ centered, you would have a love acting as a cement, that would bind men together into a brotherhood. This is the only way that true brotherhood will ever exist.

HE HELPS OTHERS MOST WHO SHOWS THEM HOW TO HELP THEMSELVES. It is much better to give hope and strength and courage, than money. The best help is not to bear the troubles of others for them, but to inspire them with courage and energy to bear their own burdens for themselves, and meet with the difficulties of life bravely. To help others is no easy matter but requires a clear head and wise judgment as well as a warm heart.

It is important, therefore, as far as possible, NOT SO MUCH TO GIVE A MAN MONEY, AS TO PUT HIM IN THE WAY OF EARNING IT FOR HIMSELF; not to give direct aid, but to help others to permanently help themselves.

The best thing to give to your enemy is forgiveness; to an opponent, tolerance; to a friend, your heart; to your child, a good example; to your father, deference; to your mother, conduct that will make her proud of you; to yourself, respect.

Charles Eliot wrote, "LIFE IS A CONTINUOUS SERVICE. TO BE OF SERVICE IS A SOLID FOUNDATION FOR CONTENTMENT IN THIS WORLD."

The greatest strength, the greatest courage, and the greatest internal security comes to each of us through service to our fellow man. Here is our peace, here is our hope, here is the thing which takes a humdrum existence, and transforms it into a splendid and useful program.

Every person has a mission to fulfill in this world. A little thinking is all that is necessary to understand why nature does not make every person a genius. People are needed for the thousands of various kinds of work to be done, and it would be unfortunate for all of us if we could not get the services of all classes of workers.

"The best service that we can do for our country and for our-selves," says Justice Holmes, "is to see so far as one may, and to feel the great forces that are behind every detail . . . to hammer out as compact and solid a piece of work as one can, to try to make it first rate, and to leave it unadvertised."

THE UNIVERSE PAYS EVERY MAN IN HIS OWN COIN. If you smile, it smiles upon you in return; if you frown, you will be frowned upon; if you sing, you will be invited to gay company; if you think, you will be entertained by thinkers; if you love the world and earnestly seek for the good therein, you will be surrounded by loving friends and nature will pour into your lap the treasures of the earth.

I expect to pass through this world but once. Any good work, therefore, any kindness or any service I can render, let me do it now, for I shall not pass this way again.

LIFE IS ONLY MADE FOR WHAT WE CAN DO FOR SOMEBODY ELSE. We are here for a purpose. We are here to help and to serve. We must give of ourselves to help. God's objective is not to merely save us from wrong, HIS GREAT CONCERN IS TO SECURE OUR SERVICE FOR THE RIGHT.

DESIDERATA

GO PLACIDLY AMID THE NOISE & HASTE, & REMEMBER WHAT PEACE THERE MAY BE IN SILENCE. AS FAR AS POSSIBLE WITHOUT surrender be on good terms with all persons. Speak your truth quietly & clearly; and listen to others, even the dull & ignorant; they too have their story. 🐚 Avoid loud & aggressive persons, they are vexations to the spirit. If you compare yourself with others, you may become vain & bitter; for always there will be greater & lesser persons than yourself. Enjoy your achievements as well as your plans. 🐚 Keep interested in your own career, however humble; it is a real possession in the changing fortunes of time. Exercise caution in your business affairs; for the world is full of trickery. But let this not blind you to what virtue there is; many persons strive for high ideals; and everywhere life is full of heroism. 🐚 Be yourself. Especially, do not feign affection. Neither be cynical about love; for in the face of all aridity & disenchantment it is perennial as the grass. 🐚 Take kindly the counsel of the years, gracefully surrendering the things of youth. Nurture strength of spirit to shield you in sudden misfortune. But do not distress yourself with imaginings. Many fears are born of fatigue & loneliness. Beyond a wholesome discipline, be gentle with yourself. 🐚 You are a child of the universe, no less than the trees & the stars; you have a right to be here. And whether or not it is clear to you, no doubt the universe is unfolding as it should. 🐚 Therefore be at peace with God, whatever you conceive Him to be, and whatever your labors & aspirations, in the noisy confusion of life keep peace with your soul. 🐚 With all its sham, drudgery & broken dreams, it is still a beautiful world. Be careful. Strive to be happy. 🐚 🐚

FOUND IN OLD SAINT PAUL'S CHURCH, BALTIMORE; DATED 1692

Segment 35

THE LAW OF MORALITY

"Right and wrong are in the nature of things. They are not words and phrases. They are in the nature of things, and if you transgress the laws laid down, imposed by the nature of things, depend upon it you will pay the penalty."—John Morley

There is an underlying pattern of law which establishes what is moral and what is not, what is good conduct and what is not. Regardless of the systems man builds up for himself nationally or religiously, (and again tears down), there is still a system of laws which work to produce penalties for unmoral action, and rewards for moral action.

"In reality," says C. S. Lewis, "moral rules are directions for running the human machine. Every moral rule is there to prevent a breakdown, or a strain, or a friction, in running that machine. That is why these rules at first seem to be constantly interfering with our natural inclinations." MOTIVES ARE INVISIBLE, BUT THEY ARE THE TRUE TEST OF CHARACTER.

"Today we are afraid of simple words like goodness and mercy and kindness," writes Lin Yutang. "We don't believe in the good old words because we don't believe in the good old values any more. And that is why the world is so sick."

A thing that will help your inner life is to set up in your mind a standard of values so that you know what is really significant, important and valuable. Conduct is life; in the long run happiness and prosperity depend upon it. External circumstances are of comparatively little importance; it does not so much matter what surrounds us, as what we are. BEHAVIOR IS A MIRROR IN WHICH EVERYONE SHOWS HIS IMAGE.

Throughout life we are constantly called upon to make decisions involving distinction between right and wrong, decisions which will in no way injure our fellow man, while producing satisfactory results for ourselves. We learn that certain laws govern our acts, and that certain results inevitably follow their performance.

Of course it cannot be denied that what is wrong or unwise is often very pleasant, sometimes even delightful for the moment. In yielding to such impulses we are buying a momentary pleasure at the expense of future sorrow; we are giving up a great deal for the sake of comparatively trivial gain; and buying the merry madness of an hour, by the long penitence of after years.

Everyone cannot be a college graduate. But everyone can have respect, high standards and values, those qualities of mind and spirit which are the true worth of every individual. MORAL SENSE IS MORE IMPORTANT THAN INTELLIGENCE. When it disappears from a nation, the whole social structure slowly commences to crumble away. History reveals Nations rise and fall, but the moral law is written on the tables of eternity. Moral rules are directions for running the human machine, and never hurting others. Everyone is indebted to the church and to every nation, organization and person who uplifts the moral standards of man. However, most of us learn our moral values in the church.

The very foundation of a man, and that which is the mightiest moving force of his life, and must be, is the moral quality of his being. Here is an illustration that shows the moral faculty is the driving force. Picture a steamship in mid-ocean; an engine in the hold is the power that moves it somewhere, that keeps it from simply drifting at the mercy of wind and wave. THIS POWER TO MAN IS ALWAYS A MORAL POWER, A MORAL FORCE. THE MOTIVE FORCE OF LIFE IS THE MORAL FORCE.

"America has cast off her moral 'guidelines' and is adrift in a sea of immorality and crime and sensuality that threatens our very permanence," writes Dr. E. R. Palen. Fundamentally, the force that rules the world is conduct, whether it be moral or immoral. If it is moral, at least there may be hope for the world. If immoral, there is not only no hope, but no prospect of anything but destruction of all that has been accomplished during the last 5000 years.

PASSIONS ARE VICES OR VIRTUES IN THEIR HIGHEST POWERS. To control our passions we must govern our habits, and keep watch over ourselves in the small details of everyday life. THE HAPPINESS OF A MAN IN THIS LIFE DOES NOT CONSIST IN THE ABSENCE BUT IN THE MASTERY OF PASSIONS. The code by which we live becomes the code which may cause our death. No one can be well or happy who is troubled by his own conduct.

Man possesses a spiritual nature, with powers to reach out and find God and communicate with Him. The intellect tells us about God; our spiritual powers find Him. There is no other form of civilization to be compared with Christian civilization as a development of human life. Humanity has its richest flavor; homes are most peaceful and happy; and human rights are most fully regarded. When any community is most completely under the power of a spiritual life, all forms of evil are lessened, and vice hides its deformed head. The reason there is so much stealing, violence, crime today, is that man has neglected his spiritual nature. In the spiritual is found man's highest excellence. This cardinal point is being overlooked today and we are dealing with effects instead of first causes. Soul cultivation is the first requisite of a stable individual or government.

WHAT DO I GET FOR BEING HONEST? YOU ARE GETTING THE CONSCIOUSNESS IN YOUR MIND THAT YOU ARE RIGHT, THE BEST REWARD THAT LIFE CAN BRING. THERE IS NO SUCCESS WITHOUT HONOR, NO HAPPINESS WITHOUT A CLEAR CONSCIENCE.

One of man's greatest dilemmas is that he is an emotional as well as a rational being. Man's behavior is greatly influenced by his impulses, and he must control his emotions and impulses. Happy indeed is the person who learns early in life to subordinate his animal impulses to his finer spiritual sentiments. MAN'S HISTORY IS INDELIBLY WRITTEN UPON HIS FEATURES. His face bears the marks of his inner character.

The evil man is a slave to the worst of masters—his own passions. Many young men today have the idea that there is something "manly" about vice. But any weak fool can be vicious. TO BE VIRTUOUS YOU MUST BE A MAN; to be virtuous is to be free; vice is the real slavery. A particular course of conduct does not degrade because it is wrong; it is wrong because it degrades. If by some extraordinary subversion of morals, or a Supreme Court decision, wrong became right (or legal), it would still be fatal to happiness and peace of mind. Life is a constant battle against evil forces. Marcus Aurelius used to say to himself each morning, "Prepare my soul, to meet today the liar, the cheat, the thief." We should add "Prepare also to meet the wise, the good, the noble."

"I do not believe the greatest threat to our future is from bombs or guided missiles. I don't think our civilization will die that way," says Laurence M. Gould. "I THINK IT WILL DIE WHEN WE NO LONGER CARE—WHEN THE SPIRITUAL FORCES THAT MAKE US WISH TO BE RIGHT AND NOBLE DIE IN THE HEARTS OF MEN. Arnold Toynbee has pointed out that 19 of 21 notable civilizations have died from within and not by conquest from without. There were no bands playing and no flags waving when these civilizations decayed; it happened slowly, in the quiet and the dark when no one was aware. If America is to grow great, we must stop gagging at the word spiritual. Our task is to rediscover and reassert our faith in the spiritual, non-utilitarian values on which American life has really rested from its beginning."

Segment 36

THE LAW OF NEEDS

You can satisfy a man's NEEDS, but never his WANTS. Man's basic needs are very small in comparison to the false standards we have set for ourselves today. Man's nature requires basic needs which include food, clothing, shelter, love, or belonging, work or some form of achievement.

Man's needs are actually few, it is his wants that complicate his life and become the millstones around his neck. Or putting it another way, his wants sometimes become the quicksands which eventually engulf him.

"Most of the luxuries, and many of the so-called comforts of life," wrote Thoreau, "are not only not indisensable, but positive hindrances, to the elevation of mankind."

Some people think they are poor just because they do not have everything they want. Most men want a million dollars, a boat, a fine home, a Cadillac, a swimming pool. Character and inner values are essential for abundant living, and are more valuable than mere material possessions. A LIFE OF LOVE, JOY: USEFUL, PURPOSEFUL, PROFITABLE, FRUITFUL —THIS IS THE GOOD LIFE.

We want more than we need, and we cause all kinds of grief getting it. Through advertising, envy, greed, self-imposed competition, we set a list of wants that even a superman could not fill. Then we proceed to kill ourselves, alienate our family, squeeze out God, to get these things; and before we realize it, what we have left is one big zero.

My wife Evelyn has the unbeatable philosophy. When asked about her personal needs she replied, "I AM RICH IN HEALTH AND INTERESTS, BUT I HAVE ALWAYS BEEN RICH, BECAUSE I NEVER WANTED ANYTHING I DID NOT NEED."

"HALF OF THE CONFUSION IN OUR LIVES COMES FROM NOT KNOWING HOW LITTLE WE NEED. I live more simply now, and with more peace," wrote Admiral Byrd. To simplify our life, first we must reduce our wants. It is not from nature, but from education and habit that our wants are chiefly derived. No one need have much anxiety about the real necessities of life. Luxuries, on the other hand, are very expensive. RICHES ARE NOT FROM THE ABUNDANCE OF WORLDLY GOODS BUT FROM A CONTENTED MIND.

It will cut down the high cost of living if we do not try to finance all our impulses. LIMIT YOUR WANTS BY YOUR WEALTH. NEVER ENOUGH, IS THE WILD GOOSE CHASE OF MOST MEN'S LIVES. Let us reserve some of our energy for enjoyment of beauty, love, service; and not all to the task of accumulation.

Viktor Frankl ties a man's love and his work together and shows that man must have meaning in life in order to go on living. A man's meaning may be love for a woman, care for a family, building a career, or a book which he feels he must write. It is a person or job to which he commits his life and toward which, in order to make such a commitment, he must feel love and concern. Ultimately, a man's meaning may even be grounded in a relationship with God.

In discussing man's needs we cannot emphasize too strongly that there must be a BALANCE in every phase of our life—physical, mental, material, spiritual. Man is body, mind, spirit, and all must be developed EQUALLY for successful balanced living. Therefore, WE MUST GIVE THE PROPER AMOUNT OF ATTENTION TO OUR PHYSICAL, MENTAL, FINANCIAL AND SPIRITUAL NEEDS. "No single way of living is exclusively right," says Sydney J. Harris. "Combination is all. Life is the art of mixing ingredients in tolerable proportions, so that all the varied needs of man are somehow satisfied, and no important hunger is neglected. This is what all extremists forget, with their too simple slogans for the good life."

"CONTENTMENT DOES NOT COME TO THOSE WHOSE MEANS ARE GREAT BUT TO THOSE WHOSE NEEDS ARE FEW," writes Manly Hall.

"Even though you have ten thousand fields," says an old Chinese proverb, "you can eat but one measure of rice a day; even though your dwelling contains a thousand rooms, you can use but eight feet of space at night."

Simplify your life. Even though you can afford everything, you should not clutter your life with non-essentials. POSSIBLY THE HAPPIEST LIFE IS THE SIMPLE LIFE—adequate, but without heavy responsibilities. Material possessions always bring responsibility. One reason why some men are always in debt is that they cannot do without the things they do not need. To some extent we are all owned by our possessions. The accumulations that weigh one down may even be of the non-material sort, like obligations, reputation or status.

According to Dr. John Schindler, every human being has the following six needs: THE NEED FOR LOVE, SECURITY, CREATIVE EXPRESSION, RECOGNITION, NEW EXPERIENCES, SELF-ESTEEM.

What is the greatest need of our generation? Here are some of the answers given by some of our greatest men: "I would answer discipline. There is almost a total lack of it." "What I need most is somebody to make me do what I can." Albert Schweitzer answered, "Man does not think." Man must learn to think for himself, not be a parrot, an echo, or a carbon copy of somebody else. Many think of the mind as a storehouse to be filled, when the mind is an instrument to be USED; practically it is both. "The need for wisdom to match our technology," another believes is the most important challenge facing man today. My deepest need, your deepest need, is for One in whose wisdom, strength, and power, our human weakness, ignorance, and feebleness can find refuge and rest. THE GREATEST NEED OF MAN IS GOD. YOU ARE COMPLETE IN HIM.

The most monumental advance of our economic-oriented civilization is the freedom from want. Man is no longer faced with fulfilling the primary physical needs of life from sunup to sundown. He now has time for self-realization and self-fulfillment, which he has been striving for centuries to attain. But he is totally unprepared for the magnificent fulfillment of his goal. He has chased the silver chalice and suddenly finds it in his lap, but does not know how to fill it.

Modern society has committed the fundamental error of disobeying the law of spiritual development. MAN'S GREATEST NEED NOW IS TO DEVELOP HIS SOUL: NEVER WAS MAN MORE IN NEED OF BEING "MADE WHOLE." With this development he is free to enjoy to the highest degree, the beauty, order, and permanence of the universe; he is free to dedicate himself in service and sacrifice to others; he is free to commune with nature and find in that communion the ties to the universal that he has always sought.

Man is on the brink of the greatest period of self-fulfillment ever imagined, yet luxury, ease, material dominating thoughts find him standing at the brink wanting. The maturity of insight that comes in an individual life should also be the same for every man collectively. Councillor describes this maturing process aptly: "With the years comes a certain ripening of the spirit. We come to see things as they are, and our mind becomes reconciled to the world as it is. Realization of the essential smallness, sordidness, and lack of completeness of the material life, turns our mind to appreciate the enduring satisfactions of the other and higher aspects of life, the spiritual life. And as, in the fullness of wisdom and experience, life stands revealed to us in its larger significances, we gain a new tranquility of spirit and our lengthening days become in their thought and in their deeds, even nobler in purpose, fuller in meaning, richer in content, and more imbued with that devotion to God and love of fellow man in which our life finds its highest sublimation."

THE LAW OF SELF-DISCIPLINE

MAN IS MADE OR UNMADE BY HIMSELF. Man controls his own passions, emotions, future. He does so by channeling his physical drives to produce mental achievement. Any animal can dissipate his strength by expending his physical drives everytime he feels them. Man's job is to channel them to more productive ends than self-indulgence.

No man ever became great doing as he pleased. Little men do as they please—little nobodies. Great men submit themselves to the laws governing the realm of their greatness.

SELF-DISCIPLINE IS ALWAYS REWARDED BY A STRENGTH WHICH BRINGS AN INEXPRESSIBLE, SILENT INNER JOY WHICH BECOMES THE DOMINANT TONE OF LIFE. Self-control is the quality that distinguishes the fittest to survive.

"THE MOST IMPORTANT ATTRIBUTE OF MAN AS A MORAL BEING IS THE FACULTY OF SELF-CONTROL," wrote Herbert Spencer. "There never has been, and cannot be, a good life without self-control; apart from self-control, no good life is imaginable. FOR MAN TO CONQUER HIMSELF IS THE FIRST AND NOBLEST VICTORY."

"One must learn little by little, by exercises repeated everyday, to establish order in one's life, to accept one's self-imposed discipline and to be one's own master," instructs Alexis Carrel. "ONE MUST ALSO TRAIN ONESELF, BY SMALL AND FREQUENT EFFORTS, TO DOMINATE ONE'S FEELINGS; one's nervousness, laziness, weariness and suffering. Such an apprenticeship is indispensable to any civilized person; the basic error of modern teaching is to have neglected it."

"MAN MUST BE DISCIPLINED, FOR HE IS BY NATURE RAW AND WILD," wrote Immanuel Kant. LIFE REQUIRES SELF-DISCIPLINE.

For the last three decades there has been a total lack of discipline taught in the home and in the schools. The "do not suppress" philosophy recommended by Dr. Spock, and the psychology of Freud and Nietzsche taught in our schools, both had as their fundamental doctrine: no part of our nature must be suppressed for fear of inhibitions. Turn it all loose. The result is being demonstrated today.

We have to conclude this civilization will destroy itself as others have before it. That leaves only one question . . . when? Pushing this nation toward its rendezvous with destruction are a host of adversaries ranging from U.S. Supreme Court decisions, to working mothers who could afford to remain home to care for their children. No matter how well meaning these adversaries, overlooked are the fundamental facts: MAN IS THE MOST PREDATORY OF ALL IN THE ANIMAL KINGDOM. HE MUST HAVE RESTRAINTS. These restraints are withering away under a widespread explosion of liberalism without restraint.

The latest annual crime statistics from the F.B.I. show us that we are actually going backward. Ask yourself, how many streets or areas of your city can you walk with safety? Pope Leo XIII said, "When a society is perishing, the true advice to give to those who would restore it, is to recall it to the principles from which it sprung." Homes without parental authority, prayer and discipline, are the workshop where future anarchists are being trained.

POWER COMES BY DISCIPLINE, AND BY DISCIPLINE ALONE. Discipline your natural desires. One can learn to manage himself as one learns to manage an airplane. "I have never met a man who has given me as much trouble as myself," wrote D. L. Moody. The only person who can hurt you, is yourself. Your capacity to say "no" determines your capacity to say "yes." You have to say "no" to lesser things, in order to say "yes" to greater things. THE GREAT REWARD IS YOU BECOME A VIRTUOSO AT LIVING.

Manly Hall writes, "There is a school of thought which says that children should not be corrected or directed by their parents. The little ones should grow and unfold like flowers in the field. Experience has proved, however, that 'wild flowers' of this nature become unmanageable because they have not learned to control themselves or accept the leadership of their parents. The neglected child becomes a problem child, and a neglected soul becomes a burden upon the body which it inhabits. There must be dedication to suitable ideals, and a willingness to sacrifice daily that which is less, to preserve that which is greater."

You cannot run away from a weakness, you must sometime fight it out or perish; and if that be so, why not now, and where you stand? We must constantly be on guard against evil and lewd thoughts, harmful attitudes, jealousy, egotism, self-importance, envy, greed, fear, worry, abnormal anxiety, anger, pessimism and hate. We must discipline ourselves. It is the bridle and the spur that makes a good horse.

"SELF-DISCIPLINE IS YOUR GOLDEN KEY; WITHOUT IT, YOU CANNOT BE HAPPY. In my lifetime," says Dr. Maxwell Maltz, "I have known many famous people—executives, statesmen, stars of stage and screen, doctors—and I have been aware of their emotional scars. Few have followed straight lines to their successes; most have blundered at times and have overcome their blunders with their persistent belief in themselves. DISCIPLINE, IN THE FINAL ANALYSIS, HAS BEEN THE TOOL WITH WHICH THEY HAVE FORGED THEIR SUCCESS; self-discipline has been their mighty weapon."

THE END OF ALL DISCIPLINE IS THAT MAN SHOULD BE TRULY HIMSELF AND ATTAIN PEACE IN HIS OWN SOUL. Happy indeed is the person who learns early in life to subordinate his animal impulses to the finer things of high spiritual sentiments. THRICE HAPPY ARE THEY WHO CARRY THEIR FACULTIES AND POWERS UP TO THE LEVEL OF GOD'S BEST THOUGHTS.

MY DAILY PRAYER

Dear LORD, may the WORDS of my MOUTH, and the MEDITATIONS of my HEART, be acceptable in thy sight.

Go with me, LORD, this day wherever I go, and be my GUIDE, my STRENGTH, and my JOY.

Fill me this day with THY INDWELLING PRESENCE, and keep me in THY WILL and THY WAY.

TEACH ME, LORD, so that I will do the IMPORTANT THINGS FIRST, each day. Help me to organize and plan my work so that I may accomplish as much as possible in the shortest possible time.

Keep me busy doing the things that are constructive, and help me to achieve my FULL POTENTIAL.

HELP ME, O LORD, to keep my nose out of other people's business.

Cultivate in me a sense of humor that will make the lives of others more pleasant. May my thoughts be good, happy, constructive, creative, pleasant and positive.

DELIVER ME from every tendency to have a criticizing and complaining nature.

KEEP ME from speaking evil of anyone.

Let MODERATION be my watchword.

And finally, O LORD, give me THY NATURE, fill me with DEEDS instead of WORDS, EXPAND MY FAITH that I may meet life's problems with CONFIDENCE and VICTORY. Help me to walk with THEE, and to BELIEVE and LIVE by THY PROMISES. Make me a USEFUL, PURPOSEFUL, and FRUITFUL servant of thine, so that when my little day is done the Master Teacher will say—"WELL DONE."

—Alfred A. Montapert

THE LAW OF PRAYER

Prayer is man's communion with God. It is releasing the energies of God. For prayer is asking God to do what we cannot do. Prayer is the effort of man to reach God, to commune with an invisible being, Creator of all things, supreme wisdom, truth, beauty, and strength, Father and Redeemer of each man.

A world famous scientist, Dr. Alexis Carrel, said, "The most powerful form of energy that one can generate is prayer. Only in prayer do we achieve that complete and harmonious assembly of body, mind and spirit, which gives the frail human reed its unshakable strength." It supplies us with a steady flow of sustaining power in our daily lives.

Abraham Lincoln said that he had been driven to his knees many times by the overwhelming conviction that there was nowhere else to go. "My own wisdom and that of all about me seemed insufficient for the day."

THE WHOLE ESSENCE OF PRAYER DEPENDS UPON OUR FAITH. IT IS THE BELIEF THAT OUR HEART EXERCISES, THAT BRINGS RESULTS.

All men instinctively pray. It is by prayer that man reaches God and God enters into him. Prayer appears to be indispensable to our highest development. Tear down the wall between God and yourself and "come alive." You can. Learn everything that is to be known about God and yourself. Learn what will make that partnership active every minute for the balance of your life, then you will tear that wall down.

"Happy is the man who has learned the secret of coming to God daily in prayer," says Billy Graham. "Fifteen minutes alone with God every morning before you start the day can change circumstances and remove mountains."

THE GREATEST THING THE GREATEST MAN EVER DID WAS TO PRAY. I know of no really great man in history who has not been a man of prayer. Any man, even the simplest of men, can establish both the fact and the necessity of and for prayer. Prayer is the one indispensable thing essential to spiritual well-being. Daily prayer is the gymnasium of the soul.

The disciples did not ask to be taught how to pray. Teach us "to" pray was their request. In order to enjoy the benefits of electricity about all one needs to know is the location and the use of a switch. The important thing is TO PRAY. "Seek and ye shall find, knock and it shall be opened unto you." By not praying we rob ourselves of the vital, essential things of life itself.

PRAYER IS AN ATTITUDE much more than it is anything else. AN ATTITUDE OF "MY FATHER KNOWETH THAT I HAVE NEED OF ALL THESE THINGS." Try that simple method of living and note the results. A thousand problems will melt away like snowbanks under a June sun. Things you now fear will be erased from your thoughts like pictures from a blackboard. Worries and burdens will drop from your life like icicles from the eaves when the sun strikes them. Clouds of depression will drift from your sky like thunderheads driven by a wind. Try it, and for the first time in your life you will know what Christ meant when He said, "Let not your heart be troubled." Trouble cannot abide if "ye believe in God." GOD HIMSELF IS THE ESSENTIAL ANSWER TO PRAYER. "HE CARETH FOR YOU," is one of the most momentous announcements in the Scriptures. It gives a sense of security not experienced by reading any other passage of Scripture.

We do not need prayer to influence God on our behalf. WE NEED PRAYER TO RAISE US UP TO THE LEVEL WHERE ALL GOD'S MERCIES AND BLESSINGS FLOW IN ABUNDANCE. On this level, prayer becomes the attitude indicated by Jesus Christ when he said, "Only believe and thou shalt see the glory of God."

The trouble is we have come to think of prayer as an act only. While prayer is an act, it is much more an attitude and a relationship. The word relationship indicates interdependence. The true relationship between God and man is not independent on either side. Man has no source of supply apart from God, and God finds what He most craves and needs in fellowship with man. On man's side, prayer is as inseparable from spiritual life as breathing is inseparable from physical life. On God's side, prayer makes access to man possible.

About the only rule I know of that is necessary for prayer is the rule of keeping our essential relationship with God in adjustment. The illustration of installing radio equipment in an airplane is not sufficient. The equipment must be kept in tune-in condition. A dead set is as bad or worse than no set. And when the pilot is in the fog that is no time to repair his equipment. He must maintain his relationship with the source of his help constantly.

What is truly effective prayer? THE ATTITUDE OF A CHRISTIAN TOWARDS LIFE ITSELF. What many of us have not seen, however, is that questioning is a form of unbelief—many times the most subtle and deadliest kind of unbelief. Once a life is fully committed to God that life is not directed by chance but by God for His purpose. If expressed gratitude is a mark of good breeding and spiritual quality, whining is a mark of bad breeding and spiritually it is a mark of downright unbelief. Nothing will so quickly and so completely ruin a true life of prayer as fretting, repining, and complaining.

TRUE PRAYER IS THE PRAYER THAT FINDS GOD AND THE PRAYER THAT MAKES IT POSSIBLE FOR HIM TO FIND US. True prayer enters into the life of God and makes it possible for Him to enter into our lives. God Himself becomes the "answer to our prayer." PRAYER IS A PATH TO POWER. IT IS THE PRACTICE OF INNER RENEWAL AND REFRESHMENT.

Understanding on our part is the prime requisite to the use of prayer. Once that understanding is attained, prayer is as easy to use as electricity—and with the same degree of certainty as to results. I do not say that our understanding is capable of encompassing all the mystery of prayer. It is not—any more than our understanding is capable of comprehending all the mystery of electricity. But comprehension of the mystery is not necessary to its use. All we need to know is that "all things are possible" to him who makes himself a conductor for the limitless energy that God puts at our command. Many psychologists realize this and prayer has effected a cure in the patient through self-therapy.

God listens only to your heart. If words voice true desire they are true prayer. Prayer is not primarily an emergency provision—not merely something to be used in case of distress or when we need something. It is the vital life of a Christian which creates and maintains fellowship with God. Prayer creates friendship—God becomes a friend to us, and we become God's friend. By cultivating a prayerful life, that guarantees my friendship for and with Him, and His friendship for and with me, God and I become good friends.

PRAYER WITHOUT FAITH IS AS IMPOSSIBLE AS LIFE WITHOUT BREATHING. Prayer will put you to work to help accomplish what you desire. And that is an important point. Many of your prayers will never be answered unless you help answer them. God is not your chore boy to be sent on missions while you conveniently sit and wait for Him to do the work.

THE OBJECT OF PRAYER IS TO EXPERIENCE GOD. Abstract truth can only be made to live, as it is translated into human experience. No matter how true a statement of fact or a doctrine may be—it is only a skeleton until wrought on by the magic of experience and made to live. MAY YOU LIVE EVERY DAY OF YOUR LIFE—WITH PRAYER.

Segment 39

THE LAW OF SEX

Next to hunger, sex is the strongest physical urge of mankind. It can be a very creative drive or a very destructive drive. It is not limited to the mere propagation of the race, but involves the entire emotional and nervous personality of the individual. Sex is a dominating force but MUST be controlled. You can't set a stick of dynamite off recklessly; neither can you fool around with sex. Discipline along this line is most needed today.

SEX IS LIKE FIRE—YOU CAN USE IT WISELY AND BE BLESSED BY IT, OR YOU CAN USE IT UNWISELY AND BE BURNED BY IT. It is a God-given power, neither moral nor immoral in itself, but moral or immoral according to its use. There is no shame in sex, there is shame in the wrong use of sex. Sex has brought more heaven and hell into life than has any other thing. And we make the heaven or the hell according to what we do with sex. THE CONTROL OF THE SEXUAL DESIRE IS ONE OF THE GREATEST FACTORS IN DETERMINING A MAN'S SUCCESS.

Every normal person has sexual desires. You should be proud to be vibrantly alive. These desires in themselves are good, but lacking in their natural outlet they frequently cause irritability, loss of poise, loss of mental equilibrium. You upset a naturally attractive personality by harboring this terrific tumult within.

Marriage usually is the solution. But there is a good substitute known as sublimation. When the hot hormones go racing through your blood you need some relief. Sublimation, which is channeling your physical and nervous energy into tennis, swimming, or some other physical exercise, helps to give partial relief. It puts the sex drive to useful work.

If you write a book, paint a picture, play a musical instrument, build a bird house, you will be using some of your creative (sexual) urge. In other words, creative work and exercise is a safety valve which will relieve an overheated condition. Sex can be used or abused; it is each one's responsibility to control and use sex constructively. Since it takes two to tango there are always social and moral implications. There is no such thing as "love 'em and leave 'em." Your entire character is a composite of your every experience.

If everyone were able to afford marriage right at maturity the problem would just about solve itself. But since biological maturity does not wait for economic maturity there is bound to be conflict in the breast of every unmarried man and woman. Sublimation is the only satisfactory answer.

The sublimation of the sex drive into other areas of activity has created some of our greatest saints, and noblest artists. It is a healthy, powerful drive if handled correctly. Channeled intelligently, it can be a tremendous spur to life and accomplishment, to satisfaction and joy of living, to sharing and building an eventful and happy marriage.

"The driving energy of the sexually mature individual is evidently a powerful force for intellectual productivity if it can be harnessed aright," says Dr. Frank Crane, M.D. "Sublimation of such inclinations probably explains a large part of the literature, art and poetry which stands in the pre-eminent class today. The ascetics and priests of the middle ages who translated their sex energy into literary and scientific products might never have attained as high a pinnacle of excellence if they had been bereft of this powerful driving force. If sex is so potent a source of motivation that it runs a close second to hunger, then we may reason quite logically that the stronger the sexual inclinations, the greater the possibility of tremendous intellectual attainment when they are harnessed in the interest of science and the arts. THE SEX GLANDS ARE, THEREFORE, BASES FOR PRODUCTION AS WELL AS REPRODUCTION."

SEX, FEAR, LACK OF SELF-CONFIDENCE ARE ALL CLOSELY CONNECTED. In fact, the school of Freud puts sex at the base of all psychological disturbances. Freud believed that sex was the main unconscious drive in human behavior. Carl Jung rejected Freud's pansexualism. He held that man's inner religious drives were at least as strong as any of his other hidden urges, and proposed that man is motivated by his goals and aspirations as well as by sex.

Many people are not mature enough to take the so-called art, sexual demonstrations, and low grade stimuli that are dished out to them on stage, screen, or TV. WE BECOME THE PRODUCT OF OUR IMAGINATIONS. THIS IS A LAW AS REAL AS THE LAW OF OSMOSIS. Violence and crime are also pictured as the way of life. To escape frustration modern youth try dope, crime, violence, and sex. DON'T EXPECT A TWENTY YEAR OLD TO HAVE THE WISDOM OF AN OLDER PERSON. THEY MAY HAVE THE PHYSICAL POWER BUT NOT THE MENTAL POWER.

Sex when healthy, in the proper institution of marriage, accepted by society and the individuals involved, can produce the most beautiful harmony and expression of inner being that is imaginable in human relationships. But true love is the basic ingredient, plus maturity which involves due consideration for the other's desires, personality, emotions, and understanding. The greatest pleasure is to give pleasure, and only the truly mature can accomplish this.

All sexual relations without love, whether under the protection of a "marriage certificate" or without such protection, are merely physical relations without spiritual union. Many so-called marriages were NEVER marriages. THERE MUST BE A HEART UNION TO BE MARRIED IN THE TRUE, DEEP, DIVINE, SUBLIME SENSE. AND UNTIL TWO PEOPLE ARE THUS JOINED, NO MAN CAN UNITE THEM. True marriage is not primarily a matter of legal law at all. The simple fact is, RIGHT needs no regulation and WRONG CANNOT BE LEGISLATED INTO RIGHT.

THE LAW OF MENTAL HEALTH

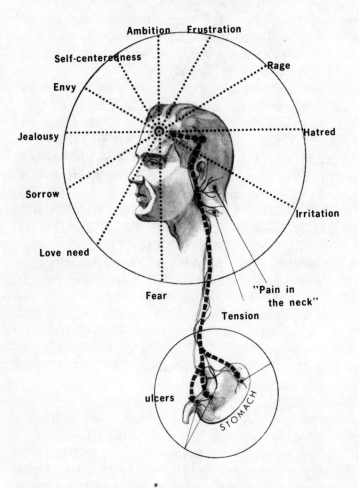

Various emotions which have their source in the brain find their way through definite pathways to the stomach. When a troublesome person can't be coped with, we say we can't stomach him" — or he gives me a "pain in the neck."

Segment 40

THE LAW OF MENTAL HEALTH

Mental health is concerned with the proper use of the mind, using our brain power, avoiding mental illness by proper adjustment to life, acceptance of life's situations. It is a law of human nature that the mind can make one well or ill, wretched or happy, rich or poor.

B. W. Bauer, M.D., says that good mental health means simply "you are able to get along with yourself. You are able to get along with others. You are able to get along with circumstances."

For health and happiness in life, the first need is a healthy mind. It is within the reach of all. We must first realize in our thoughts the existence that we would attain in actual life. The three steps in enjoying a healthy mind are: 1. The control of anger and passion of mind; 2. The conquest of fear; 3. The elimination of worry.

Fully fifty percent of the hospital beds in the United States are occupied by people under psychiatric care. The tragic waste of so many potentially productive lives is certainly one of the gravest problems confronting our increasingly complex society.

THERE IS ONE THING OVER WHICH EACH PERSON HAS ABSOLUTE, INHERENT CONTROL, AND THAT IS HIS MENTAL ATTITUDE. NO ONE CAN HURT YOU BUT YOURSELF. Please do not keep blaming other persons. It is a good day when we awaken to this fact. Mind is the master power that molds and makes man. The power of the mind is tremendous. Every act of man springs from the hidden seed of thought. LIFE IS MADE OR MARRED BY OUR HABITUAL THINKING. Man, in the final analysis, is but the incarnation of his thoughts.

Marasmus is the wasting away of life, the ability each one of us has to think himself to death. Mental gangrene. Discouraged, beaten down, morale low, the rust of life. A person can silence even the call of life itself. When life ceases to have any value for him, he kills himself. He destroys, in fact, what is already dead. "The soul and body," says a great medical authority, "live so closely together that they catch each other's diseases." In proof of his findings he says, "Eighty percent of all physical diseases have their origin in, or are enhanced by mental causes—such as worry, anxiety, fear and sorrow." He goes on to say, "Men are more sick in mind than they are in body. Men need peace more than they need a pill, a promise more than they need a plaster. The spirit is becoming an imperative in medicine."

Dr. Joe D. Nichols, M.D. writes, "If you hate me, then I become a pain in your neck. The conflict causes tension on the muscles of the neck. First, there is a drawing in the back of the neck and finally if the conflict is intense enough a tension headache is the result. The pain is not in the mind or heart; it is in the back of the neck, right where the muscles join on to the head.

"You have heard the expression, 'I am fed up with that fellow.' When you get mad at someone, then you do get a full feeling in the stomach. The conflict causes tension and then the glands in the stomach and intestines that produce the digestive juices just dry up so to speak, and you do get a full feeling in the stomach. If you eat when you are mad, then you get nervous indigestion because there are no digestive juices present. If the conflict is intense enough and goes on long enough, and some of the other factors of disease are present, especially nutritional and poisonous, then you get a peptic ulcer. We say that nervous indigestion is inorganic or functional, but the inorganic diseases are the forerunners of organic disease. All organic disease is made worse by emotional upset."

We may win the brass ring, we may get to the top of some mystical ladder of achievement. But in our deepest selves we know that the crowning achievement won't be ours if, somewhere along the way, we haven't first mastered the pounding of the tensions that send us to doctors with all kinds of complaints and ailments. FEAR paralyzes you, so you can not think straight. A lion roars to scare you, to freeze you in your tracks. Fear can kill you like a bullet, only it takes a little longer. Dr. Charles Mayo said: "Worry affects the circulation, the heart, the glands, the whole nervous system, and profoundly affects the health. I have never known a man who died from overwork, but many who died from doubt." Fear, worry, anger, depression, jealousy, hate, all these negative and destructive emotions are the great enemies of the human family and of human happiness.

Grenville Kleiser thinks "many people today need a physician of the soul. Disheartened, apprehensive, ill, they have sought surcease in drugs, diets, and other material means, but all in vain. Many have become heartsick and even rebellious. If you are in this category and should ask a physician of the soul what to do in your extremity, he would probably say to you: Your primary need is for mental poise and stability. You have mental habits of long standing that should be supplanted by right habits of thought. When you establish a calm center within yourself, you will be able to think properly and constructively. The remedy for your ailment is within yourself."

The "conclusion of the whole matter" then, as Solomon would say, is that the CAUSE of destructive moods is primarily spiritual and not physical. This determined, we are in a position to prescribe a remedy: A spiritual change is accomplished by, as the Apostle Paul would say, being "transformed by the renewing of your mind," and such a change will keep faith anchored in the deep water of abiding confidence.

Charles Kingsley wrote, "I know that what we all want is inward rest; rest of heart and brain; the calm, strong, self-contained, self-denying character; which needs no stimulants for it has no fits of depression; which needs no narcotics, for it has no fits of excitement; which needs no ascetic restraints, for it is strong enough to use God's gifts without abusing them; the character, in a word, which is truly temperate, not in drink or food merely, but in all desires, thoughts and actions; freed from the wild lusts and ambitions."

The incisive psychologist, William James, assures us that the mind, in all its moods, superimposes itself upon the physical. By "mind" Professor James evidently means "the seat and source of being" or exactly what the Bible means when it uses the word heart. "Keep thine heart with all diligence," exhorts the Old Testament writer, then adds a scientific comment to which the best science of our day will subscribe, "For out of it are the issues of life."

It is still true that God is the best cure for a troubled mind. "Thou wilt keep him in perfect peace, whose mind is stayed on thee." This is the gift that God reserves for His special protégés, talent and beauty he gives to many. Wealth is commonplace, fame not rare. But peace of mind—that is His final guerdon of approval, the fondest sign of his love. He bestows it. Most men are never blessed with it, others wait all their lives—yes, far into advanced age—for this gift to descend upon them.

These quotations from both science and the Bible are made for the purpose of showing one thing: THE "HEART," OR "MIND," OR "SEAT OF BEING," WHICHEVER WORD ONE PREFERS, DIRECTLY INFLUENCES AND AFFECTS THE WHOLE MAN. There is a you of you, and a me of me, which lies back of and dominates the physical part of us. That something is called mind by science; heart and spirit by the Bible.

Segment 41

THE LAW OF LOVE

The law of love is one of the natural laws of life. The greatest and deepest law of all. It fills the hearts of all those who seek it with kindness and compassion. It is the central theme in the laws of life, for love is cement that makes men whole.

By love we mean love of life, love of God, love of people, work, beauty, learning, nature, animals. There are two types of love. "Agappa" is the love that builds up. "Eros" is the selfish love that tears down. One is constructive, the other is destructive.

In the Old Testament everything was law, sternness, force. When Jesus came, over 2000 years ago, He brought the love which was the cement to hold men together in fellowship with God. Those that have tried God's teachings have found this to be true.

Let us apply the law of love to the prior segment 40, the Law of Mental Health. The cure for emotional disease is very simple. All one has to do is to stop attempting to violate the law of love. The law of love is divided into two parts: first, love of God; second, love of neighbor. "Thou shalt love the Lord thy God with all thy heart, and with all thy soul, and with all thy mind. This is the first and greatest commandment. The second is like unto it. Thou shalt love thy neighbor as thyself." You cannot hate your neighbor and get by with it. He will become a pain in your neck.

Now worry, fear and anxiety are also caused by emotional disease and they violate the first part of the law of love. The Sermon on the Mount teaches us not to worry about what we shall eat or wear. It teaches us to think not of tomorrow.

The cure then for the emotional cause of disease is to stop attempting to violate the Law of Love. NO MAN CAN EVER VIOLATE ANY NATURAL LAW WITHOUT PAYING A PRICE. THIS IS THE CENTRAL IDEA IN THE LAWS OF LIFE. Natural law is simple, self-evident, universal and inviolate. What is the summum bonum—the supreme good? WHAT IS THE NOBLEST OBJECT OF DESIRE, THE SUPREME GIFT TO COVET? Paul tells us, "THE GREATEST . . . IS LOVE." To love and to be loved is the greatest happiness of existence.

The words, GOD IS LOVE, do not EXPLAIN GOD, BUT THEY DO REVEAL HIM. With the revelation comes understanding—understanding, not comprehension. There is a fine distinction between the two. One may not comprehend why a mother jeopardizes her own life to save the life of her child trapped in a burning building, but her LOVE for her child does make her act understandable. Her NATURE is the explanation of her conduct. Not otherwise does one understand the acts, ways, and words of God.

How does one practice love? By kindness, respect, unselfishness, attention, patience, understanding, and trust. Each of us is born with the capacity for love, which takes many forms. It can be love for family, home, friends, country, possessions, power, fame, Divine love. The visible signs of love are without end: Love is a puppy snuggled inside of a little girl's raincoat; a blanket being tucked around a sleeping child; the Hallelujah chorus, a beam of light through a stained glass window, a lump in the throat when the flag goes by. Love is the light and sunshine of life. We are so constituted that we cannot fully enjoy ourselves, or anything else, unless some one we love enjoys it with us. Even if we are alone, we store up our enjoyment in hope of sharing it thereafter with those we love. Love lasts through life, and adapts itself to every age and circumstance; in childhood for father and mother, in manhood for wife, in age for children, and throughout life for brothers and sisters, relations and friends.

When God passed on to men and women His spiritual power, He gave the most godlike thing in His power to give, namely, power to create another creature and power to foster His own very nature—love. Love never asked anybody to do an unworthy thing. Girls, remember that if some fellow claims to be in love with you and he suggests an unworthy thing, he at once proves that he is not in love. Love never asks anybody to step down to an unworthy level. "There is the same difference in a person before and after he is in love as there is in an unlighted lamp and one that is burning," said Vincent Van Gogh. "The lamp was there and was a good lamp, but now it is shedding light too, and that is its real function. And love makes one serene about many things, and that way, one is more fit for one's work." Husband, wife, and children form the world's greatest team. Whether that team wins or loses depends largely upon whether husband and wife practice human love. Love is the greatest incentive of all. Love is the cement that binds human beings together. The strongest evidence of love is sacrifice. But it's a queer world. Many times we treat those worst, who love us best.

"For the first time in my life I saw the truth as it is set into song by so many poets. Proclaimed as the final wisdom by so many thinkers," writes the great Viktor Frankl. "The truth— that love is the ultimate and the highest goal to which man can aspire. Then I grasped the meaning of the greatest secret that human poetry and human thought and belief have to impart; the salvation of man is through love and in love. I understand how a man who has nothing left in this world still may know bliss, be it only for a brief moment, in the contemplation of his beloved. In a position of utter desolation, when man cannot express himself in positive action, when his only achievement may consist in his enduring his suffering in the right way —an honorable way—in such a position man can, through loving contemplation of the image he carries of his beloved, achieve fulfillment." Angels come to visit us and we only know them when they are gone.

In this poor, broken world the teaching of Jesus Christ is the only known philosophy of life which has never been seriously tried. Incredible as our stupidity may seem, man is still blind to the fact that the cause of all his troubles is within himself. The heart of life is love. His relationship with himself is wrong; he is divided by inner conflicts and torn asunder by the warring of his various selves.

A man contains, not only a Dr. Jekyll and a Mr. Hyde, but often in the compass of one generic personality, a saint and a devil, a believer and a sceptic, a lover and a cynic, and as many other selves as he may have roles in life. Never was man more in need of being "made whole."

Today man's relationship with God is wrong. That is the heart of the whole matter. When man really sees that with all his clever conferences, economic theories, scientific discoveries and inventions, social, national and international dreams, he just cannot deal with evil and selfishness in human hearts, he will wake up to find what has really wrecked all his schemes. THE FAILURE OF MAN TO MAKE A HAPPY WORLD IN WHICH GOD'S GIFTS ARE SHARED AND MAN LIVES HAPPILY WITH MAN, IS IN MAN HIMSELF. The power man needs is the love which is released when man is in living touch with God.

Viktor Frankl writes, "Love is the only way to grasp another human being in the innermost core of his personality. No one can become fully aware of the very essence of another human being unless he loves him. By the spiritual act of love he is enabled to see the essential traits and features in the beloved person; and even more, he sees that which is potential in him, that which is not yet actualized, but yet ought to be actualized. Furthermore, by his love, the loving person enables the beloved person to actualize these potentialities. By making him aware of what he can be and of what he should become, he makes these potentialities come true."

The most binding law in the universe is the law of love, and there is no law of man, either civil or ecclesiastical, that has authority to dictate to love. Our love is its own protection. It alone guarantees the decency of society, the perpetuity of the State, the finest inheritance to posterity, and it offers to the Church its one and only hope of recovering its lost dignity and respect. The measure of one's devotion is doing, not merely saying. LOVE IS DEMONSTRATION, NOT MERELY DEC-LARATION.

Listen to the great scientist, Alexis Carrel: "The precept of loving one's neighbor has a double aspect. Explicitly, it commands everyone to love others but, implicitly, it also commands everyone to make themselves worthy of being loved. It is beyond human powers to love the average product of industrial civilization; that is to say, an individual who is selfish, coarse, proud, lazy, envious, intemperate, ill-natured and lubricious. Mutual love will remain a Utopian ideal until we make an effort to give up the habits which render us odious to other people."

It is not by elaborating new ideologies or by reforming our political institutions that we shall build a better society. What we must do is to reform our own selves and free ourselves from those vices which separate us from one another. Then it will be possible for neighbor to love neighbor; for workmen to love their employers and employers to love their workmen. Love alone is capable of instilling in human societies the order which instinct has established for millions of years among the communities of ants and bees.

"Though I speak with the tongues of men and of angels," says the Apostle Paul, "and have not love, I am become as sounding brass or a tinkling cymbal. And though I have the gift of prophecy, and understand all mysteries, and all knowledge; and though I have all faith, so that I could remove mountains, and have not love, I am nothing."

WE IMPROVE OUR MEMORY BY:

AWARENESS   UNDERSTANDING
DEEP IMPRESSIONS   ASSOCIATION
VISUALIZATION   REPETITION
            PERCEPTION

Memory is the diary that we all carry about with us. It has been said, the things with which we store our memory will ultimately mold our character. A good memory is an essential element of genius.

THE LAW OF MEMORY

The memory is the storehouse of our experience, the diary of our lives, the journal of our accomplishments. As we grow older the things we remember grow more precious to us because there is more behind us than ahead of us.

The mind is very similar to a phonograph record on which impressions are made by five needles (sight, hearing, smell, taste, and touch). As the eye makes the deepest and longest lasting groove the impressions taken in through the eye are most durable. This is called visualization. It is also why people impress things in "the mind's eye" when they are particularly anxious to remember.

Time and circumstances can, and frequently do, dim the memory of an event, but neither time nor circumstances can, I say, write it off the record as though it had never been. Perpetuation is the common law of the universe as well as the common law of memory. It is doubtful, so psychologists tell us, if anyone ever forgets anything, in the sense of complete obliteration. Memory, they tell us, is something like a vast storage reservoir in which events, names, faces, and places are stored awaiting some circumstance, association, or suggestion to bring them up and out.

Milton, grown old and blind, drew from memory the finest things he ever wrote. Longfellow reflected that the years agone furnished him the material from which he created his finest poems. Socrates insisted that man will never outgrow his littleness until he learns to allow his memory to lead him back to yesterday. Muretus said that it was the story of Seneca's incredible memory that inspired him to his greatest achievements. Aristotle thought that memory is the measure of genius. Bacon said, "ALL KNOWLEDGE IS BUT REMEMBRANCE."

Memory and its value: There are many things in this life which everyone needs to remember, and there are, perhaps, just as many other things which everyone needs to forget. It is illogical to try to train our memories to retain everything. The successful businessman does not burden his memory with facts that may or may not be used. Record books, card indexes, and filing devices have been invented for that purpose. However, most men whose work brings them in direct contact with the general public have learned that the ability to remember names and faces and personal incidents is a real asset.

There is no need for our remembering everything. We should CONCENTRATE ON ESSENTIALS. KEEP THE BIG THINGS IN MIND, the little things on paper, is the rule. The test of a good memory is that it shall be serviceable; that the mind shall be furnished and ready with just the sort of material which it has need of, and free from encumbrances with the useless, the irrelevant, or the distracting.

All true civilization is ninety percent heirlooms and memories—an accumulation of small but precious deposits left by the countless generations that have gone before us. ONLY VERY PROUD OR VERY IGNORANT PEOPLE IMAGINE THAT OUR MUDDLE-HEADED PRESENT CAN BEGIN EVERYTHING ALL OVER AGAIN EVERY DAY—and invent a new alphabet, a new multiplication table, a new code of laws, and a new religion.

I remember many fishing trips. Long ago, I learned that catching fish is the least important part of fishing. THE THOUGHTS AND MOODS AND MEMORIES OF A FISHING TRIP ARE THE REALLY IMPORTANT CATCH THAT ONE BRINGS BACK, creeled in memory to be lived again and again. One goes back in memory to ramble aimlessly here and there, exploring secret places, climbing to the crest of a hill, following the course of a brook and experiencing again the thrill of the battle royal with the big one that got away.

The ordinary, average human memory is capable of amazing feats. Your conscious memory, if you live to be 70, will remember about 15 trillion things—that's right, 15,000,000,000,-000—from your telephone number to the shape of a watermelon. And even that huge number is small compared to the total of items stored away in your subconscious.

If you want to improve your memory, practice these things: 1. Be alert to what you want to learn—make a conscious effort to remember. 2. Be sure you understand the meaning of what you want to remember. 3. Use a trick to remember (the port side of a boat is the left side, and left and port have the same number of letters.) 4. Become interested in what you want to remember—take an interest in a person you meet and you'll probably remember his name.

Our memories are valuable because we remember the lives of those who went before. We remember our loved ones who are gone and they seem closer to us in our memory than they were in person. We remember the great men of our history that inspire us to greater ambitions and values. We remember the struggles of prior generations and strive to make our world better for their sake as well as our own.

Funny, isn't it, how trifling a thing will stir a memory that belongs to a distant past and superinduces a mood. I heard a bird sing; something in that song awakened a memory and transported me to a far place. A place which afforded me many a day of solitude and joy where I drank deeply of the tonic of strength offered by nature. The bird winged on its way. His song lingered. Twenty years it carried me back until like waters warring with confined banks, my heart, rebellious and aloof, is left warring with present restraints and limitations. BUT I'VE HAD AN HOUR OF COMMUNION WITH YESTERDAY AND IT HAS ENRICHED TODAY—thanks to a seeming trifle which, like so many little things, takes on size, as it affects and influences the heart.

The World

The Nation

The Family

Everything stems from the
individual. The world is made up
of individuals. The first unit is the
family, then the community,
then the city, then the nation, then
all other nations make up
the world . . .

So we START with the
INDIVIDUAL. The contribution of
every nation is the result of the
quality of its citizens. And where
are the citizens moulded? In the
home . . . it is our greatest
institution.

The home is the place where
plastic youth is moulded into the
finished product of citizenship.

**Come from the
INDIVIDUAL**

Segment 43

THE LAW OF HUMAN RELATIONS

"No man is an island unto himself." We cannot well live alone. A large part of the best in us must come from others. We are social creatures by nature, and the gratification of our social instinct is a first requisite for contentment, satisfaction, and emotional balance in life.

"We have been born to associate with our fellow men, and to join in community with the human race," wrote Cicero. We are not isolated individuals; both in our families and in society we are members one of another. Human relationship is a natural inherent characteristic of man.

The law is: LOVE ONE ANOTHER—PUT ANOTHER FIRST—DO FOR THE GOOD OF ALL. Everyone is sitting around waiting for the other fellow to start the doing. The law is simply help others to help themselves. This is action and involves everyone without waiting for the other person to act first.

It is not possessions or things in life that matter, the important aspect of life is people. The people you love, your friends, the people you know. Rarely do you hear anyone mention what is probably the biggest thing in his life, his family. The happiest moments of our life have been the few which we have passed at home with our family. What the world lacks most today is, perhaps, understanding and appreciation of one another, among people and nations.

Society is an extension of the individual. By society is meant the living together of human beings for their own mutual benefit. We have built an organized society which guarantees that membership of its different levels is determined solely by individual initiative. The state cannot solve our personal problems. Each individual must work out his own salvation.

Emerson said, "Everything comes out of the individual." The individual man is the basic or common denominator of society. DEMOCRACY HAS GIVEN US LIBERTY. BUT IT HAS FAILED TO DISCOVER THE LAWS OF OUR INDIVIDUAL AND COLLECTIVE LIFE. True social reform means building the kind of society man NEEDS.

You are the starting point. You and your family make up the city, the State, and the Government of the nation. The home is the foundation, where life starts and also where life ends. As the home is, so is the nation, so is the world. It is this home that is really responsible for how the world goes, whether it be good or bad.

The Chinese were very wise. They pointed out that the family relationship was a miniature of the universe. If a man is inspired to a noble reform or a desire to instruct his fellow creatures in some useful doctrine, he should first prove the value of his concepts by enriching and ennobling the life in his home. Only then should he seek a larger theatre of activity.

"Bricks and mortar do not a palace make," people do. It's not possessions or things in life that matter, the important aspect of life is "people." Go back to your home town after you have been away several years. Things are not the same. What is missing? People. Visit a home you once lived in, or a place you worked years ago. It is never the same. Why? Because the people you knew are not there. People are important to your life. Bing Crosby says, "YOUR FAMILY IS ONE OF YOUR MOST IMPORTANT ASSETS. PROBABLY IT'S THE BIGGEST THING GOING FOR YOU—although many times you may take it for granted."

We can contribute to society through building moral character, through keeping our family secure and cared for, by executing our own responsibilities, by participating intelligently in social functions that benefit man, by speaking out and standing up against the forces of evil and foreign governments that would break down our adherence to the natural law of freedom.

Man's history is indelibly written upon his features. His face bears the marks of his inner character. Wrong acts and foul deeds set their seal of ownership upon the victim of vice. "The show of their countenance doth witness against them."

"Among the disturbing signs of this time are people without faces," writes Marya Mannes. "You see them everywhere. They have features, of course, but their faces have the blankness, the total enclosure, of sleepwalkers. No feeling appears to motivate them. Part of it is the instinct of protection, a withdrawal from contact. Whatever you call it, it is both the cause and result of an immense loneliness and alienation in the midst of crowds that turns either into the passivity of nihilism or into the activity of aggression. It is clearly a process of dehumanization. Visible to anyone who walks the streets of our cities looking for a face with a soul . . . or Soul, if you will."

What a city of derelicts this is. Hollywood, the city of ambition on the rocks. If you didn't think of it before, notice tomorrow as you walk the streets that about fifty percent of all the people you meet, have faces that look like a blown-out lamp. You say that I reflect on Hollywood. No, I don't. It is just that man in his blindness, in his crass stupidity, has made the terrible mistake of investing his all in things not real. And Hollywood is just one of many places of human depravity. What wonder that a whole generation have dull eyes, muddy skins, sleepless nights, and die before the green fruit of life has had time to ripen.

We wonder why we are getting a harvest of derelicts, mental cases, drug addicts, criminals, sex maniacs, thieves. Today we are planting seeds of filth and evil under the guise of freedom of expression. These are the results of our carelessness. We are actually at war with ourselves; we are actually destroying ourselves. It is almost unbelievable that life in these United States could change so radically in a few short years. We are in the midst of a revolution, our entire system of government, education and religion is being attacked on all sides.

The United States is doomed to be captured. An army will march throughout the length and breadth of our great land. Its soldiers will march into the White House and place there, their own President. They will elect their own congress and appoint their own judiciary. They will commandeer all our resources. They will take over our mint and confiscate all our wealth. They will take over our churches and preach what they will. They will appropriate our schools and teach what they will. This vast army is on the march. It is our YOUTH. We are training them. We are the reason for the delinquency which we decry so loudly.

Blind Homer's poetic dream transformed Greece. His imagination created Achilles. Soon it became the ambition of every Athenian boy to recreate Achilles in his heart and life. When twenty thousand young Greeks became mastered by Homer's Iliad, Greece was on its way. Thus did Homer's vision turn rude tribes into intellectual giants. No less does the youth of our day need great men whose example will inspire them to climb. Thus, and only thus, will they be encouraged to transmute their highest ideals into Christian character and conduct. We need ten thousand Homers whose feet will walk our streets, but whose heads and hearts will be infinitely higher than the dirt on which they walk.

Not many of us will be known and sung as great. The centuries have only known one Plato. From him thousands of lesser minds have learned to think. Just one Dante. From him a thousand poets have tuned their harps. Only one Raphael. To him lesser artists look and are lifted up to higher levels of achievement. But all of us can be good. And finally, no greater thing was ever said of any man than that he was a good man, full of faith and of God. Such an one will wield an influence that will lift men up to higher levels of thinking long after the so-called greatness of the great has been forgotten—and that is where God fixes the price tag of highest value.

I have had plenty of occasions to experience dark days with human beings, and plenty of doubts concerning people. Now that comes from long experience. The big difference in people is not so much the color of skin, it is the difference in the level of intelligence, and characteristics they possess. I am for judging each individual on his own merits. If he is an evil doer I shun him like a bad disease. I am for personal rather than racial discrimination, whether a man's color is black, white, red, brown or yellow. The root of most of man's problems is his willingness to sacrifice human values for other objectives. The fundamental laws of Human Nature are the basis for all progress, growth, and happiness. Ignorance of these laws is responsible for one man's foot on another man's neck. Obedience to and understanding of the laws of human nature guarantees society a high degree of individual behavior.

When individuals choose the beneficial path of natural law all society grows and benefits. It is our duty to be a decent, constructive unit in the society of which we are a part. The reason our society has deteriorated is because too many of us are NOT cooperating with the basic laws of man's nature, but are working AGAINST them. Even the common law that regulates man must be founded on a knowledge of men's nature or that law leads to ruin.

Character, and not infrequently destiny, is determined by the friendships we choose. Plato said, "The measure of a man's greatness is his capacity for exalted friendship." All of our great men of history witness the truth of this observation. You will have the privilege of touching intimately only a very few really great souls during your lifetime. Ben Jonson observed, "Show me the kind of friends a person chooses and I will predict what they will do and be." Associate with great men. No man is great in and of himself. He must touch the lives of other great beings who will inspire him, lift him, and push him forward.

MAN LIVES IN TWO WORLDS

One is the material or PHYSICAL WORLD.
One is the SPIRITUAL WORLD.

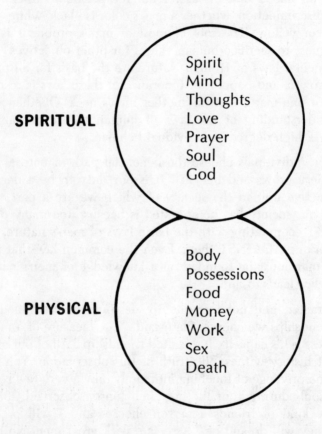

SPIRITUAL

Spirit
Mind
Thoughts
Love
Prayer
Soul
God

PHYSICAL

Body
Possessions
Food
Money
Work
Sex
Death

The mistake of men is, and ever has been, to think of the physical man as the real man and the physical world as the real world. The real man, the Scriptures insist, is the spiritual man, and the real world is the spiritual.

THE LAW OF SOUL

There are laws in connection with man's moral and spiritual nature as eternal as the law of gravity. Human laws deal with the visible side of life. Absolute justice must deal with the unseen side of life, as well as the visible things.

The Bible says, "God breathed the spirit of life into man and man became a living soul." The soul is of course the noblest part of man. THE SOUL IS THE YOU OF YOU, THE TOTALITY OF YOU, the seat of your being. The Bible calls it heart. That is where you make your decisions, from your heart, or this soul, if you please. "Keep thy heart (soul) with all diligence for from within, out of the heart, come all the issues of life both good and evil."

MAN IS BOTH A PHYSICAL BEING AND A SPIRITUAL BEING. The body is not the real man, simply the house in which the man lives. Spirit is the structure and meaning of the Universe. The body is the expression of spirit. Hence, man is nothing less than spirit incarnate. Spirit is like the radio and TV waves; you do not see them but they are there, you experience their effects. Spirit operates in the Universe and in every living man. It is God-given.

Spirit is higher than mind as mind needs some attention before it is safe to allow it to wield its mighty power over conduct. SPIRIT IS THE POWER IN MAN, just as electricity is power to the electric motor or generator. The body and the mind are only the means of expression of the spirit. The body and the mind both appear simply as mechanisms, or instruments through which the spiritual reality expresses itself. THE GREATEST CONTRIBUTION ANY OF US WILL MAKE TO THE WORLD IS TO LIVE AT OUR SPIRITUAL BEST.

Just as a candle cannot burn without a fire, men cannot live without spiritual life. The spirit dwells in all men, but not all men are aware of this. Happy is the life of him who knows this, and unhappy is his existence who does not know it. The Scriptures teach that God's spirit dwells in our bodies as in a temple. When man dies his spirit returns to God who gave it and his physical body returns to the dust.

WHAT ACTUALLY CONSTITUTES THE HUMAN ELEMENT IN MAN IS SPIRIT. YOU MUST KNOW WITH ABSOLUTE CERTAINTY THAT ESSENTIALLY YOU ARE SPIRIT. MAN IS A WORLD IN HIMSELF! The spiritual man is free to rule his world, not his world to rule him.

Billy Graham says, "You may have the glamor of the movie queen or you may have the riches of a Texas millionaire and still not find happiness, peace, and contentment. Why? Simply because you have given attention to the body and not to the soul. The INNER you is the REAL you."

Jesus said, "What does it profit a man if he shall gain the whole world and lose his own soul?" The only truly poor are the poor of soul.

The highest purpose of intellectual culture is to give a man a perfect knowledge and mastery of his own inner self. And over and above everything else, among the things that count in life, are the things of the soul and the spirit. Only a life in which heart, soul, and spirit have been allowed fullest development and expression, is a complete and worthwhile life.

"Spiritual power is a force which history clearly teaches has been the greatest force in the development of men," wrote Charles P. Steinmetz. "Yet we have been merely playing with it and never really studied it as we have the physical forces. Some day people will learn that material things do not bring happiness, and are of little use in making people creative and powerful. Then the scientists of the world will turn their laboratories over to the study of spiritual forces which have hardly been scratched."

Has our age of scientific invention, experimentation and research overlooked the most important field of all, namely, the latent possibilities, the latent potentialities of spiritual energy which, finally, are not only the individual's most priceless asset but the nation's first line of defense?

Humanity is finding out how to live the hard way. God offers us The Way. We think we know better, and take other ways of our own choosing, and are constantly getting shocks. These shocks are of various kinds—neuroses, inner conflicts, tensions, guilts, inferiorities, fear, emotionally induced illness.

Joubert wrote that "without the spiritual world the material world is a disheartening enigma." The fact is, the spiritual shows itself just as indispensable to the success of life as the intellectual and the material. Man is basically a spiritual being —his equipment for living far surpasses any visible resources available in his environment. His spirit calls out for a greater destiny. It demands a greater satisfaction than is ever possible within the confines of the physical universe.

We have an instinctive feeling that there is something sublimely beautiful in life we have never yet found, because we have never been completely satisfied. Nothing but God ever completely satisfies a man, because the soul was made for God, and without God it is restless and in secret torment. The soul is the real you of you. Your only real security is to have your soul filled with the love of the Infinite and the Eternal. A changed soul within will enrich and transform life without— enrich it for time and secure it forever.

Paul Tillich points out that "one of the unfortunate consequences of the intellectualization of man's spiritual life was that the word 'spirit' was lost and replaced by mind or intellect, and that the element of vitality which is present in 'spirit' was separated and interpreted as an independent biological force. Man was divided into a bloodless intellect and a meaningless vitality. The middle ground between them, the spiritual soul in which vitality and intentionality are united, was dropped."

The basic laws of nature are the basic laws of the spiritual realm. This must be true since God is the great First Cause in both realms. Most people consider life as a battle, but it is not a battle, it is a game. It is a game, however, which cannot be played successfully without the knowledge of spiritual law, and the Old and the New Testaments give the rules of the game with wonderful clarity.

According to Alexis Carrel, "Only spiritual values can bring light and joy. At a given moment of his life everyone must choose between the material and the human. He must refuse or accept obedience to the law of the development of the spirit." Science is the quest of truth by accumulation, comparison and classification. Philosophy is the quest of truth by analysis of mental intuitions. Education is the quest of truth by mental processes. All have their place and all are valuable, but ONE MAY BECOME A MASTER IN ALL OF THESE REALMS AND STILL REMAIN TOTALLY IGNORANT OF ESSENTIAL SPIRITUAL TRUTH.

In the human species, spiritual development is the supreme law. To convince oneself that this is so one only needs to observe the state of decline into which a population, infected at once with lack of moral discipline and intellectual infantilism, naturally falls.

There may have been a time when spiritual awakenings could be thought of as desirable but not necessarily indispensable, but not now. The whole future of civilization is in the balance. Our leaders speak of freedom, peace, security, safety and liberty as though they were detached problems. They are not and never have been. They are inseparably joined to the spiritual qualities of men. Society, government and business will rise no higher than the best spiritual life of a nation. They will sink as low. Every phase of our national life now cries aloud for a revival. The intelligent prayer for all of us to pray is, OH LORD, LET IT BEGIN WITH ME!

THE LAW OF FREEDOM

The Law of Freedom is just as much a natural law of the spiritual world as the law of growth is a natural law of the physical world. There are laws in mind, as well as in matter. There are laws of sensation, laws of feeling, laws of thought, and laws of love.

Man is free but we are not able to do all we please. In some directions we can develop ourselves; in other directions we are stopped by a barrier. Freedom, therefore, consists in this: "Of our own free will we will have to remain within the natural law of our being."

Charles Eliot wrote, "You have freedom to do right or wrong. Clearly you can go astray, for the road is not fenced. You can make mistakes; you can fall into sin. Have you got it in yourself to control yourself? Have you the good sense and the resolution to regulate your own conduct?"

Man is free, but he cannot drink a quart of scotch on arising in the morning and be at work an hour later bright-eyed and chipper, ready for work. "There are two freedoms," says Kingsley, "the false, where a man is free to do what he likes; the true, where a man is free to do what he ought."

Webster admonishes, "No man is free who cannot command himself, liberty exists in proportion to wholesome restraint."

"Have we too much freedom?" asks Will Durant. "Have we so long ridiculed authority in the family, discipline in education, rules in art, decency in conduct, and law in the state that our liberation has brought us close to chaos in the family and the school, in morals, arts, ideas, and government? We forgot to make ourselves intelligent when we made ourselves free."

Freedom will not descend to a people; a people must raise themselves to freedom. It is a blessing that must be earned before it can be enjoyed. WHEN WE LOSE OUR CAPACITY TO RESTRAIN, CONTROL, AND GOVERN OURSELVES WE ARE IN THE PROCESS OF DESTROYING NOT ONLY OURSELVES BUT OUR COUNTRY.

There is a certain "hippie" type of regressor. He cannot bear to put up with the restraints of society. He wishes to be freed from convention. But his freedom is only of the child's immature kind; it is freedom FROM something. It is not in any great human sense, freedom FOR something. One can simply regress to lower standards.

Life requires a certain amount of discipline. The old woodshed in the backyard still could be used with benefit today. Our present day youth want unlimited freedom and instant perfection. Permissiveness is not freedom. Nobody is ever going to solve any of our social, economic, or political shortcomings while sitting on a curb kicking marijuana butts with his dirty feet. The only freedom worth possessing is that which gives enlargement to a person's energy, intellect, and virtues. The hippies rattle their chains to show they are free. No one is free who is a slave to his body.

No man is free who cannot give orders to his own habits. Freedom rests, and always will, on individual responsibility, individual integrity, and individual effort, individual courage, and individual religious faith.

THOSE WHO KNOW THE LAWS OF GOD AND NATURE HAVE LEARNED THE TRUTH THAT MAKES MEN FREE—free from the ignorance of the laws, which brings about man's own destruction. The greatest freedom known to man is the freedom of an unchained soul. With the knowledge of God's lawful direction of the universe you are free to sail to the greatest heights of human achievement. This is the true and only freedom.

Men talk of world peace as if that were going to solve every problem. Well, men must move themselves over into the new world. And the average person is not fit to live in the kind of world that he dreams about. Peace surrounding a man does not assure him of peace. Fear, confusion, distress is a heart condition, much more than it is an environmental disturbance. And if we do not like our environment please remember—we made it.

"Peace on Earth." But there is no peace. There never has been. Man's entire history is one of strife, civil and national conflict, world wars, and cold war "hot spots." Economic greed and envy, exploitation of natural resources, trade imbalances, cultural differences, ambitions for power, all these will continue to create constant turmoil in international affairs. No, there is no peace possible merely through mutual desire.

ALL THINGS IDEAL MUST EXIST IN MEN BEFORE THEY CAN EXIST IN SOCIETY. PEACE, PLENTY, AND SECURITY ARE NOT DETACHED PROBLEMS. One would think so to listen to current slogans. One would think that peace, security and plenty can be had by simply waving some magic political wand, instituting some radical reform, or signing some international arms agreement. But it is not as simple as that.

There will be no peace until we "humble ourselves under the mighty hand of God." Men are reached through their hearts and not their heads. Peace can only come by way of men who have learned the art of peace from the Prince of Peace Himself —and of course that is the hard way. Our troubles can be eliminated only through the development of love, hope, sympathy, understanding, recognition and the practice of the Golden Rule. THE HUMBLE ACKNOWLEDGMENT THAT ALL PEACE PROCEEDS FROM GOD, AND TO FIND IT WE MUST FIND HIM, HAS BEEN THE SUM OF MAN'S WISDOM FROM TIME IMMEMORIAL.

Many persons absurdly associate money and goods with security. They pile them up in barns and vaults, not knowing these things are temporary symbols on a material plane where moths and rust corrupt. Security is a trait of character. Man's security comes from within himself, and the security of all men is founded upon the security of the individual.

There is the feeling that we live in a time of unusual insecurity. In the past thirty years so many long established traditions have broken down—traditions of family and social life, of government, of the economic order, and of religious belief. As the years go by, there seem to be fewer rocks to which we can hold, fewer things which we can regard as absolutely right and true, and fixed for all time.

What is ultimate security? There are several securities: global security, America's security, personal security in terms of health, financial security, and the ultimate security is security of the soul. Man's need is for more than surface security. He requires it in depth, as surely as a tree needs roots. The deeper those roots, the taller the tree, the greater its strength against the storms of life.

The struggle to become secure, and not the security itself, strengthens character. It is not by having "security" from elsewhere that happiness is assured. It is knowing that you are able to create your own security each day, that you are able to do successfully the things you have set out to do. Security is man at his best—working in freedom.

Most men strive for material security, but security of spirit is even more desirable, and we should strive for that. This is the real security, true peace of mind, which comes from within. It is having a sense of God. A SENSE OF THE PRESENCE OF GOD IS GREATER SECURITY THAN ALL THE THINGS ONE CAN ACCUMULATE. It is a priceless quality of a human soul at his highest and best state. This state is reached by those who trust in God and live by the Word.

Segment 46

THE LAW OF AGING

Aging is a natural law of life. All things are born and then begin to die. Each step of life is a further progression toward the end of the life span. All of nature ages and man is no exception.

The law of old age is an adventure—and what an adventure! It is a revelation of something new, something exciting and something wonderful. It is then that one realizes that success in life and making a success of one's life are two very different things. We are all variously gifted for success in life, but we are all equal where making a success of our lives is concerned.

Growing old has many facets—many benefits and many delights. The joy of travel, of reading old books and visiting old friends. If you love birds and animals, trees, and grass, and blue skies—if you like good humor and beautiful pictures—then the hours may be brimful of golden happiness.

Look forward to your future with enthusiasm. Remember Browning's famous lines: "Grow old along with me, the best is yet to be . . ." and the years of your life that remain including the years after you retire, can indeed prove to be your best. 'Tis eventide. Better make the most of the light.

There comes a day when the jangling telephone, the brainstorming conferences, the pressures of being a man in the jet age, have to be set aside. To know how to grow old is the master work of wisdom, and one of the most difficult chapters in the great art of living. Given three requisites—means of existence, reasonable health, and an absorbing interest—those years beyond sixty can be the happiest and most satisfying of a lifetime. Remember, everyone is not blessed with old age and age has its compensation.

When life was nearly ended, as almost his final word, Horace Greeley said, "Fame is a vapor, popularity an accident, riches take wings, those who cheer today will curse tomorrow, only one thing endures—CHARACTER!" These words but remind us there is only one thing that really matters, building a life. He who achieves character can be neither feeble in life nor forgotten in death.

Only years make men. Rarely do the great men of history distinguish themselves before they are fifty, and between fifty and eighty they do their best work—both as regards quality and quantity. Immanuel Kant did his best writing at 74. Verdi wrote Ave Maria at 85. Tennyson wrote "Crossing the Bar" at 80. Titian painted his greatest picture at 98. Goethe completed "Faust" at 82, and Michelangelo completed his greatest work at 87. Germany's Chancellor Konrad Adenauer was already 73 when he began a decade and a half of power. Pope John XXIII came in his 70's to stir the old church as few younger prelates had done. And today, at 84, Arthur Rubenstein plays to the applause of audiences of every age. Teach us to number OUR days, that we may apply our hearts unto wisdom. Old age can be the crown of man's life. I am full of years, this book is the crown of my life.

One day Michelangelo ordered the workmen to pull down the scaffolding, remove the ropes, clear away plaster, litter, and rubble, and disclose the finished work of the Sistine Chapel. Men stood in awe as they gazed upon the figures of angels and seraphs wrought into the ceiling by the Artist's Master. So one day death shall pull down the scaffolding and disclose to full view the finished work of Jesus Christ in men who have yielded their lives to Him. The sunlight of eternal years will then shine upon the structure which God shall have reared. The building material we must furnish—honesty, integrity, sincerity, truth, honor and devotion. God grant to all of us the foresight to send on good material against that day.

The words of Oliver Wendell Holmes, one of America's most distinguished Supreme Court Justices, bear testimony to the philosophy that sustained his long life of service: "The riders in this race do not stop short when they reach the goal. There is a little finishing canter before coming to a standstill. There is time to hear the kind voice of friends and to say to one's self: 'the work is done.' But just as one says that the answer comes 'The race is over, but the work never is done while the power to work remains.' The canter that brings you to a standstill need not be only coming to rest. It cannot be while you still live. FOR TO LIVE IS TO FUNCTION. That's all there is in living."

What the human race needs is a new pattern for living. Imagine the changed outlook of an individual who planned to retire at fifty or sixty and spend the next thirty years in travel, or painting, or study, or teaching. The present plan is to retire at sixty-five, then sit in the sun a few years while the body dies. Why shouldn't the body die when infested with a dying mind?

Each year, we should be more joyful than ever before, because we have fewer years ahead in which to be joyful. AS WE GROW OLDER, IT IS IMPORTANT TO US THAT EVERY HOUR SHALL BE AS RICH WITH VALUE AND BEAUTY AS POSSIBLE. We cannot afford to allow one minute to go by that does not bring wisdom, love, and beauty to our lives. Some lives, like evening primroses, blossom most beautifully in the evening of life.

When the great finals come, each one will be asked five questions. First: What did you accomplish in the world with the power that God gave you? Second: How did you help your neighbor and what did you do for those in need? Third: What did you do to serve God? Fourth: What did you leave in the world that was worthwhile when you came from it? Fifth: What did you bring into this new world which will be of use here?

FOOT PATHS TO THE BEYOND

Segment 47

THE LAW OF DEATH

Death is a law, the way of life. Death is no respecter of persons whether you are king or peasant. The greatest oak must fall. All that lives must die. "Then shall the dust return to the earth as it was; and the spirit shall return unto God who gave it."

Death is transition. Our body dies and it breaks correspondence with our physical environment. But our life is in the spirit, and this life is eternal. Life never dies. Bodies cease, but life is eternal.

Carlyle wrote, "Do we not all submit to death? The highest sentence of the law, sentence of death, is passed on all of us by the fact of birth; yet we live patiently under it, patiently undergo it when the hour comes."

We are reminded so frequently these days that our little day will soon be done. And how quickly the sun travels from the east to the west, and how quickly it travels to the horizon; the shadows lengthen, and the day is done.

Oldest question— Does human life perceive beyond the experience called death? Is that all? Is this the end of everything? Jesus said, "Let not your heart be troubled. In my Father's house are many mansions." Instincts tell men there is something beyond. A ship disappears over the horizon but it is still there. We can't see the ship, but it is still there over the horizon. The human being has its limitations. The time will come for each of us to take this trip. We will all move out of this house. Today science says there is no such thing as the destruction of matter. Death is just an experience. Death may only be the beginning of life. What appears as death is only change.

Dr. Wernher von Braun writes, "In our modern world many people seem to feel that science has somehow made such 'religious ideas' as immortality untimely or old-fashioned. But I think science has a real surprise for the skeptics. Science tells us that nothing in nature, not even the tiniest particle, can disappear without a trace. Think about that for a moment. Once you do, your thoughts about life will never be the same. SCIENCE HAS FOUND THAT NOTHING CAN DISAPPEAR WITHOUT A TRACE. NATURE DOES NOT KNOW EXTINCTION. ALL IT KNOWS IS TRANSFORMATION."

"The clock of life is wound but once . . . And no man has the power . . . To tell just where the hands will stop . . . At late or early hour." Learn to walk with death as you would a friend; you will eventually meet him. All our worldly possessions are loaned. Only our soul remains eternally our own. Death is simply a new horizon, and the new horizon is only the limit of our sight.

We are pilgrim children still on the road, and some day we shall come to that last dividing river. It may be today, tomorrow, or many years hence. But it will come. Are we prepared for it? Is God our Father? Is Jesus Christ our Savior? Is the Holy Spirit our strengthener and comforter? Is the Word of God our Guide, a lamp unto our feet and a light unto our path? Only so can we be fearless, live courageously, and die victoriously.

Death is not the enemy of life but its friend, for it is the knowledge that our years are limited which makes them so precious. It is the truth that time is but lent to us, which makes us at our best, look upon our years as a trust handed into our temporary keeping. Physical death is not the most serious thing that can happen to any person. "Fear not them who kill the body, RATHER fear him who is able to destroy BOTH SOUL AND BODY." The worst thing that can happen to us is to be separated from God.

If any one truth is made clear in the Scriptures, it is that death works no magic change in one's spiritual condition. It is the breaking of correspondence with physical environment. The simple statement of Scripture is, "Then shall the dust return to the earth as it was; and the spirit shall return unto God who gave it." Whether the released spirit is good or bad, righteous or unrighteous, it "returns unto God who gave it." Final destination, as well as the fullness of reward or punishment, will be arrived at on the basis of character and conduct; for which, in the final analysis, the individual is directly and wholly responsible.

Jesus said death is but the end of a probationary state. He lifts life out of a flat perspective to a context of reality. He gives it a wholly new dimension. Listen to His Promise:

"He that believeth on me hath everlasting life. He shall not see death." It is something more than passing strange, that our day that boasts its enlightenment, glories in its emotional maturity, and is devoted to objective reality, should more and more refuse to think on the one event that dominates all life from its very beginning: death.

Death is not the dying of the self, or the ceasing of the spirit, or even the ceasing of the purpose of the spirit, but is rather life, with mind, soul and understanding departing out of a worn-out garment or a house no longer fit for its inhabitance.

Here is the most amazing testimony ever given by a human being. It is found in the first Chapter of the Apostle Paul's letter to the Philippians, the 21st verse, "FOR ME TO LIVE IS CHRIST, TO DIE IS GAIN." I hardly need to say there are perhaps in all the range of literature, no words so profound as these. It is as though a master mind supplemented by infinite wisdom had sifted all knowledge, all eternity, and then given to us, in a word, the sum total of reality. Here is all the meaning of life and we have it in a single comprehensive word— FOR ME TO LIVE IS CHRIST, TO DIE IS GAIN.

There are eternal longings in the soul. Where or how shall they be satisfied? The longings in our heart are unsatisfiable in our immediate surroundings—so they must be satisfiable some-place else—if they were not satisfiable we would not have them. Nature does not give any property an attribute that is not used in some way. Man is overbuilt for this world.

There will be life out of death. This is the Law of the Universe. "Except a corn of wheat fall into the ground and die, it abideth alone." This is the mystery of germination. "This world is the land of the DYING," writes Tryon Edwards, "THE NEXT is the land of the living." The question, "Where will you spend eternity?" is not nearly so important as the question, "Where and how ARE you spending eternity?" Our eternal pilgrimage HAS ALREADY BEGUN. Our life and character NOW is the answer to the question of life projected into the eternal years.

Both life and death are beyond the comprehension of the human intellect. "This is life, and life eternal that you may know God." The reason that Jesus uses the word eternal is that we are built for eternal years. David was right when he said of God, "He hath set ETERNITY in our hearts."

That is the reason why you are TOO BIG FOR THIS PHYS-ICAL WORLD. You place a man on the biggest thing this world has to offer and he'd hang over on four sides. Doesn't fit him. This present world doesn't fit us, nor do we fit it. Everyone of us who is honest will own up to that truth. MAN IS OVER-MADE FOR EVERYTHING YOU FIND HERE.

I have yet to find a man who is entirely satisfied regardless of how much he possesses. Man is the offspring of God. Man has something unshared by the rest of the universe. Man thinks thoughts and sees visions infinitely beyond the mortal. The only creature that does. Have you ever noticed how triumphant the New Testament is from beginning to end? It sings about victory over death on almost every page. "I am the resurrection and the life, and who believes in me shall never die." Ageless is this message of hope to an otherwise hopeless world!

We live to serve. To God and man we must give our best. And so, dear reader, we come to the end of our little journey through this book together. We wish you God's speed in all your endeavors and hope we meet again.

Our little day will soon be done. We will, like this book, have come to the tale's end. We will have followed Life's Footpath to where sunset shadows lie softly upon autumn hills. Two worlds will blend into one, as twilight blends day and night. The fading day will burn with the golden fire of eternal sunrise.

Dreams will begin to come true and half-seen visions will begin to unfold in reality. On anxious feet, we will hurry out of hemmed-in circumstances into immortal freedom. No longer will we turn a puzzled gaze upon the pain and imperfection of life's blurred picture. We will see no longer "through a glass darkly," but face to face. Crystal clear will be the flood of light that, rolling in billowy tides, will wash life's yesterday and make it resplendent with God's unsullied beauty.

Trails end? No! It is the place where the Footpath widens into the . . . .

F-O-R-E-V-E-R.

TO SUM UP

The great laws of man's nature and the laws of the universe are eternal. These unseen forces come to our attention when we discover them and comply with the nature of their being. Nature remains a closed book until we find the key that unlocks it. From the Law of Cause and Effect to the Law of Death one truth is certain — these laws of the universe are geared to righteousness. The 47 Laws herein may well be a new expression of the basic biblical truths of man's kinship with God.

Any LAW, either civil or ecclesiastical, that does not conform to the laws of nature, must, sooner or later, become obsolete. Persons who are so lacking in their knowledge of nature and of nature's God as to conceive, enact, and seek to enforce laws which run counter to natural law, must, themselves, finally perish along with the system of pseudo-jurisprudence which they build and foster.

If man, as well as nature, is the result of a direct creative act on the part of God — and there is no scientific method of accounting for either apart from His creative act — then we may expect to find in the man the same law found in nature. To this law, he must conform in order to truly live, not merely exist.

WE NEED TO REVIEW AND OBEY THE NATURAL LAWS OF MAN'S NATURE FOR THEY ARE THE ONLY SOUND STARTING POINT TO THE RIGHT AND BASIC WAY TO EVERY MAN'S BETTERMENT! When we obey the natural laws we are rewarded with health, with happiness and success. This is Nature's reward to induce us to obey her laws. When we violate the universal laws the result is pain, disease, discontent, lack of harmony and material failure.

Even though the laws of our nature are abstract, they are still a fact. We cannot define or explain any of the real values of life, such as love, beauty, truth, friendship, creation, God. Abstract truth can only be made to live as it is translated into human experience.

THESE LAWS, THAT WE KNOW AS NATURAL LAWS, ARE THE OUTMOVINGS OF THE VERY NATURE AND PERSON OF GOD HIMSELF.

Certainly they are fixed, and certainly they are irreversible; that is because God is irreversible. He said, *"I remain the same yesterday, today, and forever."*

The Basic Laws of nature are but another name for God. In their inexorable movement, He reveals Himself in wisdom, love and power. This being true, Natural Law is the dictum of the Almighty.

Human laws deal only with the visible side of life. ABSOLUTE JUSTICE must deal with the unseen side of life as well as the visible side. There is NO WAY the individual can have a better world unless in one way or another he becomes a better person.

Few men "Know themselves." We are born a long way from ourselves. The only way we can truly know ourselves is to understand the laws of our nature. Some day EDUCATION will teach the NATURAL LAWS in school. This will be education at its best, education worthy of the name.

If we could develop some of these concepts we could solve practical issues of the hour. Man in his integrity is beautiful — if he keeps the rules. He loses this beauty when he breaks them. Most of our deficiencies are caused by our spiritual inadequacies.

The human heart is never satisfied. It seeks peace that only the love of God and the full acceptance of God can bring. In other words, only God can satisfy the soul of man. Only then is man complete, or whole, when he has this spiritual union with the Creator of life. And this belief if genuine, makes a man ten times the man he formerly was!

— *Alfred Armand Montapert*

LIFE

We are not in this world merely to get rich, or gain fame or power, or to become learned in the arts and sciences, or to build a great business.

All of these, or any of these, may be among our duties, and they may fill our hands; but in all our occupations the real business of life is to put our complete trust in God and to grow loving in disposition and noble in character.

We may learn the finest arts of life, music, painting, sculpture, poetry, or may master the noblest science, or by means of reading, study, travel and conversation with refined people attain the best culture; but if in all this we do not develop our spiritual dimension and attain a oneness with God we have missed the greatest prize of living.

If in the midst of all our duties, cares, trials, joys, sorrows, we are not day by day growing in faith, love, gentleness, unselfishness, thoughtfulness, compassion, and in all the higher branches of life, we are not learning the great lesson set forth for us by our Master in this school of life.

We cannot define or explain any of the real values of life, such as love, beauty, truth, friendship, creation, God. They are the most stable things in our lives and yet we can only experience them. We do not explain ... we can only state, and this is all we can do with a large proportion of all the facts and truths we know. No matter how true a statement of fact or Natural Law may be, it is only a skeleton until wrought on by the magic of human experience and made to live.

Since God is a God of law and order He must ever deal with His people on the highest level of intelligent logic. On the principle of cause and effect there must always be spontaneous response to an action both in kind and degree. The fact of God's eternal wedlock to Law is the only solid foundation on which our faith and hope can rest.

CHARACTER

When life was nearly ended, as almost his final words, Horace Greeley said, "Fame is a vapor, popularity an accident, riches take wings, those who cheer today will curse tomorrow, only one thing endures — character!"

These words but remind us there is only one thing that really matters — building a life. He who achieves character can be neither feeble in life nor forgotten in death. Of a noble Greek the people said, "The goodness of the man is more than the Constitution." When Paris was torn by revolution and bathed in blood it is said of Lamartine, he never locked his door for his character was his protection. Even his enemies respected his goodness.

Emerson said, "There was a certain power in Lincoln and Washington greater than their words." Their noble character was what men feared and respected. Burke, that grand old man of English history, was mightier by far by virtue of what he was than what he said. Character — true, sterling, Christian character — is in itself success. Without it even the millionaire is a failure.

Character is best formed in the stormy billows of the world. The grand aim of man's creation is the development of a beautiful character. Listen to the admonition of Lt. Gen. A. G. Trudeau: "Character is something each one of us must build for himself, out of the laws of God and Nature, the example of others, and most of all, out of the trials and errors of daily living. Character is the total of thousands of small daily strivings to live up to the best that is in us."

The earth holds many wonders but the greatest wonder of them all is the man who makes it his first business to walk with God and fill his niche in the purpose of the Infinite. Well did Milton exclaim, "A good man is the ripe fruit our earth holds up to God." Character is everything to a man!

LESSONS IN LIFE

In my striving and reaching I have learned that I don't get paid for having a brain...I get paid for USING my brain. Expand your MIND—increase your horizons. A person gets paid for USING his brain, not just for having one.

THOUGHTS . . . . My present thoughts determine my future.

FUTURE . . . . . . This is the kind of thinking you have to engage in—figure out what is going to happen in the future, and figure out how you can participate in it.

ATTITUDE . . . . . The quality of your life depends upon your attitude. It is not how much you do, or what you do, it is HOW you do it. Your attitude rules the HOW. You can make it difficult or you can make it a breeze.

CONTENTMENT . Most of us are more in need of a deeper sense of CONTENTMENT with life as it is than we are of a deeper understanding of life.

HARDSHIPS . . . . Hardships and adversity build strong men. Great people never have it easy, that is why they become great. Not infrequently does adversity make a greater contribution to us than comfort.

NATURE . . . . . . Those who cannot see God in nature are not very likely to find Him in grace—for nature is the visible garments of the invisible God.

PRAYER . . . . . . It may be true that prayer is not intended to make God willing to bless us, but it is true that it is intended to make us FIT TO BE BLESSED.

SELF-IMAGE . . . Think WELL of yourself, as the world takes you at your own estimate.

SERVICE . . . . . . YOU serve God best by serving your fellow man.

—*Alfred Armand Montapert*